# JONSON'S
# *Masque of Gipsies*

# JONSON'S
# *Masque of Gipsies*
## IN THE BURLEY, BELVOIR, AND WINDSOR VERSIONS

AN ATTEMPT AT RECONSTRUCTION
BY
W. W. GREG

London: *Published for*
THE BRITISH ACADEMY
*by* GEOFFREY CUMBERLEGE
OXFORD UNIVERSITY PRESS, AMEN HOUSE, E.C. 4
1952

*Oxford University Press, Amen House, London E.C. 4*

GLASGOW NEW YORK TORONTO MELBOURNE WELLINGTON
BOMBAY CALCUTTA MADRAS CAPE TOWN

*Geoffrey Cumberlege, Publisher to the University*

PR
2624
.M3
1952

PRINTED IN GREAT BRITAIN

# PREFACE

*The Gipsies Metamorphosed*, though the longest, is not usually reckoned among the greatest of Jonson's masques. Despite the haunting music of 'The faery beame upon you' its lyrical quality is not on the whole of the highest, and while recognizing the happy fecundity of the invention, we may agree with Herford that in matter of sculduddery Jonson misses the enormous *entrain* and gusto of Burns. At the same time the social historian will find the work an illuminating document for the tastes and manners of the court of the first Stuart.

But, however this may be, an editor can hardly fail to discover a peculiar fascination in the masque. Performed in three different versions and preserved in five independent texts, it presents to the critic a problem that is certainly unusual and may be unique. Hitherto editors have been content to follow the majority of the early authorities in presenting readers with a composite text. Here, although sensible how much must depend on conjecture, I have attempted for the first time a detailed reconstruction of the several versions. This has called for methods, if not of investigation, at least of presentation that are new in my experience and must be regarded as in some measure experimental.

I am aware that my treatment of the text may not meet the approval of conservative critics; indeed the edition is intended as in a minor way a challenge and a manifesto. At the same time I have not sought to advertise this aspect of my work, and while concealing nothing, I have for the most part been content to leave those with different critical opinions to find out for themselves what I have been up to. Anyone who happens to be interested in editorial method will find my position set out in a paper entitled 'The Rationale of Copy-text' in the Virginia *Studies in Bibliography* for 1950–1, a paper that was the direct outcome of the present work.

I have received kind assistance from several quarters, but it is right that one name should stand alone. I need hardly draw attention to the constant use I have made of Dr. Percy Simpson's edition of the masque in the monumental Oxford Jonson, for my indebtedness is manifest, if only in the record of points on which I happen to disagree with Dr. Simpson's findings. But my obligations are not confined to his published work. Far from resenting my intrusion in a field so peculiarly

his own, Dr. Simpson from first to last placed his unrivalled knowledge and accumulated materials freely at my disposal. For his generosity I can only offer him my cordial thanks.

And here I may mention that the notes at the end of this edition are mainly confined to what concerns the distinction of the versions and the establishment of the text. To have attempted anything of an exegetical nature would have been an impertinence, in every sense of the word, at a moment when we are eagerly awaiting Dr. Simpson's commentary.[1]

Through the courtesy of the authorities of the Huntington Library, and the generosity of the Rockefeller Foundation, I was able to get photostats of the Heber manuscript; to the authorities of the British Museum, the Bodleian Library, and the Public Record Office I am indebted for permission to have other manuscripts photographed, and to those of the Cambridge University Library for facilities in obtaining photostats of their unique copy of the Duodecimo in its unpublished state.

TANNER'S KNAP  
PETWORTH, 1950

W. W. G.

## REFERENCES

SIMPSON. *The Gypsies Metamorphosed*, edited by Percy and Evelyn Simpson in vol. vii of Ben Jonson's Works (pp. 539–622). Clarendon Press, 1941.

COLE. *The Gypsies Metamorphosed*, edited by George Watson Cole. New York, for the Modern Language Association of America, 1931.

MCCLURE. *The Letters of John Chamberlaine*, edited by Norman Egbert McClure. 2 vols. Philadelphia. The American Philosophical Society, 1939.

[1] This appeared after my work had gone to press.

# CONTENTS

## INTRODUCTION

I. VERSIONS AND TEXTS . . . . . 1

    The performances, p. 1. The two states of the Duodecimo, p. 3. The Heber–Huntington manuscript, p. 6. The Folio of 1641, p. 7. The Newcastle manuscript, p. 7. Partial texts, p. 9. Symbols used, p. 10. (James's verses to Buckingham, p. 12.)

    DESCRIPTIVE NOTE ON THE FIVE PRINCIPAL TEXTS . . 13

    Characteristics of $D^1$, p. 13; of $D^2$, p. 15; of F, p. 15; of N, p. 17; of H, p. 18.

    NOTE ON THE NAMES OF THE CLOWNS AND WENCHES . 21

II. MAIN DIFFERENCES BETWEEN THE VERSIONS . . 25

    The Belvoir Version, p. 26. The Windsor Version, p. 29. Contents of the Missing Leaves of $D^a$, p. 36.

III. DIFFERENCES BETWEEN THE TEXTS OF THE COMPOSITE VERSION 39

    The four sections of the text, p. 39. Section (A), p. 39. Section (B), p. 40. Section (C), p. 42. Section (D), p. 44. Summary, p. 46. [Table of main revisions.] The dances, p. 46. [Table of the dances.] The songs, p. 51. [Table of the songs.] Relation of the texts in respect of revision, p. 52.

IV. EVIDENCE OF THE SCRIBAL VARIANTS . . . 53

    (1) Evidence for the independence of $D^1$, p. 54. (Evidence of contradictory groupings, $D^1D^2$, p. 58; $D^1H$, p. 59; $D^1f$, p. 60.) (2) Evidence for the group NF, p. 64. (Contradictory evidence, p. 65.) (3) Evidence for the group $D^2f$, p. 65. (Contradictory evidence, p. 68.) Stemma and editorial implications, p. 68. Diagram of combined revision and variation, p. 70.

    NOTE ON SOME SUBSIDIARY TEXTS . . . 71

    1. The Conway manuscript, p. 71. 2. The Tanner and Rawlinson manuscripts, p. 75. 3. The Chilmead manuscript, p. 77.

V. ANALYSIS OF THE VARIANTS . . . . 77

    Object of the analysis, p. 77. Revisional variation, p. 78. Apparent revision in β, p. 80. Apparent revision in γ, p. 80. Apparent revision in f, p. 81. Distribution of errors, p. 81. Length of the several texts, p. 83. Definition of 'errors', p. 84. 'Intrinsic' and 'inferential' errors, p. 84. Errors in α, p. 85. Errors in $D^1$, p. 86. Errors in β, p. 87. Errors in H, p. 88. Errors in γ, p. 89. Errors in $D^2$, p. 90. Errors in f, p. 91. (Apportionment of errors between γ and f, p. 92.) Errors in N, p. 93. Errors in F, p. 94. Relative accuracy and reliability of the texts, p. 95. Residual variants, p. 98. Variants between $D^1$ and β, p. 99. Variants between H and γ, p. 100. Variants between $D^2$ and f, p. 101. Variants between N and F, p. 101.

    THE PRESENT EDITION . . . . . 102

THE PARALLEL TEXTS . . . . 117

NOTES . . . . . . . 204

INDEX . . . . . . . 233

# LIST OF ILLUSTRATIONS

*between pages* 116 *and* 117

I. Duodecimo of 1640: Engraved title, variant states; from copies in the Huntington and Cambridge University Libraries.

II. Duodecimo of 1640: General title and Special title to the Masque.

III. Duodecimo of 1640: Page 59 in the original setting (sig. D6) and in the cancel (sig. d1).

IV. Folio of 1641: Special title to the Masque.

V. Chilmead's setting of the Patrico–Jackman duet, from the British Museum MS. Add. 29396 (fols. 71$^b$, 72$^b$).

VI–IX. Heber–Huntington Manuscript, pages 3, 22, 48, 49.

X. Verses by James I, from the Newcastle Manuscript (fol. 1$^a$): British Museum MS. Harley 4955 [see p. 20].

XI. Newcastle Manuscript, folio 6$^a$.

XII. Conway Manuscript, page 4, from State Papers, Domestic, James I, vol. cxxii, art. 58.

# INTRODUCTION

## I. VERSIONS AND TEXTS

BEN JONSON's masque of *The Gipsies Metamorphosed*, to give it the title he appears to have intended, was presented before James I and his court on three occasions in 1621: first on Friday, 3 August, at Burley-on-the-Hill in Rutland, the seat of his favourite, George Villiers, Marquess (later Duke) of Buckingham; again the following Sunday, 5 August, at Belvoir Castle, Leicestershire, the seat of Francis Manners, sixth Earl of Rutland, Buckingham's father-in-law; and lastly at Windsor, probably some time early in September.[1] At each repetition alterations were made in the text, slight no doubt for the performance at Belvoir since there was little time for revision,[2] substantial for that at Windsor a month or so later. For our knowledge of these alterations we are mainly dependent on a manuscript of the masque in the Huntington Library, which formally records several, though certainly not all, instances of revision. From the evidence there supplied we are able to infer that one of our authorities, namely the Duodecimo of 1640 as originally printed, represents the early

---

[1] The date of the Burley performance is given in a letter of 4 Aug. from John Chamberlain to Sir Dudley Carleton (S.P.D., James I, cxxii. 60; McClure, ii. 395–6; Cole, p. 3): 'as yesterday the ·K· was to be entertained by the ·L· of Buckingham at Burly in Rutlandshire ... where was great prouision of playes maskes and all maner of entertainment; and this day the court remoues to Beauuoir.' Reporting from London he gives no details, but writing again on 27 Oct. (see p. 36) he mentions 'a ballet or song of Ben Iohnsons in the play or shew at the lord marquis at Burly'. The date of the Belvoir performance appears in the text (B 908[1]). Our only direct evidence for the date of the performance at Windsor is the special title to the masque in the 1641 Folio of Jonson's works, according to which all three performances were in 'August, 1621.'—and this appears to be an error. According to Nichols's *Progresses* (iv. 715) James's peregrinations lasted throughout August: on the 31st he was at his hunting-box at Easthampstead, Berks., a patent of nobility dated 4 Sept. at Westminster presumably implies his presence there; on 9 Sept. he knighted Sir Edward Leech at Windsor, and on 11 Sept. Sir Maurice Berkeley at Whitehall. The performance of the masque must, it would seem, have been between 5 and 10 Sept., perhaps on the 9th. The earliest mention of the Windsor performance is in Chamberlain's letter of 27 Oct. (see p. 36).

[2] In fact this argument has little weight, for the Belvoir performance must have been designed from the start, and any necessary alterations could have been, and indeed probably were, prepared beforehand (see note on B 924). Thus, had the change of local demanded extensive modifications (which it did not), there would have been no difficulty in making them. What the shortness of time does exclude is any extensive literary revision, if only for fear of disturbing the actors' parts.

## Introduction

version of the masque performed at Burley.[1] All our other authorities represent the revised text, but none of them attempts to give the version presented either at Belvoir or Windsor, for all contain a composite or conflated text consisting of the Burley version (substantially complete) together with the Belvoir and Windsor revisions, whether these took the form of additions or substitutions. The details of the revision are considered in Sections II and III of this Introduction.

A rough outline of the masque may help the reader to follow the further account of the texts. The speech 'At the Kings Entrance' is not properly part of the masque, but was spoken by the porter on James's arrival at Burley-on-the-Hill. The masque itself opens with the appearance of the Gipsies, and after some introductory speeches the Jackman invites the spectators to have their fortunes told. The Captain tells the King's and another Gipsy the Prince's. These were followed at Burley and Belvoir by fortunes of six of the principal ladies present, and at Windsor by those of eight chief officers and nobles. These concluded, enter eight country clowns and wenches, who supply what may be called an antimasque. They discuss the Gipsies and collect money among themselves for the music that accompanies their rustic dance. The Patrico proposes that they too shall have their fortunes told, and this is done in a series of ribald couplets while the Gipsies pick their pockets and then make off. Left alone, the clowns (Burley) or the clowns and wenches (Windsor) discover and lament their loss; but the Patrico restores their property. After this, in reply to an inquiry by the clowns, is sung the ballad of Cock Lorel, to which, at Windsor, were added three stanzas in abuse of tobacco. In the Windsor version (at least) the clowns are so delighted by the tale that they beg to be allowed to join the company of the Gipsies; but the Patrico explains the difficulty of the calling and the training it needs. The rest of the company now reappear, 'changed' from their Gipsy disguise to their own fashion of lords and gentlemen of

---

[1] Simpson's statement (p. 541) that it gives 'the Burley and Belvoir versions' ignores the fact that, as he elsewhere recognizes, alterations made at Belvoir do not appear in the original Duodecimo text. (The allusion to 'the Beaver-kin' at B 132 belongs to Burley and was in fact omitted at Belvoir.) Doubts whether it is a pure Burley text expressed in a review in *R.E.S.*, Apr. 1942, xviii. 156, rested on errors or confusions in Simpson's collations. Other doubts, arising out of the names of the Clowns and Wenches of the antimasque, are discussed (and dismissed) in the Note at pp. 21–5.

# Versions and Texts 3

the court. At this point the Windsor version introduces the Patrico's blessing of the King's five senses, in which the clowns bear the burden. The conclusion in praise of King and Prince consists of verses by the metamorphosed Gipsies alternating with songs by the Jackman. A prologue and epilogue were added at Windsor.

The only authority that presents any bibliographical problem of importance is the one I have referred to as the Duodecimo, which has come down to us in two strikingly different states. The masque here forms the third item in a little collection entitled,

> Q. Horatius Flaccus: His Art of Poetry. Englished By Ben: Jonson. With other Workes of the Author, never Printed before. London: Printed by J. Okes, for John Benson. 1640.[1]

The masque originally occupied the last three leaves of quire C (C10–12) and the whole of D and E with the exception of E12, which was blank. It has a title-page of its own on C10 (verso blank):

> The Masque of the Gypsies. Written by Ben: Jonson. London: Printed by J. Okes, for J. Benson, and are to bee sold at his shop in St. Dunstans Church-yard in Fleet-street. 1640.

There is also a head-title, 'The Masque of the Gypsies', above the entrance speech; but the masque proper is headed 'The Gypsies Metamorphos'd', as in all the other texts: there is no running-title. The text, as I have said, is that of the original Burley version, and it was set up from a good manuscript, possibly one prepared for presentation on the occasion of the first performance.[2] But before the book was issued, Benson,

---

[1] After the preliminaries, which include an engraved title with a portrait-bust, re-engraved by William Marshall after the portrait by Robert Vaughan originally published by Humble c. 1625 (a title found with two forms of the imprint), the sections are (1) 'Quintus Horatius Flaccus his Book of the Art of Poetry to the Piso's' (this is Jonson's first draft of his translation, later superseded by the revised version printed next year in the Folio), (2) 'Ben: Ionson's Execration against Vulcan', (3) the masque, (4) 'Epigrams to Severall Noble Personages in this Kingdome. The Author Ben: Ionson': each of the later sections has a special title. In spite of the statement that these works had been 'never Printed before', Benson had himself published, and Okes had printed, the *Execration* and the *Epigrams* in quarto earlier in the year: only the Horace and the masque were new. Benson entered 'Ben Iohnsons Execration against Vulcan with other his smaller Epigrams' in the Stationers' Register on 16 Dec. 1639, 'Quintus Horatius Flaccus his booke of the Art of Poetry to the Piso's translated into English by Ben: Iohnson' on 8 Feb. 1640, and 'The Masque of the Gypsies by Ben: Iohnson' on 20 Feb. following.

[2] Simpson (p. 553) suggests that 'it may even have been autograph', but I can find no definite indication of this. He appears to have been influenced by the fact

the publisher, somehow acquired[1] a manuscript of the fuller composite version, and though this was in fact a rather inferior copy, he decided to amplify the already printed text in accordance with it. To do this he cancelled the leaves D6–10 and E5–11[2] and replaced them by two newly printed quires, d12 and e12.[3] This brought his edition into substantial agreement with the fuller version. But it was only where the difference between the versions was marked that Benson went to the trouble of reprinting: we must not, for instance, conclude that because the Windsor prologue (w 1–20), the Windsor

that it often retains the Jonsonian spelling ''hem' where other texts have ''em' (see p. 550); but ''hem' is also found in the later state of the Duodecimo, which we cannot suppose to have autograph authority, and even once in the Huntington manuscript.

[1] Simpson (p. 552) says 'certainly by dishonest means', and he elsewhere (viii. 3) speaks of all Benson's manuscripts as 'surreptitiously acquired'. Benson's publications were no doubt 'surreptitious' in the sense that they were not authorized by Jonson or his executor, but that would not, according to the notions of the time, imply any dishonest dealing. So far as I am aware, the only reason to question whether Benson acquired his manuscripts honestly in the ordinary course of business is an allegation by Thomas Walkley that Benson and Crooke 'obtayned by some casuall or other indirect meanes false & imperfect Copies' of certain works of Jonson's. But this is an *ex parte* statement made in the course of a bill in Chancery filed by Walkley on 20 Jan. 1640/1, and should be accepted with reserve. In any case the words would apply rather to Benson's original manuscript of the masque than to the one he later acquired, and the earlier Simpson admits to have been 'a good one'. Even Benson's final edition is superior to Walkley's in the Folio. (It is true that Benson only got hold of the unrevised text of the Horace, whereas Walkley had the corrected version, and it is probably to this fact that Walkley's words properly apply.) Walkley's Chancery bill was printed in *The Library* in Dec. 1930 (xi. 226–9) and discussed in the issue of Mar. 1931 (xi. 461–5). Simpson (vi. 146) misdates it 'January 1640', which would make it earlier than Benson's entrances in the Register to which it refers. In *The Times Literary Supplement* for 14 Mar. 1935 A. G. Chester showed that Walkley was still seeking redress in 1648, as appears from documents in the House of Lords calendared by the Historical Manuscripts Commission. In the course of his communication he represents Walkley as alleging in his Chancery bill that the copies in question 'had been stolen from his shop'. So legend grows.

[2] Not E9–11, as stated by Simpson, p. 552.

[3] It naturally required some adjustment to make the new quires fit exactly into the place of the cancelled leaves. In d the compositor found his material rather scanty: he left several pages short and set the first of the Ladies' fortunes in large type instead of in small (as in the cancelled leaves). In e, on the other hand, there are signs of crowding: the blessing of the senses and the conclusion are set solid, whereas earlier all verse is leaded. The insertions of course disturbed the pagination: we find the numbers 69–82 and 95–104 repeated (E12, blank, and F1, the title to the *Epigrams*, were from the first omitted from the reckoning). The make-up of the two states may be represented in tabular form as follows:

| | C10–12 | D1–5 | D6–10 | D11–12 | E1–4 | E5–11 | E12 (blank) |
|---|---|---|---|---|---|---|---|
| First state | pp. 43–8 | pp. 49–58 | pp. 59–68 | pp. 69–72 | pp. 73–80 | pp. 81–94 | (unpaged) |
| Second state | (same) | (same) | d1–12 pp. 59–82 | (same) | (same) | e1–12 pp. 81–104 | (same) |

variant at w 104, the Belvoir variant at B 130, the Windsor variants at w 175 and 190, and the rewriting in the antimasque between w 568 and 766, do not appear in his edition, they were therefore absent from the manuscript from which the cancels were printed—he may have overlooked them or not thought them worth worrying about; indeed, the important addition to the King's fortune (w 301–18) was the first variant to which he paid attention.

It is only by accident that the cancelled leaves have survived, and that imperfectly. In one copy, preserved in the Cambridge University Library (formerly Y.5.66, now Syn.8.64.13), the process of cancellation was not completed: the leaves E5–8 were indeed removed, but D6–10 and E9–11 were only slashed, and the cancelling sheets were never inserted.[1] To this fortunate chance we owe our knowledge of almost a third of the text as originally printed, for out of the twenty-five leaves occupied by the text of the masque (that is excluding the title and the final blank) only thirteen were retained in the published state; twelve were cancelled, and of these eight survive in the Cambridge copy.

Thus the Duodecimo as published consists of two quite distinct portions. Thirteen leaves (C11–D5, containing B 1–267, and D11–E5, containing B 497('any Gypsies ...')–758) survive from the original state and were printed from a good manuscript of the Burley version; twenty-four leaves (the two inserted sheets: $d^{12}$, containing w 262–548('... never see'), and $e^{12}$, containing w 811–1291) are new and were printed from a less good manuscript representing the common composite version. Since it is natural to refer to the Duodecimo

---

[1] We might have expected leaves D6–7 as well as E5–8 to have been bodily removed, since these were the one or two innermost folds of their respective quires, and were not needed for the sewing. The explanation, however, is obvious. The leaves E5–8 are the four leaves of the inner third of a duodecimo sheet, and as such they would (according to the usual method of duodecimo imposition) be detached from the rest of the sheet before folding: they could, therefore, be readily discarded. To remove D6–7 would mean opening the edges of the leaves. The other leaves to be cancelled were only slashed and it was left to the binder to cut them out after sewing and leaving stubs. These stubs are visible in several copies and sometimes preserve sufficient traces of printing to be identified (cf. p. 54, note). For the same reason of security the blank E12 was left, though in some copies the binder appears to have removed it. There can be little doubt that in the Cambridge copy E5–8 were purposely removed, but it also suffered the accidental loss of C3–10. Another anomalous copy is that formerly in the Beverly Chew collection and now in the Huntington Library, in which the cancelling sheets were duly inserted, but the binder omitted to remove the slashed leaves E9–11. These agree with those in the Cambridge copy.

as 'D', the two *states* may be conveniently distinguished as D$^a$ and D$^b$. But for reasons by now apparent these symbols cannot be used to distinguish two different *texts*. To this point I shall return.[1]

Much the best authority for the composite version is a manuscript that once belonged to Heber and is now in the Huntington Library (HM 741). It is clearly and carefully written, but not in an altogether calligraphic manner, and the untidiness of the irregularly shaped leaves makes it uncertain whether it can have been intended as a presentation copy. It is also the only known text that attempts to distinguish the successive revisions in any systematic manner, though its record is certainly not complete. The hand has a general resemblance to Jonson's, but is not his;[2] nor is the almost total lack of punctuation in his manner; nor, according to Simpson, does the spelling resemble his. A couple of early press-marks enable the authorities of the Huntington Library to identify the manuscript as having been in the Bridgewater collection about 1640, and they have confidently identified a marginal note as being in the hand of the second Earl, at that date still Viscount Brackley.[3] His father, John Egerton, Baron Ellesmere and (from 1617) first Earl of Bridgewater, was a man of literary tastes and like his father, Thomas Egerton the Lord Chancellor, a collector: he lived till 1649. Though he held no office at court and is not known to have been present at any performance of Jonson's masque, he is likely enough to have obtained a copy privately. But the manuscript did not remain in the Bridgewater collection. It is known to have been in the possession of the antiquary Peter le Neve (1661–1729) and was in the Heber sale in 1836

---

[1] Cole published a complete facsimile of D$^b$ from the Chew copy in the Huntington Library (pp. 55–95), and another of the three leaves of D$^a$ (E9–11) preserved in the same copy (pp. 259–64). The Cambridge copy of D$^a$ (complete but for the title C10 and E5–8) has never been reproduced: Simpson, of course, collated it, and it is here reprinted for the first time.

[2] I am ashamed that in a brief note published in 1934 I casually stated that it was.

[3] Since the Bridgewater collection is now in the Huntington Library, the authorities there are in the best possible position to pronounce on these points. I have not myself been able to confirm the identification. Simpson writes (p. 546): 'As proved by the old shelf-mark "8.2." and by a note in the handwriting of the Earl of Ellesmere [meaning 'Bridgewater'] . . . this manuscript was once (*circa* 1640) in the Bridgewater library.' This is misleading, for in 1640 the first Earl was still alive, and the note is certainly not in his hand.

Fuller particulars of the manuscript will be found in the Descriptive Note on the Texts, p. 18.

(catalogue pt. XI, lot 603),[1] when, through the bookseller Thorpe, it passed into Sir Thomas Phillipps's collection (MS. 10100; catalogue 1836, no. 721): sold again in 1897, it passed, through Quaritch, to A. W. White (handlist 1914, p. 51), and from him about 1916 to Henry E. Huntington.[2] It might be legitimate to connect this manuscript with the great name of Bridgewater, but it is perhaps safer to call it the Heber–Huntington manuscript.

The masque was included in what came to be known as the 'third volume' of Jonson's works, the Folio published by Thomas Walkley in 1641 under the nominal editorship of Sir Kenelm Digby,[3] who probably did no more than select from Jonson's papers those suitable for publication. The edition is important as being presumably printed from a manuscript found among the author's remains, but the text is neither as accurate nor as well presented as that in the Heber–Huntington manuscript. It seems, however, to represent a later stage in the revision.

So closely associated with the Folio text that it must be assumed to have been transcribed from the same original,[4] is a copy in the British Museum MS. Harley 4955 (fols. 2–30). 'This manuscript, as its contents show, was made for the Newcastle family, probably for the Earl, who was Jonson's patron', Simpson remarks (p. 560). It was for Sir William Cavendish, later first Earl (1628) and Duke (1665) of Newcastle, that Jonson was to write the Welbeck and Bolsover entertainments on the occasion of visits by Charles I in 1633

---

[1] While in Heber's possession it was used by Gifford for his edition of Jonson's works in 1816.

[2] These particulars, from Simpson (p. 546), are based on information supplied by the authorities of the Huntington Library. Cole gives a complete facsimile of the manuscript, pp. 100–213.

[3] In his first address to the reader prefixed to *The Last Remains of Sir John Suckling*, 1659, the publisher, Humphrey Moseley, writes concerning his inclusion of the unfinished piece *The Sad One*: 'Nor are we without a sufficient President in Works of this nature, and relating to an Author who confessedly is reputed the Glory of the English Stage (whereby you'll know I mean *Ben: Johnson*) and in a Play also of somewhat a resembling name, *The Sad Shepherd*, extant in his Third Volume; which though it wants two entire *Acts*, was nevertheless judg'd a Piece of too much worth to be laid aside, by the Learned and Honorable Sir *Kenelme Digby*, who published that Volume.' Moseley was in a position to know the facts of the case, seeing that he had lately acquired the rights in the volume in question from the original publisher. That Digby was Jonson's literary executor is confirmed by Walkley's bill in Chancery (cf. p. 4, note 1).

[4] In this blunt statement I follow Simpson, whose account is here rather summary (cf. p. 8, note 3). There are advantages in making the assumption at the start. The evidence on which it is based will be found in Section IV.

and 1634; and it was for another Sir William Cavendish, afterwards (1626) second Earl of Devonshire, that he had already written the so-called Blackfriars entertainment on the occasion of the christening of his second son, Charles, in 1620. Texts of all three pieces are in the manuscript; written in the same calligraphic hand.[1] The style in the Blackfriars entertainment and in the masque is also similar—the performances were within eighteen months of each other—that in the Welbeck and Bolsover entertainments a dozen years later is in some respects different.[2] This and the general make-up of the volume prove that the texts were not all copied at the same time and suggest that the copies may have been roughly contemporary with the performances. The transcript of the masque, though elaborately written and fully punctuated, shows none of the editorial care and knowledge apparent in the Huntington manuscript; at the same time it reproduces its exemplar more faithfully than does the Folio, and is indeed the best copy we possess of the final text. It is not, of course, a presentation copy, but one made by a scribe in the employ of Sir William Cavendish from a borrowed original, and its close textual resemblance to the Folio allows us to assume that the original was provided by Jonson himself.[3]

[1] The Blackfriars entertainment occupies fols. 48–52, the Welbeck entertainment fols. 194–8, and the Bolsover entertainment fols. 199–202. It will be noticed that the masque, though in fact a year later than the Blackfriars entertainment, was transcribed first.

[2] With the facsimiles in the present volume compare those from the three entertainments given by Simpson at pp. 768, 790, and 806 respectively.

[3] MS. Harley 4955 was examined and described by W. D. Briggs in 'Studies in Ben Jonson. I', *Anglia*, 1913, xxxvii. 463–93: the bulk of his article is devoted to collations. Simpson's treatment of the manuscript is hasty and misleading. On p. 560 he asserts that 'it follows the . . . Folio in all its errors', which is incorrect and is contradicted by what he says later. On p. 541 he writes: 'The fourth text is that of the . . . Folio, badly printed from an independent manuscript. A slavish copy of this text is preserved in Harley MS. 4955 in the British Museum: from the textual standpoint this manuscript is negligible.' From this a careless reader might assume that the manuscript was copied from the Folio. What Simpson really meant appears on p. 561: 'The explanation of this manuscript text appears to be that the scribe took it from the Folio copy before it went to press.' He adds, however: 'After the Folio had been printed there would be no point in copying out this masque from it: there is no evidence that members of the Cavendish family took part in any of the performances; if they had done so, the Earl[-to-be] could have secured a sounder text.' This is surely fanciful. It is clear that the compiler of the manuscript was interested only in certain particular works of Jonson's, and transcription from the Folio would have been the natural course, if the Folio were already in existence. It is the text of the manuscript that proves that by no possibility can it derive from the Folio, and it may have been written nearly twenty

There exist a number of manuscripts of or including particular portions of the masque. Three preserve some of the fortunes. Of these the most interesting is one preserved among the Conway papers in the Public Record Office (S.P.D., James I, vol. cxxii, art. 58) and endorsed 'The Gypsies Maaske att Burley'. A cataloguer's note states that it is in the hand of Sir Henry Goodyer (1571–1627), who was one of the Knights of the Barriers at the marriage of the Earl of Essex (see Jonson's *Hymenaei*, 4°, 1606) and the subject of one of Jonson's *Epigrams* (no. 85).[1] A single sheet of four pages, it contains the fortunes of the King and Prince (in the shorter versions spoken at Burley) followed by those of the Ladies, including the Countess of Exeter's, in an order different from that of the complete texts. The manuscript is of importance historically, since it gives the names of three of the speakers, and textually as presenting a purely Burley text independent of the original state of the Duodecimo. (See further in the Note to Section IV, pp. 71–5.)

The other two are in the Bodleian: MS. Tanner 306 (fol. 252) and MS. Rawlinson Poet. 172 (fol. 78). Both contain the fortunes of the Lord Keeper, the Lord Steward, the Lord Treasurer, and the Lord Chamberlain, in that order. They thus agree with the Huntington manuscript in omitting the Earl of Buccleuch's fortune and in placing the Lord Chamberlain's last; but this is of little significance, since they also omit the fortunes of the Lord Privy Seal, the Earl Marshal, and the Marquess of Hamilton, and differ from all other authorities in placing the Lord Steward's before the Lord Treasurer's. Textually the two manuscripts are closely related, but their readings are of little interest. In the Rawlinson the fortunes are followed by extracts from the Cock Lorel ballad; in the

---

years earlier. What sort of text Sir William might have been able to obtain at a performance I really cannot say; but I would point out that the copy he, or his secretary, actually did obtain was the very one that Jonson appears to have preserved among his own papers. 'Slavish' in a sense the scribe certainly was, for he reproduced some manifest errors, but, as will appear later, he transcribed his original more accurately, and made in it more intelligent emendations, than did the scribe of the Huntington manuscript. Simpson did not collate the Newcastle manuscript, or at any rate has not published any collation: he cites it only sporadically in his apparatus, and not always correctly—for example he twice reports in it errors it does not contain (l. 531 of his text, and l. 1432, where $C$ is a slip for $N$), and he once (l. 201) cites it as correct where in fact it shares the error of the Folio.

[1] Comparison with letters of Goodyer's in the Record Office makes the identification to my mind probable, though I find in them little trace of the peculiar spelling of the verses.

Tanner there follow two poems addressed by King James to Buckingham on the occasion of his visit to Burley, poems also found in the Newcastle manuscript (see pp. 12–13). (See further in the Note to Section IV, pp. 75–7.)

Of less importance are certain other extracts. A manuscript formerly in the possession of Mr. Bertram Dobell, and believed to be now in America, contained a copy of the blessing of the senses (w 1129–89), a very loose version apparently written down from memory and of no textual value.[1] The British Museum MS. Add. 29396[2] (fols. 71$^b$–72$^b$) has the Patrico and Jackman's duet (w 508–33) with a musical setting by Edmund Chilmead;[3] and Robert Johnson's setting of the first dozen lines of the Jackman's opening song (w 89–100) is printed in *The Musical Companion*, 1672–3 (pp. 88–9):[4] in neither case are the few variants of any importance.[5] There are also a score or more texts in print or manuscript of the Cock Lorel ballad, some fragmentary, some expanded, and some with music,[6] for a list of which I am indebted to Dr. Simpson. They often show individual peculiarities, but are probably of no textual value: I have not attempted to examine them.

I may now summarize our authorities for the text of Jonson's masque and give the symbols by which I shall refer to them. But first I must clear up the complication caused by the two states of the Duodecimo. We have:

D$^a$ = Benson's Duodecimo of 1640 as originally printed, and preserved (imperfectly) in the Cambridge copy.

D$^b$ = the same as modified by cancellation and insertion before publication.

But this bibliographical distinction is inadequate, and the symbols therefore misleading, for textual purposes. D$^a$ does, indeed, contain a homogeneous text, which we may call D$^1$;

---

[1] Dr. Simpson most kindly allowed me to see the transcript that Dobell made for him.

[2] A collection of English songs made by, and mostly in the hand of, Edward Lowe, who was organist at Christ Church, Oxford, 1630–56, became Professor of Music at Oxford in 1661, and died in 1682.

[3] Facsimiled by Cole, pp. 16–18.    [4] Ibid., p. 15.

[5] Chilmead was not born till 1610 and his setting of the song can hardly be the original. Johnson was musician to Prince Henry in 1611 and to Charles I in 1625–6, and is known to have composed music for plays. He is likely enough to have been employed on Jonson's masque.

[6] Cole, p. 19, facsimiles the opening of one with musical setting from *Wit and Mirth, or Pills to Purge Melancholy*, pt. ii, 1700, and refers, p. 14, for further information to Playford's edition of *The Musical Companion*, pp. 160–1.

## Versions and Texts

but $D^b$ is made up of certain leaves of $D^a$ interspersed with others newly printed and containing a text of a wholly different character. The text of $D^b$, therefore, is in part $D^1$ and in part another, which we must call $D^2$.[1] It may be well to point out here that though Bentley must have possessed two complete manuscripts (one of the Burley and one of the composite version) we are only imperfectly acquainted with the contents of either. Our knowledge of his first manuscript (Burley) is limited by the fact that of $D^a$ four leaves are, it seems, irretrievably lost; our knowledge of the second (composite) by the fact that Bentley contented himself with printing from it, for insertion in $D^b$, only those sections of the text in which it differed most widely from the first. In fact our knowledge of his second manuscript is more restricted than our knowledge of his first.

Our textual sigils will therefore be as follows:

$D^1$ = the Duodecimo text as originally printed, whether preserved (imperfectly) in our only copy of $D^a$ or partially surviving in $D^b$: Burley version.

$D^2$ = the text of the two Duodecimo sheets specially printed for insertion in $D^b$: composite version.[2]

H = the Heber–Huntington manuscript (HM 741 in the Huntington Library), *c.* 1621?: composite version.

N = the Newcastle manuscript in the British Museum (MS. Harl. 4955), *c.* 1621?: composite version.

F = the closely related text printed in the Folio of 1641: composite version.

When, as sometimes happens, it is necessary to refer to the manuscripts that served as copy for the three printed texts, I use the symbols $d^1$, $d^2$, and $f$. It is assumed that N was directly transcribed from $f$. Hypothetical manuscripts

---

[1] Simpson makes his symbols 'D1' and 'D2' do duty both bibliographically and textually, and he is thus led to use a symbol 'D' where only one Duodecimo text is available. But in so doing he uses 'D' in two textually different senses. In lines 1–292 and 747–999 (of his edition), the sections retained in $D^b$ from $D^a$, his 'D' means $D^1$; in lines 1000–1273, where our only copy of $D^a$ is defective, his 'D' means $D^2$. This inevitably misleads the student unless he bears constantly in mind the limits of these sections. It is only slowly and painfully that I have extricated myself from the confusion. The symbol 'D', if used at all, should mean the agreement of $D^1$ and $D^2$ where both texts are extant; and this is just the sense in which Simpson does not use it, except occasionally and it would seem by inadvertence. It is safer to eschew the symbol 'D' altogether.

[2] For the modified symbols *$D^1$ and *$D^2$, see the description of The Present Edition, p. 106.

in the transmission of the text will be referred to by Greek minuscules.

To these may be added the four most important manuscripts containing extracts only:

Con = the Conway manuscript of the King's, Prince's, and Ladies' fortunes, at the Record Office: Burley version.

Tan = the Tanner manuscript (306) of four of the Lords' fortunes, in the Bodleian Library: Windsor version.

Raw = the Rawlinson manuscript (Poet. 172) of the same four Lords' fortunes, also in the Bodleian: Windsor version.

Add = the Chilmead manuscript of the Patrico–Jackman duet in the British Museum (MS. Add. 29396): Windsor version.

The Newcastle manuscript (fol. 1) prefaces the masque with some verses addressed by James I to Buckingham on the occasion of his visiting Burley, and another copy of the same is appended in the Tanner manuscript to its selection from the Lords' fortunes. These verses are mentioned in a letter from Chamberlain to Carleton on 18 August 1621 (S.P.D., James I, cxxii. 77; McClure, ii. 397; Cole, pp. 3–4): 'The ·K· was so pleased and taken w$^{th}$ his entertainment at the lord marquis that he could not forbeare to expresse his contentment in certain verses he made there to this effect, that the ayre, the weather, (though yt were not so here [sc. in London]) and every thing els, even the staggs and bucks in their fall did seeme to smile, so that there was hope of a smiling boy w$^{th}$in a while, to w$^{ch}$ end he concluded w$^{th}$ a wish or votum for the felicitie and fruitfulnes of that vertuous and blessed couple, and in a way of Amen caused the bishop of London [George Montague] in his presence to geue them a benediction.' The Newcastle manuscript affords the better text; it runs as follows.

Verses made by king Iames at Burley in the hill.<br>Aug: 1621.

The heauens that wept perpetuallie before,
   since we came hither shewe there smilinge cheere
This goodlie house it smiles; and all this store     5
   of huge provision, smiles vppon vs heere,
The bucks, and stags, in fatt they seeme to smile
   God send a smyling boy within a while.

## Versions and Texts

Votum :·

If euer in the Aprill of my daies,    10
  I satt vppon Pernassus forked hill,
  and there inflam'd with Sacred furie still
  by pen proclaim'd our greate Appollos prayse,
Grant glistering Phæbus w$^{th}$ thy golden rayes
  my earnest wish which I present thee heere.    15
  beholdinge of this blessed coople deere,
  whose vertues pure no pen can dulye blaze
Thou by whose heate the Trees in Fruite abound,
  blesse them with Fruite delitious sweete, & fayre,
  that may succeede them in theire vertues rare    20
firme plant them in theire natiue soyle, & ground,
  Thou Ioue that art the onlye God indeed,
    my prayer heare Sweete Iesus interceede.
      Pro fertilitate et fælicitate

Tan omits the heading and the necessary subscription, which should be read in conjunction with the intermediate heading 'Votum'. Line 7: Tan mis-emends *fatt* to *faith*; indeed, without Chamberlain's letter it might not be obvious that it is a misreading of *fall*. Line 11: Tan reads *Parnassus*. Line 17: for *pen* Tan has *tongue*. Line 20: for *that* Tan has *w$^{ch}$*. Line 21: Tan omits *& ground*, but adds *& grant* at the beginning of the next line. Lines 22–3: there should, of course, be some stop after *heare*: misunderstanding this, Tan alters *heare* to *here*; hence, in an attempt to make sense, its misplaced substitution of *& grant* for *& ground*.

There are doubtless other copies of these verses.

### DESCRIPTIVE NOTE ON THE FIVE PRINCIPAL TEXTS

There are points in the texts that merit closer attention, and a study of their formal characteristics may throw light on their relationships and on the nature of the manuscripts from which they were printed or transcribed. Naturally we shall expect the three printed texts to exhibit some common features, and the two manuscript texts others; still, while we must not rashly infer any direct relation between them, resemblances must be given their due weight.

### *Characteristics of* D$^1$.

From certain peculiarities in the setting of the masque Cole (pp. 29–30) concluded that Benson divided the copy for his volume in two, and having calculated that the masque would fill sheet E, began printing the *Epigrams* on F1. Then, when the *Horace* and the *Execration* were completed, he found that he had allowed too much space for the masque, and he was forced to print parts of it in larger type, to resort to heavy leading, to leave some pages short, and finally to admit a blank leaf at the end.[1] I believe this to be completely mistaken. The fact that a blank leaf was left at the end of the masque is discounted by another being left at the end of the *Execration*.[2] The first two sections (the *Horace* and the *Execration*) were printed in small type in order to avoid over-running the long decasyllabic lines; it was only natural that larger type should be used for the short measures in which much of the masque is written, and for the prose in which the problem of over-running did not arise, and small type be reserved for the longer measures where it might be serious. In fact we find large type similarly used in some of the *Epigrams* that happen to be in shorter lines. The few short pages that occur near the end seem due to a desire to avoid beginning a fresh song or speech near the foot of the page: the text could have been spread out as well or better by a freer use of large type. I can see no reason whatever to suppose that the book was not printed straight ahead.

Typographically the text presents few unusual features. The casual use of italic is on the whole sparing and normal, as, for example, in stage directions, speakers' names, proper names in the text, Latin words, and so on.[3] The only passage wholly italicized is four lines of verse that conclude a prose speech (B 62–5); these may

---

[1] Or rather, of course, we are to suppose that Okes adopted these devices to rectify an original error of Benson's. In support of his theory Cole pointed out that the *Epigrams* were registered two months earlier than the masque; the implication being, I suppose, that Benson was held up for the licence of the latter. But he had already printed, with the date 1640, a separate quarto edition of the *Execration* and the *Epigrams* (entered 16 Dec. 1639), so that it is in fact unlikely that he began work on the Duodecimo collection till some time after he entered the masque on 20 Feb.

[2] It is true that, as Cole pointed out, the blank E12 (at the end of the masque) was not allowed for in the pagination, whereas the blank C9 (at the end of the *Execration*) was. But this fact is fatal to his own argument, for had Benson been calculating beforehand on what page to begin the *Epigrams*, he would, of course, have assumed that E12 would contain the end of the masque, and he would have included its pages in his count. Actually the title-leaf of the *Epigrams* (F1) is also excluded from the reckoning, though those of the *Execration* and the masque are included. I can offer no explanation of these abnormalities. We might also wonder why blank leaves were left before the masque and the *Epigrams*, though not before the *Execration*. But for this the reason is obvious. Benson, or rather Okes, wished to have a blank *page* facing each of his special titles; in which he showed his taste and care. The *Horace* ended on a recto, so that he already had the blank verso to face the title of the *Execration*. But both the *Execration* and the masque ended on a verso, so that the only way to get a blank *page* to face the following title was to leave a blank *leaf*. This, too, points to the book having been printed straight ahead.

[3] Cole (p. 51) remarks on the general absence of italics in D1 compared with the other texts, and thinks that the latter agree more closely with Jonson's practice as seen in the holograph of *The Masque of Queens*. The judgement is perhaps a little sweeping.

## Versions and Texts

have been sung, but songs are not elsewhere italicized, at any rate in the extant portion (the Cock Lorel ballad is lost). The first of the long verse speeches by the Patrico, that of entrance (B 121–207), is divided into paragraphs or stanzas of varying length, in which the compositor was undoubtedly following his copy, since some such division is found in all the texts: this is, however, the only text in which there is no indentation. The second, which may be called the restitution speech (B 716–73), is printed without break (but the end is lost). In regular stanzaic speeches or songs the stanzas are separated in the Jackman's first song (B 96–119), and the fortunes of the Prince (B 312–35) and the Countess of Buckingham (B 421–44), but not in that of the King (B 288–308). In the case of verse speeches (and at the beginning of sections of prose) the speakers' names are centred, even in the case of the single-couplet fortunes of the antimasque (in B 582–637) and the single lines of a song divided between several singers in the conclusion (B 985–92). If this feature was in the copy, this must have been of some graphic elaboration. Lastly, all verse speeches and songs (except single couplets), and sometimes sections of prose as well, begin with plain two-line initials.

### Characteristics of $D^2$

Naturally, when setting up the cancel sheets from a fresh manuscript, Okes's compositor generally followed the style of $D^1$. There are, however, some differences that may be credited to the influence of the copy. Casual italicizing may be a little heavier throughout, but only noticeably so towards the end. What is remarkable is the use of italic through long passages of the text, as in the Cock Lorel ballad (not in $D^1$) and the songs of the conclusion (B 62–5 are not in $D^2$). Neither of the Patrico's long speeches is present, nor is the first song by the Jackman. The Cock Lorel ballad is divided into stanzas, as it always is: stanzas are separated in the Countess of Buckingham's fortune, but not in the King's or Prince's. Speakers' names are centred much as they are in $D^1$, but not in the case of the divided song (the couplet-fortunes do not appear). Two-line initials are used, but there is only one (instead of ten) in the conclusion. Both these differences may be due to the fact that towards the end the compositor found himself rather pressed for space. The introduction of an alternative passage due to revision at Belvoir (B $908^{1-12}$) is rather awkwardly managed. There is no indication that the manuscript used was calligraphic, though the italicizing of the songs suggests some elaboration.

### Characteristics of F

The printer of F may, of course, have been acquainted with $D^b$, and the slight textual indication that he was (see notes on W 264–7 and W 1243) is at first sight borne out by certain typographical resemblances between the two editions. It should be the easier to decide which of them are due to imitation in that the close relationship between F and N often helps us to determine in what respects F was following its source. There are, however, limits to the inferences we can draw. One in particular concerns the use of italic, when this is more than incidental. For the heavy script adopted in N for purposes of differentiation was not suited to extended use, and we cannot, therefore, argue that because the lavish use of italic in F finds no counterpart in N, it was not a feature of their common original. It is true that in their use of italic $D^b$ and F are very similar. Like $D^b(D^1)$, F italicizes the four lines B 62–5, and like $D^b(D^2)$ it italicizes the songs in the conclusion (with the probably accidental exception of the fourth) and the Cock Lorel ballad. It even carries the practice further, for it prints in italic the Patrico's speeches of welcome (B 551–71) and farewell (B 639–49) in the antimasque, which $D^b(D^1)$ prints in roman. But here we come across a remarkable peculiarity. Although both the Cock Lorel ballad and the Patrico's speeches are italicized, yet in the former the first word or two of each stanza and in the latter most of the rime-words are roman; and we find a corresponding distinction in the script of N. There is nothing analogous in any other text. There can be no doubt that in this peculiarity F was following its source, and it follows that it was most likely following it likewise in italicizing the passages, and if these passages, then probably the other verses similarly treated. There seems, therefore, no reason to suppose that in its use of italic F was imitating, and extending, the practice of $D^b$. And the same is true in respect of two-line initials, in the use of which F is again more lavish than any other text. There are occasionally larger initials in N, but they are too sporadic to give any indication of the practice of the source. Two-line initials are, of course, a feature both of $D^1$ and $D^2$; but we note that in the conclusion, whereas the initials of $D^1$ were discarded in $D^2$, they were restored by F, and moreover that F introduced initials of its own in the numbered stanzas of the blessing of the senses and likewise in its arbitrary divisions of the entrance and restitution speeches. So far as the evidence goes F might be imitating and extending the practice of $D^b$, or following that of its source. Perhaps, however, it is sufficient to remark that in the matter of initials, and incidentally of italics too, F is only carrying on a typographical practice already established in the earlier masques of the collection. Nor elsewhere is there any specific evidence of the influence of $D^b$. F introduces the Belvoir alternative at the end of the antimasque in the same clumsy manner as $D^2$; but N does so too, and in the introduction of two earlier Windsor alternatives (not in $D^b$) F shows itself clumsier still. F does not centre the speakers' names either in the fortune-couplets (as does $D^b(D^1)$) or in the broken song (where they are centred in $D^1$ but not in $D^2$), and there are a few other instances in which it departs from the practice of the other printed texts. F and N alike recognize only the first three of the eight paragraphs into which $D^b(D^1)$ divides the entrance speech: the restitution speech, continuous in $D^b(D^1)$, is divided in two by F and N, perhaps merely representing the turn of a page in the source (in H a fresh page happens to begin at the same point). In both speeches some lines are indented (which they are not in $D^b$), and some similar, but not identical, indenting appears both in N and H. Full stanzaic division is found only in the Cock Lorel ballad: the stanzas of the Jackman's song are indicated by indentation but are not separated; there is no stanzaic division in the fortunes. In these respects both N and H agree with F.

## Characteristics of N

MS. Harley 4955 is a folio volume filled with transcripts of various items in verse and prose, evidently prepared for some member of the Cavendish family, probably William, later Earl of Newcastle. It contains many compositions by Jonson, masques, poems, and letters, which fall into three sections separated by other matter: fols. 2–55, including the Gipsy masque and the Blackfriars entertainment, and fols. 173–82 and 192–204, including respectively the entertainments at Welbeck and Bolsover. The earliest items that can be dated belong to 1620, the latest to 1634: the volume was probably completed before 1640. There is more than one hand in the manuscript, but all the Jonson items were written by the same scribe, who was responsible for the bulk of the collection. While, however, all are in the same hand, and this shows no appreciable variation, the calligraphic style of the earlier and later items differs in that the clumsy Italian lettering used for purposes of differentiation in the former is in the latter replaced by a much more elegant semi-gothic script, though this is still a little too heavy for the accompanying text.

The manuscript is calligraphic, and it has some peculiar features. Intersecting rules make a wide margin at the head and on the left of each page. The latter is usually blank, but is used for speakers' names in prose and on the rare occasions in verse when they are not centred. The top margin usually contains the name 'Beniamin Iohnson' in the large Italian script (gothic in the case of the later entertainments), and when, as occasionally happens, this is displaced by a heading or direction of some sort, the name is written in lighter script in the top left canton. The hand is a very regular and rather beautiful one, purely Italian (except for final secretary -*e*) and eminently legible (except for the close resemblance of certain letters, particularly *o* and *r* and *v* and final *e* and *t*).[1] In the masque

---

[1] The writer had the not altogether unusual peculiarity of using the contraction 'p̃', not only correctly for *per* and *par*, but also incorrectly for *pre* and *pro*. Thus he writes: w 41, 210 p̃seru'd *for* preseru'd, 346 p̃mise *for* promise, 430 p̃uided *for*

the script used for differential purposes (where italic would be employed in print) is also Italian in character, but much larger, heavier, and more formal. The manuscript would be an extremely handsome one were not its appearance marred by this inordinately prominent 'italic', which gives the page a blotchy look and often shows through the paper, obscuring the writing on the other side.

Another hand has added in the left margin a curious numeration, which runs as follows from fol. 3$^b$ to fol. 29$^a$:

3. 51 *to* 8. 56; I. p. 57, 2. 58 *to* 8. 64; K. pma. 65, 2. 66 *to* 8. 72; L. pma. 73, 2. 74 *to* 7. 79.

The second numerals correspond with the page-numbers of the 1641 Folio (F) and the letters show the first numerals to be the page-numbers of the several quires (H–L in fours) of the same, 'p' or 'pma' standing of course for (*pagina*) *prima*. The writing seems later than that of the text, but the form of the abbreviations shows that it is not modern, and the manuscript must have been compared with the Folio at some time probably before the end of the seventeenth century. There is, of course, no possibility of the Folio having been printed from the manuscript, still less of the manuscript having been copied from the Folio.

The features that persist throughout the volume cannot, of course, derive from the original of the masque. It is otherwise with those that N has in common with F, and these have been already sufficiently discussed in dealing with that text. The earlier revisional alternatives are written in the margin much as they are in H, but lack the explanatory headings there supplied. The last one (B 908$^{1-12}$) is inserted in the text as it is in F. In both cases N doubtless reproduced its copy exactly. The general impression we get from a comparison of N and F is of a rather elaborately, if not very intelligently, written original, possibly of a calligraphic character.

## *Characteristics of* H

I have reserved to the last our most important authority, the Heber-Huntington manuscript. This is misbound, and the quires seem to have been in their present incorrect order when it was in the Bridgewater library, for on what is now the first page, at the head of which stands the direction 'The Gypsyes chang'd' (W 1087), there is a note believed to have been written by the second Earl of Bridgewater *c.* 1640, 'This should have been bound at y$^e$ end of y$^e$ Gypsies Metamorposed' (*sic*). On the same page is the press-mark '|8.|2|$^b$' (repeated on the verso), but on what is now page 17, which bears the heading 'The Gypsies metamorphos'd' (W 21), there is another press-mark

prouided, 967 pferre *for* preferre, 1069 ptest *for* protest. I record these in the collations, but take no further notice of them. In general his use of contractions is not only frequent but loose, e.g. 'y$^e$' and 'y$^{ee}$' commonly stand for 'ye' and 'yee' instead of 'the' and 'thee', and 'y$^r$' may mean 'your' or 'their'.

# Versions and Texts

'⌊8.⌋ᴸ·ᴵ·'. Evidently there was at some time a confusion between the heading and the direction, and the two parts were apparently once treated as separate tracts and later bound up in reverse order. But the confusion is, in fact, much greater than this would indicate. There is a pencil numbering of the *pages* (5 to 61) in the order in which they now appear, and also a pencil numbering of the *leaves* (1–29) in the correct order of the text. The correspondence between the two is shown in the accompanying table. From this it is easy to deduce that the manuscript was written on seven quarto sheets (or at any rate on seven four-leaf quires) with one odd leaf at the end, which we may designate as a–g and (g)+1, and that these actually occur in the order g(+1) a b f e d c. Thus only one pair retain their original order: the last (with its odd leaf) stands first, then come the first and second, followed by the four others in reverse order. All that the note on the first page attempts to do is to correct the position of g(+1). The leaves vary appreciably in size and in an apparently arbitrary manner,¹ in height from a little over 18 to a little over 20 cm. and in width from under 14 to nearly 18 cm.

The manuscript is carefully written in a clear but current hand.² It is ostensibly a secretary hand but has a large admixture of Italian forms. For purposes of differentiation an elegant and purely Italian script is used, which, however, in single words is not always

---

¹ In some cases, but not all, the wider leaves are designed to accommodate marginal additions.

² It seldom presents any difficulty to the reader, but one or two points deserve notice. The letters 'n' and 'u' are on the whole fairly well distinguished; but the scribe occasionally writes what appears to be a distinct 'n' in place of 'u', as in w 901 'clouen' and w 913 'caruer'. I have taken no notice of such aberrations. For final -(e)s he uses four distinct symbols. The secretary and Italian forms of -s are used indifferently (in words not otherwise 'italic') and he also uses the contractions 'ʃ' and 'ę' fairly consistently for -es. But neither contraction is carefully formed. The 'ʃ', though sometimes clear, tends to be truncated and merges imperceptibly into the Italian -s, so that it is sometimes doubtful which was intended, and doubtful whether the writer was fully conscious of the distinction. Similarly 'ę' tends to be written small, in which case it comes to resemble an Italian -e. This is not of much consequence, since the scribe hardly ever uses the Italian -e, though there is one clearly formed example at w 410 'bringe'. It is possible that he himself occasionally got confused, for at w 752–3 he wrote 'handkercheifę' where the singular is clearly intended.

| Pagination | Foliation | Foliation | Pagination |
|---|---|---|---|
| 61 | 12 | 29 | 13 |
| 59 | 11 | 28 | 11 |
| 57 | 10 | 27 | 9 |
| 55 | 9 | 26 | 7 |
| 53 | 16 | 25 | 5 |
| 51 | 15 | 24 | 37 |
| 49 | 14 | 23 | 35 |
| 47 | 13 | 22 | 33 |
| 45 | 20 | 21 | 31 |
| 43 | 19 | 20 | 45 |
| 41 | 18 | 19 | 43 |
| 39 | 17 | 18 | 41 |
| 37 | 24 | 17 | 39 |
| 35 | 23 | 16 | 53 |
| 33 | 22 | 15 | 51 |
| 31 | 21 | 14 | 49 |
| 29 | 8 | 13 | 47 |
| 27 | 7 | 12 | 61 |
| 25 | 6 | 11 | 59 |
| 23 | 5 | 10 | 57 |
| 21 | 4 | 9 | 55 |
| 19 | 3 | 8 | 29 |
| 17 | 2 | 7 | 27 |
| 15 | 1 | 6 | 25 |
| 13 | 29 | 5 | 23 |
| 11 | 28 | 4 | 21 |
| 9 | 27 | 3 | 19 |
| 7 | 26 | 2 | 17 |
| 5 | 25 | 1 | 15 |

clearly distinguishable from that of the text. In this are written the sometimes elaborate headings and directions, speakers' names, and many words in the text. Among the last are, of course, proper names and the like, but also a wide range of other words: indeed, the distinction is arbitrary and even haphazard, and seems devoid of significance. In keeping with this is the almost complete lack of punctuation. In spite of the beauty, in parts, of the writing and the elaborate display of the directions, the manuscript is not markedly calligraphic, and the want of care shown in punctuation, combined with the untidiness of the oddly shaped leaves, make it doubtful whether it can have been intended as a presentation copy. It was undoubtedly transcribed (not always accurately) from a good original; otherwise the chief characteristic of the text is its careful editing, as in the assignment of the revisional passages to the occasions for which they were written, and in the note respecting the substitution of the Lords' fortunes for the Ladies'. These do not appear to derive from the copy, but were probably added by the scribe from his own knowledge of the circumstances, and he seems to have edited some of the directions in a like manner (see w 501–6, note). There were, however, limits to his editorial knowledge and care, for he certainly misplaced the Lord Chamberlain's fortune, bungled the beginning of one of the speeches (w 838, note), omitted to correct two lines that he had copied in the wrong order (w 186–7), and left out a couplet necessary to the sense (w 1149–50).

In the casual use of 'italic' H is more lavish than any other text: on the other hand (as in N), no longer passages are italicized. It agrees with $D^1$ in the paragraphing of the entrance speech and in making the restitution speech (apparently) continuous: on the other hand, it agrees with N and F in indenting some, though not always the same, lines in these speeches.[1] In its division of stanzas and its treatment of speakers' names H agrees with N and F.[2] There are some larger initials, but they are neither frequent nor prominent, and have no obvious relation to those of the printed texts.

The edges of some of the leaves have been trimmed and letters or even words lost at the end of certain lines. On one occasion at least this was done before the manuscript left the hands of the writer, for he repeated a mutilated word (see w 121–2, note).

Not much, it would seem, can be inferred regarding the character

---

[1] In the entrance speech the indenting is identical in N and H; in the restitution speech the relation is much more complicated, though there is a general similarity.

[2] HNF tend not to centre speakers' names in the later portions of the text. Instances are w 767 (centred in $D^1$, omitted in NF), w 838 (centred in $D^2$, omitted in NF), w 849 (centred in $D^2$), w 952 (centred in $D^2$), w 984 (centred in $D^2$), and w 1071 (centred in $D^2$). This must be a feature of the source of the composite texts, and the persistent centring in $D^2$ is presumably due to the compositor's following the practice of $D^1$.

# Versions and Texts

of any of the manuscripts used as copy. N is certainly calligraphic, and even allowing that some elaboration in F may be due to imitation of $D^b$, there remains sufficient likeness between it and N to suggest that their common source $f$ may have been of like character. It is clear that some peculiar features, such as the paragraphing and indenting of at least one of the longer verse speeches, must go back to an early, though not perhaps to the earliest, stage. The general centring of speakers' names was the usual practice in masques, and is doubtless original. The length to which it is carried in $D^1$ may have been an individual peculiarity.[1]

NOTE ON THE NAMES OF THE CLOWNS AND WENCHES

In his introduction to the masque Simpson writes as follows (p. 558):

> The Folio and Duodecimo texts differ in their treatment of the Clowns and Wenches, who supply something in the nature of an antimasque. Originally they paired off as Prudence and Francis, Cicely and Harry, Roger and Mary, Peg of the dairy (who is not provided with a partner), Maudlin and Thomas; these names survive in the text at lines 814–18 [i.e. B 562–6 = W 616–20]. At Windsor they become Tom Clod, Dick Townshead, Jack Cockrell, and Paul Puppy, and the wenches are localized as Prudence of the Park, Francis of the Castle, Long Meg of Eton, and Christian of Dorney. The original version is preserved in the Duodecimo.[2]

Now this is, to say the least, misleading. Apart from the 'localization' of the Wenches, an obvious Windsor modification, and the fact that at Windsor they were given speaking parts, the Duodecimo ($D^1$) agrees substantially with the Folio (and indeed with all the other texts) and does not differ, as implied, in the names and numbers of the Clowns and Wenches introduced. At W 504–5 H has 'enter y$^e$ Clownes. Cockrell. Clod. Towneshead Puppy', and the other texts have a corresponding direction at a slightly later point: these names are, moreover, confirmed and the Christian names supplied in the text in all authorities alike. At Windsor the entry of the Wenches is thus described in H (W 581–6):

*Clod* ... see where the minstrell$_e$ come [*read* minstrell comes] ...
*Coc* I and all the good wenches of windsor after him   yonders
   Prue ô the parke
*Town* And Francis ô the Castle

---

[1] It should, however, be noticed that in N the speaker's name to the first of the couplet-fortunes is centred, and that to the fourth is written as though it were part of the text. It would be curious if these irregularities were accidental, and it is at least possible that $f$ retained traces of an arrangement such as we find in $D^1$, traces that have been completely eliminated in H and F.

[2] Simpson presumably means the Duodecimo as originally printed ($D^a$), not as later published ($D^b$).

## Introduction

*Pup* And longe Meg of Eaton
*Clod* And Christian ô Dorney . . .

This, peculiar to the Windsor version, appears also in N and F (D² is absent) and the names (but not the localizations) are confirmed in the text, in which the Wenches have speaking parts. In D¹ the Wenches are not formally introduced at all, and they take no part in the dialogue, but they are all named in the text, and their names are the same as in the distinctively Windsor texts.[1] Thus the evidence for the names of the Clowns and Wenches is the same in all texts, and the fact that they were already assigned before any of the distinctively Windsor alterations were introduced affords a strong presumption that they remained unchanged throughout.

What, then, is Simpson's ground for supposing that the characters were renamed when the Windsor version was prepared? It is to be found, as he indicates, in a passage of the Patrico's speech of welcome to the country lads and lasses. This is substantially the same in all texts: H reads:

> and tell you some chances
> in midst of yo$^r$ dances
> that fortune aduances
> to Prudence or Francis
> to Sisley or Harry
> to Roger or Mary
> or Peg of the Dairie
> to Maudlin or Thomas . . .

In place of 'Peg', D¹ has 'Meg'. It is argued that these must have been the names originally borne by the Clowns and Wenches, since it is to them that the speech is addressed.[2]

Now, although rigid logical consistency should not be sought in compositions of this kind, let us for a moment look at the matter from the dramatic point of view. In D¹, so far as the text is concerned, only two Christian names have been mentioned up to this point, Tom and Dick, and no hint has been given even of the presence of the Wenches.[3]

---

[1] Concerning the anomalous 'Maudlin' in D¹ (B 690) see below, p. 24.

[2] Cole (p. 237) has another explanation. Rejecting Gifford's identification of the names as those of 'other Clowns' and 'other wenches', he suggests that they may be those of lords and ladies of the court: 'it is noteworthy that "Sisely" corresponds to Cecily Manners, Countess of Rutland, and "Frances" to either Frances Coke, Lady Purbeck, or Frances, Countess of Exeter . . . Cecily's husband was "Roger," but the name suggests rather Roger Palmer, cupbearer to Prince Charles. Considering the allusion in "the Kate and the Mary" [B 203] to the Marchioness and Countess of Buckingham, and the Patrico's line about making the court ladies "turn Gipsies" [B 193], it is possible that the song [? speech] represents a design abandoned in the final stages of preparation.' Ingenious, but hardly worth serious consideration. I think he comes nearer the mark when he suggests that the names in the list probably 'indicate an original cast for which other names in part were substituted' in the course of composition.

[3] Cockrell has also been named, and so have Tom Ticklefoot and Cheeks, but

It is therefore dramatically impossible that the Patrico should know the names of more than two of the country folk, unless the Gipsies are a local band already acquainted with the neighbouring yokels. But this they cannot be, for Townshead is the only one who recognizes them for Gipsies at all. It would appear, then, that in his list the Patrico is merely stringing together names that might fit his audience, and this is confirmed by his addressing the girls (w 605–6) in obviously generic terms as

>Sweet doxies and dells
>My Roses and Nells . . .

Notice, too, that he promises fortunes, not to Prudence *and* Francis, but to Prudence *or* Francis, and so on: he might have added 'or whatever your names may be'.

It might further be objected that if the list was intended to give the actual names of the Clowns and Wenches, and that these were altered between the Burley and Windsor performances, the list, too, would have been altered or suppressed. This argument, however, is weakened by the fact that several passages that we know must have been omitted at Windsor, yet appear without indication of the fact in the composite texts.

It is clear that if Simpson's view is correct D¹ does not faithfully reproduce the text of the original performance. This is, of course, inconsistent with what he himself says of it. In one place (p. 541) he writes (not quite accurately) that D¹ 'gave the Burley and Belvoir versions' and that 'Virtually the text of the first two performances must have been the same'; and in another (p. 552) that 'Benson began by securing the text of the original performance at Burley-on-the-Hill'. And this view is borne out by the evidence. D¹ contains none of the passages that H assigns to Windsor or that internal evidence connects with it, and generally offers a manifestly earlier state of the text than any other authority. Indeed, its text appears to be even earlier than that of the Burley–Belvoir performances, since it omits the fortune of a late arrival, the Countess of Exeter, which was certainly spoken at Belvoir and probably at Burley. Thus the manuscript from which D¹ was printed was almost certainly written before the Burley performance and very likely as a presentation copy on that occasion. How, then, should it contain an early revision of the antimasque made for the Windsor performance? It would seem that Simpson failed to consider the implications of his theory.

We should have to suppose that this early copy of the original version remained in Jonson's hands, or else was returned to them, and that he used it as the basis for a first draft of the Windsor version of the antimasque, while leaving it otherwise untouched. This revision

these last are out of the picture. What has happened in the Windsor version is irrelevant, since it is at Burley that the Clowns and Wenches are alleged to have borne the names mentioned by the Patrico.

presumably involved more than the pointless substitution of one set of names for another, mostly different; for the numbers of the Clowns and Wenches were altered, and incidentally reduced. At the same time the Patrico's speech was left standing though it had become inconsistent with the dialogue. The assumption cannot, of course, be disproved; but it appears rather far-fetched, and it is, I believe, unnecessary. Incidentally, I would point out that it is much more likely that a presentation copy should many years later have found its way into Benson's possession, than that he should have had access to a manuscript that remained in Jonson's hands.

Let us look closer at the Patrico's list and get the facts clear. He mentions five girls' names, Prudence, Cecily, Mary, Peg (or Meg), and Maudlin, and four boys' names, Francis, Harry, Roger, and Thomas; but he leaves Peg unpaired, so that—if they are really the names of characters, but not otherwise—there was probably a fifth boy unnamed. In the text there are only four pairs, and the directions leave no doubt that these were all that appeared. All authorities agree upon their names: there are the girls, Prudence, Francis, Meg, and Christian, and the boys, Tom Clod, Dick Townshead, Jack Cockrell, and Paul Puppy.

There is no disguising the fact that there is some resemblance between the two groups. Among the girls there is a Prudence (a relatively uncommon name) in both, and among the boys a Thomas (a relatively common name). There is also a Francis in common, but in the list it is the name of a boy and among the characters that of a girl. There is also a Peg in the list (actually Meg in $D^1$) and a Meg in the text, both of course pet forms of Margaret. Lastly, a Maudlin appears in the list, and once inconsistently in the text of $D^1$ (B 690). The correspondence is not very impressive, but is hardly likely to be due to chance coincidence. Undoubtedly the most striking point is the last, and it would afford strong support to Simpson's case if we could argue that in this instance the name Maudlin was accidentally left standing in the text when the others were altered. But we cannot so argue; for the character called on a single occasion Maudlin in $D^1$ is the one elsewhere, both in that text and the others, called Meg, and if we are to equate the characters with the names in the list at all, Meg must be identified with Peg (actually called Meg in $D^1$). It follows that in $D^1$ Maudlin cannot be a survival from the original version, but must owe its appearance to some confusion—presumably a subconscious reminiscence of the list. It is therefore without evidential value.

How, then, are we to account for the occasional similarity of the names of the characters and those mentioned in the list? The explanation I suggest is this. We must not assume that the text was always written straight ahead in the order in which it now appears. Jonson may have composed the Patrico's speech before the prose portions of the antimasque had taken shape. He may have meant the speech, addressed to the Clowns and Wenches, to give their actual names, or he may have merely intended that it should supply a list of likely names from which he could later choose any he might require. When he came to write the prose portions he, in fact, chose for the most part different names; but he left the Patrico's speech standing with a list of fanciful but plausible names reeled off by the speaker on the spur of the moment when he could not in the nature of things know the real names of those he was addressing. The alternatives Peg and Meg and Francis's change of sex are suggestive of some such semi-dependence. Maudlin in $D^1$ I take to be an original slip, corrected in the archetype of the composite texts. Jonson, having decided to call the character Meg, in a moment of confusion accidentally substituted another name from the list. And in much the same way Meg replaced Peg in the list, either in $D^1$ itself or in its copy.

On this view the change from the names in the list to those found in the text occurred, not in the preparation of the Windsor version, but in course of the original composition. Simpson would not be by any means the first to have mistaken inconsistencies of composition for evidence of subsequent revision. That Jonson sometimes altered his intention in the course of writing, or that he did not trouble to change what he had written when circumstances altered, is shown by the name Charles given to the Gipsy Captain (w 74), presumably in expectation that the part would be played by the Prince, whereas it eventually fell to George Villiers.

I therefore see no reason whatever to doubt that in $D^a$, so far as it survives, we have the original text of the masque as it was performed at Burley on 3 August 1621, with the sole exception probably of its omission of the Countess of Exeter's fortune.

## II. MAIN DIFFERENCES BETWEEN THE VERSIONS

The only surviving text of the masque as originally presented at Burley is that preserved in $D^a$, and this is imperfect owing to the loss of four leaves from the unique Cambridge copy. All the other authorities, $D^b$, H, N, and F, include alterations made in the text for the Belvoir and Windsor performances, and it is only after we have ascertained at least the general nature and scope of these alterations that we can hope to form an idea of the probable contents of the missing leaves of $D^a$.

The text of the masque, in all authorities except $D^a$, is a composite one, in which the original Burley version has been expanded and overlaid by subsequent additions and alterations, so that besides the later accretions it includes the whole of the original version with the exception of a few passages that were recast in such a manner that it would have been difficult to retain both drafts. Sometimes, as I have said, the original passage is suppressed in favour of the revision; sometimes, it would appear, passages of the original are allowed to stand that cannot have formed part of the later performances; sometimes the original and revised versions appear side by side (or in the inferior authorities conflated into a continuous text). The most important substitution, that of the Lords' fortunes for the Ladies', is notified only in H, and H is likewise the only authority that is at all explicit concerning other alternatives.

For the detection of additions and alterations we have three sources of information: (1) specific statements in H, supported as a rule by less clear indications in N and by confused hints in $D^2$ and F; (2) differences between $D^1$ and the composite texts amounting to more than mere verbal variants (unavailable, of course, where $D^a$ is defective); and (3) internal evidence where the composite versions have taken over without alteration passages containing allusions only appropriate to Burley or Belvoir, or alternatively where they contain allusions only appropriate to Windsor. All evidence concurs to indicate that the alterations made for the Windsor performance were far more extensive than those at Belvoir, and we may as a rule assume that unassigned alterations were first introduced in the Windsor version.

### THE BELVOIR VERSION

We naturally open our inquiry with the alterations made for the production at Belvoir. $D^1$ begins with a speech by the Porter headed simply 'At the Kings Entrance',[1] which is not, strictly speaking, part of the masque at all. It is Buckingham's personal welcome to James and obviously can only have been spoken at his house at Burley.

In $D^1$ the Patrico's entrance speech includes the lines (B 130–40):

> There's a Gentry Cove here,
> Is the top of the shire,

---

[1] H specifies 'at Burly'; F has 'The Speech at the Kings Entrance at Burleigh', but N reverts to the simple form of $D^1$, which suggests individual elaboration in H and F. $D^2$ is absent.

> Of the Beaver-Ken,
> A man amongst men:
> Yee neede not to feare,
> I've an eye, and an eare,
> That turnes here and there,
> To looke to our geere:
> Some say that there be
> One or two, if not three,
> That are greater than he.

Opposite the beginning of this passage, which forms a distinct paragraph or stanza in all texts, H adds in the margin, and with the heading 'At Beauer', the couplet:

> There be Gentry Coues here
> Are the Cheife of the shire.[1]

These two lines must be meant to replace the first four of the original version, since 'A man' cannot refer to the plural 'Coves'; furthermore, the last three lines of the stanza also require a singular antecedent, and must have been omitted when the alteration was made.[2] The original version refers, of course, to the Earl of Rutland; the revised version refers to the local magnates generally, and thus finds its parallel in the 'Room-morts' or great ladies of the next stanza (B 141). The point of the allusion at Burley and the reason for its alteration at Belvoir (where the original would seem more appropriate) are not altogether clear, and are discussed in the notes; but of the fact and nature of the revision there is no doubt.

The Countess of Exeter's fortune (B 406–17) is not in $D^1$. Admittedly her arrival was unexpected and a fortune had to be provided for her at short notice. Simpson (p. 542) thinks this was added at Belvoir; but, as Cole (p. 23) observes, its absence from $D^1$ is, in the circumstances, no proof that it was not spoken at Burley. Certainty is not possible, but the appearance of the fortune in Con, which purports to represent the Burley performance, is in favour of its having been spoken there.[3]

---

[1] The lines are also in N, written in the margin, but without heading: F omits them: $D^2$ is still absent.

[2] These three lines are indented in H, N, and F; but there is no significance in this, for a number of other lines are similarly indented in the same texts.

[3] According to Simpson (p. 542) the Countess of Exeter's fortune 'is not found in either state of [the Duodecimo] text', but this is an error disproved by his own collations. Equally mistaken and at variance with his collations is his further statement (ibid.) that the Countess of Rutland's fortune (B 388–405) is not in $D^1$, an oversight on which he bases the picturesque theory that 'As hostess during the second party she had naturally stayed at home to prepare for it' (see, however, the note on B 393).

Just before the Gipsies' metamorphosis the Patrico has a passage of fifteen lines (B 908–22: the first five are lost in D¹) 'For he we call chiefe ... We are one mans all', in praise of their Captain and enlarging on Buckingham's hospitality. (That Buckingham played the Captain, implicit in these lines, is explicitly stated in Con.) These lines, we learn from H, were replaced at Belvoir by nine others, recording the date, 'The fifte of August', and instead praising Rutland, 'the good man of Beuer, our Buckinghams father', father-in-law, that is. Moreover, the lines that follow, spoken on Friday,

> Make it a jolly night,
> If not a Holly night,

were on Sunday replaced by

> then so much the rather
> make it a iolly night
> for t'is a holie night

a version so much more to the point that we cannot but suppose it to be the original, and the Burley an adaptation; which means that the Belvoir variants must have been written as part of the original draft, as is indeed inherently probable.¹

These are the only Belvoir alterations recognized in H or the other composite texts. But earlier in the same speech of the Patrico's occurs the line (B 897),

> Here at Burlye o'th' Hill,

which obviously can have been spoken nowhere else, though it is found, without note, in all the composite texts (D¹ is here defective). It is, however, a parenthetical line, and there are several riming with it, so that it could be omitted without disturbing the text. Similarly unnoticed, we find at the end of the Jackman's first song the lines (B 118–19),

> For though we be here at Burly,
> We'd be loath to make a Hurly.

(So D¹, but all texts agree.) These lines too can only have been sung at the first performance. The couplet can be

---

¹ In H the 12 (9+3) substitute lines, headed 'At Beuer' and with '&c'.' at the end, are written in the margin opposite B 908–20. The close repetition of B 923–4 marks the end of the passage to be replaced, and the position of the heading in fact corresponds to what internal evidence suggests must have been the beginning. N inserts the first 10 lines into the text as a new paragraph after B 922, with a marginal 'Beuer' opposite the third and fourth; after which it continues with the Burley text, but brackets B 923–4 and adds in the margin 'Be: for tis a holye night'. D² and F have the same arrangement, except that they centre 'Bever' as if it were a speaker's name and substitute the Belvoir for the Burley variant in B 924.

omitted without damage to the text, but since it might be more difficult to fit the truncated stanza to the music, it is possible that the whole of the last quatrain was sacrificed at Belvoir. It is the more remarkable that this allusion to Burley should have been left unnoticed, since only a few lines before a trifling Windsor variant at B 111 was duly recorded (see p. 30). We may perhaps conclude that in the original of the composite version certain lines were marked as having been omitted either at Belvoir or Windsor by some sign that was consistently ignored in preparing the extant texts.

### THE WINDSOR VERSION

We now pass to the more extensive changes made in preparation for the performance at Windsor. The double performance at Burley and Belvoir must clearly have been provided for when planning the progress, and the necessary alternatives were presumably written at the time of the original composition. The only later addition was the Countess of Exeter's fortune, and this may actually have been written between the performances, supposing it to have been first spoken at Belvoir. The later performance at Windsor was probably no part of the original plan but a repetition by royal command.[1] We may conclude, therefore, that the revised version was taken in hand in the latter part of August. The revision, however, does not appear to have been carried out all of a piece. The bulk of it appears in H, but as we shall see in the next section, further alterations seem to have been made that are found only in $D^2$ and N and F, and yet others confined to N and F. Here we are only concerned with the main revision as it appears in H.

Naturally the passages peculiar to Burley, which were omitted or altered at Belvoir, must also have been omitted or altered at Windsor.

It will be convenient to deal first with the most important change introduced at Windsor, since several other minor alterations follow from it. H alone, in a note after B 480, records that

> At Windsor in place of the Ladies
> fortunes were spoken theise following
> of the Lordes.

We know, of course, from their absence from $D^1$ that the Lords' fortunes were not in the original version of the masque,

[1] See, however, p. 32, note 2.

but this note is our only direct evidence that they were a substitute for, and not a supplement to, those of the Ladies.[1]

The rest of the changes may be taken in order. The Porter's speech of welcome, already no doubt omitted at Belvoir, was replaced by the 'Prologue at Windsor' that follows it in H but precedes it in N and F.

The next change is in the Jackman's opening song. The original text has (B 108–11):

> Knacks we have that will delight you,
> Slights of hand that will invite you,
> To endure our tawny faces,
> And not cause you cut your laces

that is to say, without fainting—cutting the laces of an Elizabethan bodice being the equivalent of unfastening Victorian stays. Of course, when the Lords' fortunes replaced the Ladies', the phrase no longer applied, and the line was altered to read

> And not cause you quit your places

that is, run away for fear—a few lines below the Jackman begs his audience to 'sit still, we will not fray you'.[2] At the end of the song the allusion to Burley must, of course, have been suppressed at Windsor as well as at Belvoir.

In the Patrico's speech that follows several changes were made. At B 130 ff. the alternative that H ascribes to Belvoir would fit as well, or almost as well, at Windsor, and we may perhaps conclude that it was made to do duty again with the same consequential omission. Two later passages allude specifically to the Ladies and were altered when the Lords took their place. The first runs in D¹ (B 187–93):

> Or what will you say now,
> If with our fine play now,

---

[1] The fact could indeed have been inferred, if obscurely, from the confused record of the dances (see pp. 46–9) and from certain of the other changes made at Windsor.

[2] In H the words 'cut your laces' are underlined (not italicized as they are by Cole and Simpson) and in the left margin is written

> {windsor quit yo$^r$ places}

The alternative is similarly placed in N, but reads

> : wo: quit y$^r$ places:

and there is no underlining, so that the meaning is less clear. In F the readings have been conflated into one unintelligible line:

> Wo. Quit your places, and not cause you cut your laces.

## Main Differences between the Versions

> Our Knackets, and Dances,
> We worke on the fancies
> Of some o' these Nancies,
> These Trickets, and Tripsies,
> And make 'hem turn Gipsies.

For these lines H provides the following marginal substitute (w 173–80):

> At windsor
> or what will you say now⟨e
> if w^th o^r fine play nowe
> o^r feates and o^r fingering
> here without lingering
> cousening the sight℮
> of the lords & the knigh⟨ts
> some one of theire Georges
> come of to saue charges[1]

The Patrico's speech concludes in D¹ as follows (B 201–7):

> But be wise and wary
> And we may both carry
> The Kate, and the Mary,
> And all the bright Aery
> Away to the Quarry,
> If our brave Ptolomee
> Will but say follow me.

(Kate and Mary were the names of the Marchioness and Countess of Buckingham.) Of this paragraph the first two lines were allowed to stand: for the rest H provides the substitute (w 190–201):

> At windsor
> the George & the garter
> into o^r owne quarter
> or durst I goe farder
> in methode & order
> theres a purse & a seale
> I'haue a great minde to steale
> that when o^r trick℮ are done
> wee might seale o^r owne pd⟨on
> all this we may doe
> and a greate deale more to⟨o

---

[1] These lines are written, rather small, in the right margin opposite B 187–93, with the heading on a line with 186. The identity of the first couplet confirms the point at which the substitution should begin: the extent of the cancelled passage depends on internal evidence, but evidently the whole of the paragraph or stanza was meant to go. In N the marginal passage, without heading, is written opposite B 181–8: in F it is clumsily inserted into the text immediately before the lines it should replace. D² is absent.

> If o<sup>r</sup> braue Ptolomęe
> will but say followe me[1]

The next two alterations reveal themselves only through comparison between D¹ and the later texts (D² is now available), for these contain no indication that their text is not original. There is no proof that the additions were not made at Belvoir, but probability is in favour of Windsor. In the Burley version the second part of the King's fortune, after the song, consists of three six-line stanzas (B 288–305) followed by a triplet:

> This little from so short a view,
> I tell, and as a teller true
> Of Fortunes, but their Maker, sir, are you.

In the later version these three lines are replaced by a further three stanzas (w 301–18). In like fashion the Prince's fortune, which originally occupied four six-line stanzas (B 312–35), was extended to eight (w 322–69: only completely preserved in H).[2]

Next follow the remaining fortunes, those of the Ladies at Burley and Belvoir, those of the Lords at Windsor. These in turn are followed in the composite texts by a duet between the Patrico and the Jackman (w 508–33): it is not in D¹, and

---

[1] These lines are again written small in the right margin: the heading is opposite B 198, and the writing runs to the foot of the page, about two lines below B 207. The repetition of the final couplet shows where the substitution ends, and the point from which it carries on is indicated by a dash at the end of B 202. In N the marginal passage, without heading, is written opposite B 197–204, but again there is a line connecting it with 202: in F it is inserted in the text after B 205, and 206–7 are omitted to avoid duplication. D² is absent.

[2] There is something rather strange about these alleged additions to the King's and the Prince's fortunes, and it could quite plausibly be maintained that the fuller version of the composite texts is, in fact, original, and that given in D¹ an abridgement. Certainly no one reading the longer versions would suspect that they were not written all of a piece. The longer version of the King's fortune is in regular stanzaic form throughout, whereas the shorter breaks off midway, summarizing in an anomalous triplet the thought that is developed in the remaining stanzas of the other. Of course, compression and expansion are equally possible, but it is curious that the stanzas supposedly added in the Windsor version seem, in fact, particularly appropriate to Burley. The Prince's fortune ends very abruptly in the shorter version: the longer carries on not only the thought, but the sentence, without a break. Can there have been some reason why the fortunes as first written had to be curtailed at the original performance? Whatever the truth about the composition, the agreement of D¹ and Con makes it certain that it actually was the shorter version that was spoken at Burley, and it is most unlikely that any change was made at Belvoir. The fuller version was doubtless used at Windsor, where elaboration of the royal fortunes would be appropriate. We need not, however, conclude that the Windsor performance was part of the original plan.

internal evidence shows that it was written for the Windsor performance:

> Come Windsor the Towne
> w<sup>th</sup> the Maior and oppose
> weel put 'em all downe ...

We now come to the antimasque, the most minutely revised portion of the work, as is evident from a comparison of $D^1$ with H (supported in the main by N and F : $D^2$ is for the most part absent). None of the alterations are indicated in the composite texts, and only the most striking can be noticed here. In the Burley version the Wenches had no speaking parts, and though they certainly appeared in time for the Country Dance (B 548) they were not formally introduced and less was made of their presence. In H their entry, which is substituted for a rather colourless passage in $D^1$ (B 530–40) and was clearly written for Windsor, runs as follows (W 581–91):

> *Clod* ... see where the minstrelle come [*read* minstrell comes] ...
> *Coc* I and all the good wenches of windsor after him   yonders Prue ô the parke
> *Town* And Francis ô the Castle
> *Pup* And longe Meg of Eaton
> *Clod* And Christian ô Dorney
> *Town* See the Miracle of a Minstrell
> *Coc* Hee's able to Muster vp the smocks ô the two shires
> *Pup* And sett the Codpeices and they by the eares at pleasure

The end of this passage is adapted from an earlier one that was cut out in revision. In $D^1$, after his call for 'Cheeks upon the Bag-pipes, & Tom Ticklefoot with his Tabor', Puppy continues (B 521–3):

> he could have mustred up the smocks o'th two shires; and set the Codpeices and they by the eares, I wusse ...

Here the two shires are naturally Rutland and Leicester, in which the Burley and Belvoir performances respectively took place. In the revised version the allusion is forced, and is indeed only justified by the fact that some of the Wenches come from Windsor (Berks.) and others across the river from Eton and Dorney (Bucks.).[1] The elaboration of the part played by the Wenches is the outstanding feature in the revision of the antimasque. It is prepared for at W 568–9,

---

[1] Simpson is not quite correct in implying (p. 545, note 3) that the allusion had no point at all at Windsor.

where to his original remark, 'We must have some musick then', Cockrell is made to add 'and take out the wenches' to the dance. And whereas, when the yokels are lamenting their losses, those of the girls were originally described by the Clowns in speeches at B 686, 690, 697, and 701, in revision these speeches were, with the necessary modification, transferred to the Wenches themselves. Not all differences, however, are, it would seem, due to revision. Consider the passage in D¹ (B 674–8):

> *Cock.* What was there i' thy purse? was the Lease of thy house in it?
> *Pup.* Or thy Granams silver Ring?
> *Clod.* No, but a Mill-sixpence of my Mothers, I loved as dearly——

In H (and substantially in the other texts) this reads (w 725–9):

> *Coc* what was there i' thy purse thou keepest such a whimperinge was the lease of thy house in it?
> *Pup* Or thy Grannams siluer ringe
> *Clod* No but a Mill sixpence I lou'd as dearlie . . .

In the first of these speeches 'thou keepest such a whimpering' ('whining' in N F) is an admirable revisional touch, but in the last there can have been no possible reason for cutting out the words 'of my Mothers', and it is safe to assume that their omission in the later texts was accidental. (Simpson very properly restored them.)

The loss of four leaves from Dᵃ deprives us of our basis of comparison from w 811 to 1085: what these leaves may have contained and in what manner the Windsor version may have been expanded (as it certainly was) we shall inquire later.

The survival of B 913–26 after the hiatus in D¹ shows that the Burley version contained the speech by the Patrico immediately before the Gipsies' metamorphosis with which the antimasque concludes; and we may infer that it contained it in substantially the same form as the composite texts, since the mention of 'Burlye o'th' Hill' (B 897) suggests that these reproduced the original version.[1] This line must, of course, have been omitted at Windsor as at Belvoir; but it is not possible to tell for certain what happened to the end of the speech. Neither the original laudation of Buckingham, nor that of Rutland substituted at Belvoir, was suited to the

---

[1] See, however, p. 37, note.

## Main Differences between the Versions

Windsor performance. The words 'he we call Chiefe' (B 908) contain too obvious a reference to the Captain (i.e. Buckingham) for the address to be respectfully transferred to the King, their new host; and though some of what follows might have been made to apply, there is no break in the text where a fresh start could conveniently be made. Most likely the whole passage from B 908 to 926 (as well, of course, as the Belvoir alternative) was omitted. It will be noticed that this meant sacrificing B 919, which at Burley led up to the cry for 'a hall' (that is room for dancing) at B 927 (W 1086); but this had already, it would seem, been sacrificed at Belvoir (see p. 28).

The further speech by the Patrico after the metamorphosis and the dance (W 1090–1118) is not in D¹ and was doubtless a Windsor addition: it explains not only that the Clowns had been played by knights, but also how the parts of the 'lasses' had been taken by 'pages', which is in keeping with the more prominent part played by the Wenches in the Windsor version.

The blessing of the King's senses (W 1119–89) is another addition, doubtless made at Windsor, which does not appear in D¹.

The conclusion of the masque is the same in the two versions; but the Epilogue is an avowed Windsor addition and is of course absent from D¹.

These are the main alterations that can now be detected as having been made in preparation for the performance at Windsor. Cole, impressed by the length of the Windsor additions, suggested (p. 23) that the Cock Lorel ballad was left out, its coarseness making it unsuitable for recitation at the royal court, and that Puppy's words at W 954, 'Sʳ. you are a Prelate of the order', which introduce the Clowns' proposal to join the Gipsies, were written to connect with his earlier question at W 837, 'What sort or order of Gypsie I pray Sʳ', though the two passages do not, in fact, join up very neatly. Now it is true that the performance at Windsor was probably a more public and formal affair than those at Burley and Belvoir, and we shall see (p. 46) that there actually is reason to suppose that two of the dirtier passages in the antimasque were suppressed on that occasion. Nevertheless, it is very unlikely that this immensely popular song, which seems to have proved the main attraction of the masque at Burley, should have been sacrificed. That it was, in fact, retained is also probable from a letter of 27 October 1621, in which Chamberlain, enclosing a copy to Carleton, wrote: 'for lacke of better newes here is likewise a ballet or song of Ben Iohnsons in the play or shew at the lord marquis at Burly, and repeated again at windsor, for w^ch and other goode service there don, he hath his pension from a 100 marks increased to 200^li per annum, besides the reuersion of the mastership of the revells. there were other songs and deuises of baser alay, but because this had the vogue and generall applause at court, I was willing to send yt.'[1] Moreover, if the ballad was not sung at Windsor, for what occasion were the three additional stanzas written (see p. 45)?

Treatment of the Windsor recension must remain incomplete without an analysis of the dances, but this cannot be undertaken till we have considered some further details of revision in the next section (pp. 46–9).

### CONTENTS OF THE MISSING LEAVES OF D^a

Having now got a general picture of the alterations the masque underwent in preparation for the performance at Windsor, we are in a position to inquire into the contents of the four leaves, E5–8, missing from our only copy of D^a. The first point to determine is approximately how many lines they contained. The printing of D^a is far from uniform, and no very close estimate is possible. But we may note that the first four leaves of sig. D contain 162 lines of print, the last four 182, and the first four of sig. E 195;[2] and it will therefore be reasonable to conclude that the missing leaves contained between 150 and 200 lines of print. It might be argued that they are likely to have resembled D9–12 and E1–4 more closely than the remoter D1–4, and that the number of lines they contained is therefore likely to have been nearer the upper than the lower limit. On the other hand, there are usually more lines to the page in prose than in verse, so that if the lost leaves should prove to have been occupied mainly with verse it would tend to reduce the number.

---

[1] S.P.D., James I, cxxiii. 62; McClure, ii. 404–5. Chamberlain does not indeed specify the 'ballet or song' he encloses, but Cock Lorel is the only one to which the description can apply. Simpson, who quotes the letter (p. 546: he misdates it 1622, and indeed in Chamberlain's hand, as in some others of the time, 1 looks very like 2), remarks that it 'explicitly says that the song was repeated' at Windsor. This is not, perhaps, quite true, for Chamberlain may only have meant that the masque was repeated: however, I have no doubt that his assumption is correct.

[2] I take no account of the last four leaves of sig. E since the last two pages are blank and several others short.

There is one important consideration to be borne in mind. For convenience of insertion Benson and Okes would be likely to make their cancels consist, if not of whole sheets (twelve leaves)—as in fact they did—at any rate of complete thirds of a sheet (either four or eight leaves). In the first cancel, $d^{12}$, new matter is found on $d1^v$ and new matter fills $d12^r$: nothing less than a whole sheet would have sufficed. In the second cancel, $e^{12}$, which includes the end of the masque, the Epilogue on $e12$ is new. The first four leaves of this cancel include, on $e4^r$, the end of the Cock Lorel ballad, and of this we know that the last four stanzas were a late addition (see p. 45). It follows that two-thirds of a sheet would just not have sufficed for this cancel. And since this cancel begins just where the leaves are missing in $D^a$, the important conclusion follows that for all we know or can surmise the first six pages of the cancel may be an exact reprint of the first three of the four leaves missing from $D^a$.

Now the text of $D^2$, in the section corresponding to the leaves missing from $D^a$ (that is w 811–1085 and b 908–26), runs to 294 lines of print, so that, if no lines of $D^1$ were omitted in revision, the new matter must have amounted to between 100 and 150 lines. Our problem is to identify these lines in $D^2$. It does not, in fact, appear very difficult to do so.[1]

We know that the Cock Lorel ballad figured in the Burley version: that much at least is clear from John Chamberlain's letter (p. 36). But, as we shall shortly see (p. 45), the last three quatrains are not in H and have every appearance of being an addition, no doubt written for the Windsor performance. They were almost certainly not in the Burley text. In $D^2$ they occupy 13 lines of print.

The next most obvious passage to pick out as possibly additional is that in which the Clowns seek admittance into the 'order of Gipsies' and the Patrico explains to them the 'misterie' of the calling. Moreover, it is tempting to connect Puppy's words at w 952–3,

> An excellent song and a sweet songster & would ha done rarelie in a Cage

with the later dialogue (w 1065–70):

> *Coc* Oh he would Chirpe in a paire of stocks sumptuouslie  I'ld

---

[1] For reasons explained in the notes it is probable that w 865–6 were absent from $D^1$, but we must not reckon their omission here, since they are also absent from $D^2$, which we have taken as the basis of our computation.

> giue any thing to see him play loose w<sup>th</sup> his hands when his feet are fast.
>
> *Pup.* Ô my Conscience he feares not that and the Marshall himselfe were here   I protest I admire him

It would, however, require some adapting. The allusion to playing fast and loose evidently refers to the feats of which the Patrico has been boasting, and the Earl Marshal was among the Lords who first appeared at Windsor. I suggest that the passage originally ran:

> *Pup.* An excellent song and a sweet songster & would ha done rarelie in a Cage.
>
> *Coc* Oh he would Chirpe in a paire of stocks sumptuouslie.
>
> *Pup.* Ô my Conscience he feares not that: I protest I admire him.

Then, as we know, followed the speech by the Patrico leading up to the metamorphosis. It is true that as it stands his offer to show 'more of my skill' (w 1074) appears to refer to the display he has already made of it, but in fact what he goes on to promise is a feast, thus carrying on the Cock Lorel theme rather than that of his juggling tricks.[1] Allowing for the adjustment, the passage in D² occupies 121 lines of print.

Together the two passages account for 134 lines, which is well within our limits and would mean that the four leaves of Dᵃ contained 160 lines. This is perhaps a few lines less than we should expect, but is near enough for our purpose.[2]

If the above argument is correct the Windsor revision in this portion of the text consisted in the addition of Cockrell's speech at w 865–6 and the last three stanzas of the Cock Lorel song (w 940–51), and the introduction of the theme of the Clowns' proposal to become Gipsies (w 952–1070, incorporating a few lines of the earlier version).

---

[1] There may have been some revision here: for instance w 1072–4 may be new, and their insertion may be the cause of the obvious corruption in w 1075. But this is not really necessary. Above I have only been refining on a suggestion put forward by Cole (p. 49). But he confined his attention to the addition of the proposed enrolment of the Clowns.

[2] It is always open to conjecture that some lines in D¹ were cancelled in revision. For example, if the opening of the Patrico's speech (w 1072 ff.) was altered, the original version may have been a trifle longer.

## III. DIFFERENCES BETWEEN THE TEXTS OF THE COMPOSITE VERSION

We have now taken a general view of the differences that distinguish the original Burley version of the masque (only slightly altered at Belvoir) from the version later performed at Windsor, as they emerge from a comparison of the earlier form of the Duodecimo ($D^1$) with the Huntington manuscript (H). But the four authorities that preserve the Windsor version, or more precisely that include the Windsor alterations in a composite text—namely the Huntington and Newcastle manuscripts, the Folio, and the cancel sheets of the Duodecimo ($D^2$)—do not always agree in their evidence. It goes without saying that they present many verbal variants—these will be examined in the next section—but they also reveal certain major differences, most of them clearly the result of revision, and these it is the purpose of the present section to analyse.

The cancels in the Duodecimo—$D^2$ as we have agreed to call them—furnish, of course, only an incomplete and discontinuous text. It follows that (neglecting minor differences) we have for the composite version sometimes four and sometimes only three authorities, a fact that divides the text into four sections that for critical purposes it is necessary to distinguish. These sections are: (*A*) B 1–27 and W 1–261, before the first cancel; (*B*) W 262–369, B 336–480, and W 370–548 ('... didst thou never see any'), corresponding to the first cancel; (*C*) W 548('any Gypsies ...')–810, between the cancels; and (*D*) W 811–1085, B 908–26, and W 1086–1291, corresponding to the second cancel. In sections (*A*) and (*C*), where $D^2$ is absent, $D^b$ of course preserves the $D^1$ or Burley text, and is therefore not an authority for the revision.

(*A*) In this section, since there is no $D^2$ text, we cannot tell, when H differs from N F, whether this is due to variation in *f* or in a common source of *f* and $d^2$. The differences, however, are unimportant, and it matters little where we assume them to have originated.

(1) In N and F the Windsor prologue (W 1–20) precedes the Porter's speech at Burley (B 1–27). This order, though illogical, is in fact the natural one, since it would be easier to prefix the newly written leaf to the manuscript than to insert it in its proper place. H has the historical order, Burley–

Windsor, but this is probably due to editorial rearrangement, and it is reasonable to assume that $d^2$ agreed with $f$.

(2) F omits the Belvoir variant at B 130; but since the lines appear (though without heading) in N, the omission must have been due to carelessness on the part of the compositor and not to their absence in $f$. We may assume, then, that the variant was present in $d^2$. But the absence in N of any heading to the variant here, and again to those at B 189 and 203, makes it likely that these headings were supplied by the scribe of H from his own knowledge rather than copied from the original.

Neither of these variants suggests that either the source of $d^2f$ or $f$ itself underwent any revision subsequent to the production of H, and they may be dismissed as irrelevant to our present purpose.

(*B*) This is the first section for which $D^2$ is available, and throughout it $D^2$ and N F are in close agreement, all differences from H being apparently due to variation in the source of $d^2f$.

(1) The three lines w 367–9, which form the second half of the concluding stanza of the Prince's fortune in its longer form, are found only in H: evidently an accidental omission in the source of $d^2f$.

(2) H alone has a note after B 479 stating that at Windsor the Lords' fortunes replaced those of the Ladies (cf. p. 29). This might, of course, be another case of common omission in $D^2$ N F, but in view of the headings also peculiar to H (see *A*2), there is a strong presumption that it was an editorial addition in H for which there was no formal source.

(3) A clear case of alteration is the position of the Lord Chamberlain's fortune (w 371–89), which is the last of the Lords' fortunes in H but the first in $D^2$ N F. There can be no doubt that the latter are correct in beginning with the six great officers of state, and ending with the Lords Hamilton and Buccleuch, who held no position at court. Cole (p. 44) pertinently remarks that 'For the Lord Chamberlain to follow the Lord Hamilton, a young man and popular but not comparable with the great Earl of Pembroke, appears a gross violation of precedence'. There can be little doubt that this fortune (and probably each of the others) was written on a separate leaf, and that this leaf had been carelessly placed at the end when H was transcribed, but was later moved to the

## Differences between Texts of Composite Version 41

beginning. (We shall find confirmation of the shift when we come to examine the dances, p. 50.)

(4) A small variant in the Lords' fortunes is the absence in H of four lines (w 402–5) from that of the Lord Keeper, John Williams, the newly appointed Bishop of Lincoln. They run in $D^2$:

> Ile venture my life,
> You never had wife,
> But Ile venture my skill,
> You may when you will.

There would be no impossibility in supposing an accidental omission, for we know that H did leave out a couple of lines near the end (w 1149–50, ($D_7$) below); but on the whole the variant seems more likely deliberate. Cole (p. 44) remarks that 'The lines ... may not have pleased the Bishop of Lincoln', implying that they were removed; but that would make H represent the later state of the text, which is contrary to the rest of the evidence. Simpson, on the other hand, writes (p. 557): 'Williams did not marry: were there rumours of an abortive engagement in 1621, which suggested a compliment otherwise pointless? The context runs smoother without it'. This implies, I think correctly, that the lines are an insertion. They have no connexion with what comes before or after.

(5) The Earl of Buccleuch's fortune (w 485–500) is not in H. It too may, of course, have been accidentally omitted, but that is very unlikely in so carefully prepared a text. More probably it was (like Lady Exeter's at Burley) a late addition to the original after H had been transcribed; in which case $D^2 N F$ go back to a more completely revised form of that original than does H.

(6) Lastly, the direction for the entry of the Clowns is in H placed before and in $D^2$ N F after the Patrico–Jackman duet (w 507–33). Now the dance that accompanies their entrance originally linked the Ladies' fortune with the antimasque, the duet as well as the Lords' fortunes being a Windsor addition. It is clear from $D^2$ N F that the whole of this addition must have been inserted in the original manuscript in front of the entrance direction: this becomes particularly clear when we compare $D^2$ with $D^1$. It is therefore probable that both the amended position and the elaborated form of the direction in H are due to the editorial activities of the scribe.

Thus, of the six variants in this section, two (2, 6) are to be credited to the scribe of H, one (1) is an error in the source of $d^2f$, whereas one (3) is a transposition and two (4, 5) are additions made in the original after H had been transcribed.

(*C*) In this section $D^2$ again fails us, and we cannot, therefore, be certain whether the important differences between H and NF originated in *f* or whether they were already present in the source of $d^2f$. Since, however, some similar though less extensive variants in the final section (where $D^2$ is again present) are confined to NF, it is legitimate to suppose that some at least of the variants in the present section may also have been first found in *f*.

(1) First, the passage (w 573–81) that in H runs, 'Clod will you gather the pipe monie ... see where the minstrelle come i' the mouth on't', some of which, inherited from Burley, is of a particularly unsavoury nature, is omitted in NF, which in place of it have only the innocent phrase 'see where he comes'.

(2) In H Jack Cockrell's fortune (w 644–5) reads:

2. *Gip.* you'll steale yo$^r$ selfe drunke I finde here true
as you rob the pot the pot will rob you

a couplet, intelligible no doubt if rather lacking in point, that survives from the original version preserved in $D^1$. In NF we find, without speaker's name:

you'le ha good lucke to horse flesh ô my life,
you plow'de soe late w$^{th}$ y$^e$ vicars wife

to us perhaps obscure, but said to be proverbial and doubtless having some more or less indecorous point for the audience. Clearly in the original both couplet and speaker's name were struck out, and when Jonson wrote the new couplet, probably in the margin, he forgot to specify the speaker.

(3) Another unsavoury passage inherited from Burley concerns and includes the fortune of Long Meg. The lines in H (w 664–9), 'shee hangs an arse terriblie ... as good for a Sowe as a pancake', are omitted in NF, and for the following speech by Townshead,

Harke nowe they treate vpon Tickle foote

they substitute one by Puppy,

They slipp her, and treat vpon Tickle foot

an amusingly barefaced evasion.

## Differences between Texts of Composite Version

(4) At w 735 H (following D¹) makes Puppy say, 'he can ill pipe that wantȝ his vpper lip'—a doubtless true but seemingly irrelevant observation.[1] NF, reading 'his vpper lippe; Monie', supply the explanation. The saying, which was cited by John Heywood as proverbial as early as 1546, implies that nothing can be done lacking the necessary means, and NF, make the application clear, that money is needed for a piper to 'wet his whistle' (w 733). No doubt we have here a slight but significant revision.

(5) The lines w 741–3 show progressive revision. In D¹ we learn that Meg (there miscalled Maudlin)

> has lost an inchanted Nutmeg, all guilded over, she had to put in her Sweet-hearts Ale . . .

In H she herself says:

> I haue lost an inchanted Nutmeg all guilded ouer inchanted at Oxford I had to putt i' my sweet hartȝ ale

and finally in NF:

> I haue lost, an inchanted Nuttmegge all guilded over, was inchanted at Oxforde for mee, to put i' my sweete harts Ale . . .

This shows the minuteness of some of the revision: we may suspect, however, that it was by oversight that the first 'inchanted' was left standing.

(6) Lastly the words in H (w 748–9), 'and Francis Adlebreech has lost somewhat too', themselves an expansion of D¹, are further expanded in NF to read 'Francis Addlebreech has lost somwhat too, besides her Maidenhead', and a slight consequential alteration is made in the girl's reply.

Here we have six clear cases of revision in *f* subsequent to the preparation of H. Two (1, 3) are unquestionably for the sake of decorum, the others seek to add point or definition to the dialogue. They are not, indeed, the only variants between H and NF that may be due to revision—note for example, the omission of 'if I' in w 596 and the insertion of 'daintye' in w 737—but it is not always easy to distinguish with certainty between minor revisions and scribal variants, and the matter will claim further attention at a later stage (see pp. 78 ff.). Meanwhile the evidence here collected is ample to establish the fact of revision in this section.

---

[1] In D¹ Townshead replies, 'Yes, a Bag-piper may want both'; but this had already been cut out in H, perhaps as manifestly untrue.

(*D*) In the final section D² again becomes available. Three main variants are peculiar to NF, and justify—or at least supply a basis for—our former conclusion that at any rate the more extensive revisions of the previous section probably also first appeared in *f*.

(1) At w 829–32 a rather pointless passage that H had probably inherited from Burley (for D¹ fails us here), 'for the hob nailes are come to me . . . trust my Iudgm$^t$ in a Gipsie agen', is also present in D² but is omitted in NF.

(2) Just below, at w 835–6, H supported by D² reads: 'The kinge has a noise of Gypsies aswell as [of] Bearewards.' To this NF add 'and other Minstrells'—a reasonable supposition.

(3) Later, at w 978–83, there was some progressive and rather extensive recasting. In H the passage reads:

> *Pup.* Tutt they haue other manner of guiftes then telling of fortunes or picking of pockettş
> *Coc* I an if they please to shewe them or thought vs poore Contrie folks worthy of them
> *Pup.* What might a man doe to be a gentleman of yo$^r$ Companie S$^r$.
> *Coc.* I a Gipsie in ordinarie or nothing

In D² certain modifications appear. In the first speech the second and third 'of' are omitted, and the second speech runs:

> *Cock.* I, and they would bee pleased to show 'hem, or thought us poor mortall country folkes worthy of them.

In NF the whole is rewritten thus:

> *Pup:* Tut, they haue other manner of guifts, then pickinge of pockets, or tellinge fortunes, If they would but please to shewe='em, or thought vs poore Cuntrye mortalls, worthye of them, what might a man doe, to be a Gentleman, of your Companie S$^r$:
> I, a Gipsie in Ord'narye or Nothinge:/

The first three speeches have been run together, but the last stands separate both in N and F, though it has lost its prefix in the course of revision.

A minor peculiarity of NF may be mentioned, namely the writing or printing of the words 'Aske him;' (w 835) and 'the Diuells Arse?' (w 847–8) as separate lines in the text. This must have been a feature of *f*, but its significance is not apparent.

There are four variants from H that are common to D²NF.

(4) At w 837–9 H alone makes the words 'a flagonfleakean' part of Puppy's speech instead of the first line of the Patrico's

## Differences between Texts of Composite Version

verses.[1] There can be no doubt that $D^2NF$ are right and that the error arose through the misplacing of the prefix to the verses in the original. Of this we have confirmation in its absence in NF and in the writing of the line in N as though it were a sort of title or heading. In $D^2$ the name 'Patrico' is duly placed at the head of the verses.

(5) In H the speech by the Patrico that introduces the Cock Lorel song is interrupted by the lines (w 865-6):

> *Coc.* O. I. the song the song in any Case if you want Musique wee'll lend him o<sup>r</sup> mistrell

which are not in $D^2NF$. We cannot suppose them to have been added by the scribe of H, nor can we imagine any reason for their omission. They are doubtless an insertion, for they interrupt not only the speech but the rime-sequence, and were introduced to allow Cheeks and Ticklefoot to accompany the 'clarke' who sings the ballad. Supposing them to have been part of the earliest Windsor revision and rather obscurely written into the manuscript, we can imagine them to have been overlooked by the writer of the source of $d^2f$ though preserved by the more careful scribe of H. If this conjecture is right the speech cannot, of course, have been in $D^1$, which is here defective.

(6) At the end of the Cock Lorel ballad three stanzas (w 940-51) pandering to James's well-known dislike of tobacco and pork and salted fish are found only in $D^2NF$. They are clearly an addition made after H had been written. Their distinct origin is confirmed by a trifling peculiarity in N, where they are the only stanzas of the song in which alternate lines are indented.

(7) Lastly, a couple of lines in the blessing of the King's hearing (w 1149-50) are also peculiar to $D^2NF$:

> Or a long pretended fit,
> Meant for mirth, but is not it:

that they are original is proved by the next line, which is also in H:

> onelie time and eares out wearinge

for while the metal-workers of Lothbury and the Puritans of Banbury might wear out long-suffering ears, only a tedious narration could be said to outwear time. The couplet must

---

[1] Simpson, holding himself bound to follow his copy-text H, endeavoured to make sense of it by putting a question-mark after 'flagonfleakean', but this is more botching.

therefore have been accidentally omitted in H. It may be added that whereas in H the stanzas of the blessing are unnumbered, in the other composite texts they bear the numbers 1 to 5, and D² alone carries the numbering further, prefixing '6' to w 1182.

In this section then we find three instances of revision in $f$ (1–3) and two of revision in $d^2f$ (3, 6): two variants are due to error or omission in H (4, 7) and one to omission in $d^2f$ (5).

We have examined twenty-one cases of variation between H, D², N, and F, and the results may be summarized as follows. Error in H accounts for two ($D$ 4, 7), error in $d^2f$ for two ($B$ 1, $D$ 5), error in F for one ($A$ 2). Editing in H accounts for three ($A$ 1, $B$ 2, 6). The other thirteen are due to revision. In one case there was successive revision in $d^2f$ and $f$ ($D$ 3). In four other instances the revision was certainly in $d^2f$ ($B$ 3–5, $D$ 6) and in two certainly in $f$ ($D$ 1, 2). In no less than six instances ($C$ 1–6) the revision, for all we can tell, may have been either in $d^2f$ or in $f$, though analogy points to the latter, at least in the more important cases. One of the motives of revision, showing itself most probably in $f$, was a sense of decorum ($C$ 1, 3). This may seem unlikely on the face of it: Dr. Simpson asks, 'why should Windsor have been more sensitive than Burley?' (p. 546) and privately protests that if some revisions reduced, others heightened the indelicacy of the performance. Impropriety, however, is a matter of taste, and an audience that sniggered over the vicar's wife may have frowned on *Tartaretus de modo cacandi*.[1]

I here add a table giving a conspectus of the main Windsor revisions and showing the manuscript in which each first appeared, so far as this can be ascertained. (For the meaning of the symbols see p. 68.) The table takes no account of presumed omissions or of isolated words and phrases.

This will be a convenient place to consider the dances indicated in the various texts, an analysis of which should throw some light on the alterations made in the structure of the

---

[1] I suppose that the Master of the Revels, Sir George Buc, who must presumably have sanctioned the masque for performance at Windsor, if not for the private shows at Burley and Belvoir, may have insisted on these passages being removed. The revision at w 670 to my mind suggests that Jonson made it in submission to authority and with his tongue in his cheek. In tidying up the cuts he may have made a few revisions elsewhere. I do not think there is any doubt that even the latest revisions are Jonson's.

# Differences between Texts of Composite Version

## Scheme of the Main Windsor Revisions

| Ref. w | Passage | β | γ | f |
|---|---|---|---|---|
| 1–20 | Prologue | addition | | |
| 104 | 'cut your laces' | alteration | | |
| 175–80 | ⎫ in the Patrico's address to | substitution | | |
| 190–9 | ⎭ the Lords and Ladies | substitution | | |
| 301–18 | to King's fortune | add. (om. B 306–8) | | |
| 346–69 | to Princes fortune | addition | | |
| 371–484 | Lords' fortunes for Ladies' | substitution | | |
| 371–89 | Lord Chamberlain's fortune | | transposition | |
| 402–5 | in Lord Keeper's fortune | | addition | |
| 485–500 | Lord Buccleuch's fortune | | addition | |
| 507–33 | Patrico–Jackman duet | addition | | |
| 568–9 | ⎫ 'and take out the wenches' | addition | | |
| 572 | Ticklefoot's entry | omis. (B 521–3) | ? | alteration |
| 573–81 | 'claw a churl' | | ? | omission |
| 580–98 | Entrance of Wenches | alteration | | |
| 644–5 | Cockrell's fortune | | ? | substitution |
| 664–9 | 'hangs an arse' | | ? | omission |
| 670 | 'treat vpon Ticklefoot' | | ? | alteration |
| 724 | Antimasque 'Much good doe 'hem' | omis. (B 670–3) | | |
| 725 | 'such a whimpering' | addition | | |
| 736 | The piper's lip | omis. (B 685) | ? | verbal add. |
| 737–56 | The Wenches' losses | alteration | | |
| 741–3 | The enchanted nutmeg | | ? | alteration |
| 748–9 | Frances's loss | | ? | alteration |
| 829–32 | Townshead's hobnails | | | omission |
| 940–51 | Cock Lorel, 3 stanzas | | addition | |
| 953–1064 | ⎫ The Clowns and the | addition? | | |
| 978–82 | ⎬ [Gipsy gifts] | | alteration | alteration |
| 1065–70 | ⎭ Company of Gipsies | alteration? | | |
| 1089–1189 | Blessing the King's senses | addition | | |
| 1270–91 | Epilogue | addition | | |

masque. It is, of course, in the main a matter of differences between the Burley–Belvoir version on the one hand and the Windsor version on the other, but there are nevertheless some points of divergence in the several composite texts. In the accompanying table I first give the dances as recorded in H, since this is the text that affords the fullest information, after which I indicate in several columns the differences observable in $D^2$ and in NF (which are throughout in agreement): finally, I give the dances as recorded in $D^1$. A blank in these columns indicates that the text in question is not available, a dash that it agrees (substantially) with H, and brackets that though present it contains no record of the dance.

In $D^1$, in which the dances before the antimasque are regularly numbered 1 to 6, the arrangement seems at first sight quite straightforward. Closer examination, however, and comparison with H suggest doubts whether this is so. $D^1$ has only six dances where H has seven, and it is difficult to believe that there was not always a dance separating the Prince's fortune from those of the Ladies. It will be remembered that there can be no question of revision here, for at Windsor the Ladies' fortunes did not appear. It is true that H, since it includes Lady Exeter's fortune, must represent a later stage in the preparation of the Burley version than that represented by $D^1$, or even perhaps a state first reached at Belvoir. But it is most unlikely that any alteration was made in the number of dances between the Burley and Belvoir performances, still more unlikely that any last-minute changes were made at Burley. It is also true that the actual form of the directions preserved in H may be due to an editor (not the scribe of H, since the directions are substantially the same in NF, but some earlier scribe) but still they must have been based on indications in the original manuscript. These indications I believe to have been substantially, if imperfectly, preserved in $D^1$. I think that what happened was this. In $d^1$ (or else in the original from which $d^1$ was copied) the entry dance was unnumbered as it still is in NF. The fortune dances (Ladies') were six in number, as in H, and the numbers indicated figures rather than separate dances, again as in H. The printer of $D^1$ (or perhaps the scribe of $d^1$) having not unreasonably added '1' to the direction of the entry dance (as also did the editor of H) erroneously carried on this numbering, changing 1 to 2 and 2 to 3 in the next two directions, thus treating the several figures as distinct dances: but he accidentally

# Differences between Texts of Composite Version

## Disposition and Numbering of the Dances

| | Ref. | H | D² | N F | D¹ |
|---|---|---|---|---|---|
| | w 85 | Introduction<br>Dance 1. (Entry)<br>Song and verses | | Dance | — |
| | w 229 | Dance 2. 1 straine<br>The King's fortune with songs | | — | Dance 2 |
| | w 319 | Dance 2. 2 straine<br>The Prince's fortune | 3. 2 | — | Dance 3 |
| The Ladies' fortunes at Burley | B 336 | Dance 2. 3 straine<br>Lady Marques Buckingham | — | — | [ ] |
| | B 387 | Dance 2. 4 straine<br>Countess of Rutland<br>Countess of Exeter | — | — | Dance 4<br><br>(omitted) |
| | B 418 | Dance 2. 5 straine<br>Countess of Buckingham<br><br>Lady Purbeck<br>Ladie Eliz: Hatton | —· | | [ ]<br><br>Dance 5 |
| The Lords' fortunes at Windsor | w 370 | Dance 2. 3 siraine<br>Lo: Keeper<br>Lo: Tresurer<br>Lo: Priuie Seale<br>Earle Marshall<br>Lo: Steward | Lo: Chamb.<br>— | Lo: Chamb.<br>— | |
| | w 468 | Dance 2. 4 straine<br>Lo: Marquess Hamilton<br><br>Lo: Chamberlaine | [ ]<br><br>Buckcloug<br>(omitted) | [ ]<br><br>Buckcloug<br>(omitted) | |
| | w 501-2 | Dance 2. 6 straine→Dance 3<br>Antimasque begun | ——* | ——* | Dance 6 |
| | w 602 | Contry Dance<br>Antimasque concluded | — | — | — |
| | w 1088 | Dance (at the metamorphosis)<br>Conclusion | — | — | — |

\* After, instead of before, the duet (w 507-33)

omitted the direction for the dance after the Prince's fortune, so that with 'Dance 4' he came again into agreement with the original. The change in position of the fifth dance is easily explained, since before Lady Exeter's fortune was inserted the natural position of this 'straine' would be after rather than before that of the Countess of Buckingham, with two fortunes before it and two after it. The position to which it was moved after the insertion would give greater prominence to the Countess of Buckingham and so make up for placing her after the Countess of Exeter.

In H, thanks to careful editing, we have a perfectly regular series, so far as the Ladies' fortunes are concerned. The entry is called 'Dance 1' by the scribe, and the six fortune measures arc numbered, not as separate dances, but as several 'straines', that is tunes or figures, of one second dance: the last of these 'straines', still no doubt a courtly measure, merges on the entrance of the Clowns into a third dance, presumably of a more rustic character. But the numbering is carried no farther: the 'Contry Dance' and the final measure are in no way related to the others. This suggests that the whole numbering originated with the measures of the fortune dance, and that the description of this as a second dance was an afterthought due to the ingenuity of the editor of the composite version.

Compared with this orderly sequence, the record H gives of the measures accompanying the Lords' fortunes is sketchy and, I think, demonstrably wrong. We may reasonably assume that these fortunes were written on separate leaves inserted into the original manuscript. We have already seen that when H was transcribed the leaf containing the Lord Chamberlain's fortune, which should have stood first, came, in fact, at the end. This was doubtless the order in which the original of the composite version was put together. The Lord Keeper's fortune was thus left at the beginning, and at the head of this leaf the editor quite properly repeated the direction, 'Dance 2. 3 straine', which had originally introduced the Ladies' fortunes. Then after the Lord Steward's fortune H has 'Dance 2. 4 straine': this was probably introduced by the scribe since it is not in $D^2NF$. There is no indication of a fifth strain in any text, though of course the '6 straine' still introduces the antimasque. There may, of course, have been fewer dances at Windsor than at Burley, though why it would be hard to conjecture. But when H was transcribed the Lord Chamberlain's

## Differences between Texts of Composite Version 51

fortune was misplaced and the Earl of Buccleuch's had not yet been added. It follows that if the '4 straine' really came where indicated, there were six fortunes before it and only one after. This is frankly incredible. The true arrangement is not difficult to conjecture. The fourth straine must have come after the fortune of the Lord Treasurer, thus dividing the six high officials into two equal groups; then after the Lord Steward's fortune must have come the fifth straine, separating the officers of state from the two unofficial lords. The loose papers of the Lords' fortunes evidently did not provide sufficient indications of the dances to allow the introduction of necessary directions.

Before $d^2$ and $f$ were prepared the fortune of the Earl of Buccleuch had been added at the end and the leaf bearing the Lord Chamberlain's had been moved to the beginning. But since the direction for 'Dance 2. 3 straine' had already been written at the head of the Lord Keeper's fortune, which now stood second, the shift resulted in the absurdity of making the Lord Chamberlain's fortune precede the measure that should divide the royal fortunes from those that follow, and so it stands in $D^2$ and $NF$.[1] This is indeed the only dance that these texts connect with the Lords' fortunes, for they omit that after the Lord Steward's. No difficulty arises in these texts over the measures associated with the Ladies' fortunes: the only point to notice is that in $D^2$ the direction for the second is misprinted 'Dance 3. 2 Straine' in imitation of $D^1$.

The textual results of these considerations may be seen in the parallel texts printed in this volume, for which the present analysis supplies the justification.

A word may be added respecting the songs, though textually the differences between the texts add nothing to our knowledge. The facts are given in the accompanying table. But for a few trifling errors all texts agree in numbering the songs before the antimasque 1 to 3, leaving the duet and the Cock Lorel ballad unnumbered, and numbering the songs of the conclusion 1 to 5.[2] These last, though they differ in stanzaic form, might be regarded as strophes of a single ode (one consists of two lines only) which would account for their

[1] The absurdity is to some extent concealed in the composite texts by the intervention of the Ladies' fortunes.

[2] NF omit the number of the first song and N alone that of the first of the second series. $D^2NF$ omit the heading to the duet: indeed, the 'Song' of H is probably due to the scribe. $D^1$ omits to number the last two songs.

separate numbering. In the first series the second and third, which are in the same stanzaic form, could, and perhaps should, be regarded as one, but the first is clearly a separate poem. In any case the present numbering must derive from the original manuscript.

### Numbering of the Songs

| Ref. | First Line | H | D² | NF | D¹ |
|---|---|---|---|---|---|
| w 88 | From the famous Peake of Darby | Songe 1 | | Songe | —— |
| w 230 | The faery beame vppon you | song 2 | | —— | —— |
| w 270 | To the old longe life and treasure | Song 3 | —— | —— | —— |
| w 507 | why this is a sport | Song | [ ] | [ ] | —— |
| w 875 | Cock-Lorell would needes haue the Diuell his guest | Song | —— | —— | —— |
| w 1191 | The sports are done yet do not let | Song 1 | —— | ——* | —— |
| w 1207 | vertue! his kinglie vertue w^ch did merrit | Song 2 | —— | —— | —— |
| w 1215 | Looke looke is he not faire | Song 3 | —— | —— | —— |
| w 1231 | Good Princes sore aboue theire fame | Song 4 | —— | —— | Song |
| w 1253 | O that we vnderstood | Song 5 | —— | —— | Song |

\* N Songe (no number)

We have reached a point at which we may profitably ask what inferences can be drawn from the evidence so far examined. The fact that the texts containing the Windsor version are not pure Windsor texts but composite ones, retaining almost all the distinctively Burley and Belvoir matter, of course proves that they do not go back to anything of the nature of a Windsor prompt-book. They might rather be supposed to derive more or less directly from the original manuscript upon which successive revisions had been carried out by means of marginal alterations and inserted leaves. Omissions must have been somehow indicated, but whatever indications there may have been were evidently disregarded in preparing the extant texts—doubtless deliberately, since the object seems to have been to produce a literary record, one therefore as complete as possible. Thus the picture we get is that of an original manuscript, α, from which $d^1$ was derived, and which underwent, first some slight revision for the performance at Belvoir,[1] and later more extensive revision in preparation for that at Windsor. It was from the manu-

---

[1] In fact, the Belvoir alternatives may have been in the manuscript from the first and have been deliberately omitted in preparing $d^1$; but the Countess of Exeter's fortune, whether it was first spoken at Burley or at Belvoir, must have been added to the manuscript after $d^1$ had been transcribed.

script in this state, which we may call α', that H was copied or derived. Next it received certain specific additions, an important transposition, and an uncertain amount of revision, which produced state α", a state that gave rise to $d^2$. Lastly it underwent some final polishing, including the removal of two of the more disagreeable passages, and was left in state α‴, represented by *f*. That this last revision was authoritative and not the work of an irresponsible bowdlerizer appears to be guaranteed by its having been selected for publication by Sir Kenelm Digby from among the author's own papers. Simpson, in spite of his contempt for F, the text of which he describes as 'execrable', recognizes the essential character of *f* when he describes it as 'Probably . . . an official copy' (p. 555); and when he writes (p. 548) of H that 'It reads like a first attempt at the Windsor text, perhaps a copy written for presentation before the readings were finally adjusted', he seems to imply that it is in *f* that those final adjustments are to be sought.

Although we have already had hints that such a simple scheme as that outlined above may not cover all the facts, yet as a provisional presentation I may be allowed to put it into diagrammatic form thus:[1]

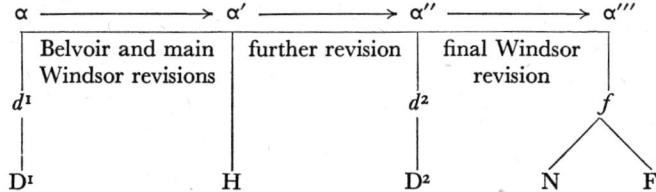

## IV. EVIDENCE OF THE SCRIBAL VARIANTS

So far we have considered only such differences between the texts as appear to be due to deliberate revision, and indeed only the more important of these. Later (pp. 78 ff.) we shall find that there are a number of merely verbal alterations that may be reasonably classed as revisional, and that it is not always easy to distinguish them from scribal variants. The latter are, of course, frequent, and in considering them we shall do well to set aside any differences that might be due to revision.

[1] Cole (p. 43) prints a stemma that I confess I do not understand. It appears to imply that H includes only the Belvoir and not the Windsor revisions. Of course this cannot have been his intention.

If the diagram at the end of the last section truly represented the facts, the texts $D^1$, H, $D^2$, and $f$ would be each independently derived from successive states of α and apart from revision their readings would not fall into groups. This, as we shall see, is not borne out by the evidence, which on the contrary points to very definite grouping. It is the purpose of the present section to carry out a preliminary analysis of the readings of the texts, with a view to establishing the groups into which they do, in fact, fall. I shall not at this stage attempt to deal with all variants, but shall confine attention to a number of the more striking, sufficient to establish a prima facie case that can be further tested, and will I hope be confirmed, by the full analysis of all actual and hypothetical texts attempted in the final section. The analysis is based on my own collation of the several authorities, but in making this I have had the great advantage of comparing it with Simpson's apparatus; and if, as I hope, my own is the more reliable, this is due to the constant check such comparison afforded rather than to any greater accuracy on my own part.[1]

### (1) EVIDENCE FOR THE INDEPENDENCE OF $D^1$

Not as the most obvious, but as the most important textual feature, I propose first to consider the independent position of $D^1$, or rather of the common derivation of the other texts, $HD^2 f$. The number of readings in which $D^1$ differs from all other texts is considerable, and a fair proportion of these are due to obvious errors in $D^1$: these prove nothing; it is only if we can show that some of the variants are due to errors common to $HD^2 f$ that we can infer a source for these texts independent of $D^1$.

---

[1] Simpson, who collated more copies of some texts than I have had the opportunity or the patience to do, records six variants between different copies of F: B 118 heare : here, W 445 ow : owne, W 466 ado : adoe, W 893 Tyrcwomen : Tyrewomen, W 894 perfumes : perfumers, W 1061 defedendo : defendendo. Four of these are press-corrections, two are due to faulty impression. At B 908[1] (Belvoir variant) he reports F as reading 'fist', but two copies in my possession read 'fift' with the second 'f' broken. He also reports one variant between copies of $D^2$: W 351 laughte : laughter; this he treats as a press-correction, though it looks more like faulty impression (he does not say whether the following period is present in both). There is another at W 266 where some copies read 'Bountifull,' and others 'Bountifu l' (an 'l' and a comma having dropped out). I am able to add a curious little variant between copies of $D^1$. In the Cambridge copy the first word of B 377 (on sig. D8 recto) is 'Preserving'. In my copy of $D^b$ the stub of this leaf remains and bears sufficient traces of printing to show that the word began with a lower-case 'p'. None of these variants affect the analysis attempted in the present edition and I take no further notice of them.

# Evidence of the Scribal Variants

What evidence is there, then, of common corruption in H D² ƒ, or in H ƒ where D² is absent? We can, I believe, adduce seven instances.[1]

The most important is at w 227–8. Immediately before the dance and song that introduce the fortunes all texts give the Captain the line (H)

> well, dance another straine & wee'll thinke howe

but D¹ alone supplies the riming line

> Meane time in song doe you conceive some vow.[2]

We can hardly suppose that an original defect was conjecturally remedied in D¹, and both lines are needed to introduce the dance and song that follow.[3]

Less obvious, but I think hardly less certain and significant, is an instance at w 690 ff., where, in fact, no text can be accepted as correct. In D¹ we find:

> 4 *GYPSIE*
>
> Yet look to your selfe, you'l ha' some ill luck
> And shortly, for I have his purse with a pluck,
>
>     Away Birds mum,
>     I heare by the hum . . .[4]

This must be wrong, for the short verses are certainly spoken by the Patrico. This was realized in the other texts, which substitute 'Patrico' for '4 Gypsie'. But it seems unlikely that the Patrico himself picked Puppy's pocket before calling off

---

[1] There is an eighth error at B 413, where 'one' ought certainly to be 'ones', as Simpson was the first to point out. But this is in the Countess of Exeter's fortune, which is not in D¹, and since the error also appears in Con, it may have been a slip in Jonson's autograph. In what follows I usually mention how each variant is treated by Simpson, as a warning that his interpretation of the evidence sometimes differs from my own.

[2] D¹ assigns this line to '1 Gypsie', which cannot be right, for the First Gipsy is the Captain. Simpson, who introduces the line into his text, makes the simplest correction to '2 Gypsie', but it is more likely that '1' is a graphic error for '4', since this confusion is found elsewhere (cf. w 655, 671). It is worth noting that the last speaker before the Captain was the Third Gipsy. A note in Simpson's apparatus implies that the line may have been lost because it comes at a turn of the page in H. But this is impossible since the line is also missing in N F (D² is absent), and ƒ cannot possibly be dependent on H.

[3] By 'vow' is meant prayer, and the song is the beautiful invocation, 'The faery beame vppon you'. Though neither line is more than hackwork, they appear genuine enough.

[4] D¹ and H both happen to begin a page with 'Away Birds mum', so that it is impossible to say whether they meant to leave a space or not. There is no space in F, a rather uncertain one in N. D² is again absent. Simpson follows H and leaves a space.

his gang. There can be no reasonable doubt that D¹ accurately represents the original, in which the Patrico's name was accidentally omitted before the short verses, and that the passage has been wrongly emended in H*f*.

The other five cases concern only verbal variants, but are not therefore less significant. The first is perhaps the most interesting. At B 187 ff. D¹ reads:

> Or what will you say now,
> If with our fine play now,
> Our Knackets, and Dances . . .

For the last line H has

> oᵣ knackes and dances

and *f*(N)

> Our knackes, and our dances

D¹ and *f* are metrically correct, which H is not. Simpson follows *f*, and if this is original, H merely has a small omission of its own: on the other hand, if H reproduces an original error, *f* makes the obvious emendation. But neither assumption will explain 'Knackets', which no scribe or emendator would be likely to invent. The only reasonable supposition, it seems to me, is that the reading of D¹ is original. It is true that no such word as 'Knacket' is recorded in *O.E.D.*, but that does not prove that it did not exist. I suggest that 'Knackets' is what Jonson wrote, knowing (or believing) it to be a cant variant of 'knacks' in the sense of tricks (cf. w 101, 1037).[1] If so, nothing would be more likely than for one scribe to substitute the more familiar, but metrically impossible, form (as in H), and for a subsequent scribe to restore the metre in the easiest manner possible (as in *f*).

Another interesting case, which also seems to involve emendation in *f*, is found at w 678–9. On hearing the Patrico's ribald fortune for Christian, Puppy exclaims in D¹:

> Is that a fortune for a Christian? a Turke Gypsie could not have told her worse.

It should probably be 'a worse' as in HNF, but otherwise no fault can be found with this. 'Turke' (qualifying 'Gypsie') is antithetical to 'Christian', and it commonly means cruel, barbarous, unfeeling, especially towards women. On the other hand, the reading of H, 'A Turke wᵗʰ a Gypsie', is to

---

[1] Jonson may even have invented the word as a variant of 'knack', just as at B 192 he appears to have invented 'tricket' on the basis of 'trick'.

me unintelligible (though Simpson retains it), and so it seems to have been to whoever substituted 'a Turke or a Gypsie' as in $f$.[1] The reading of H can only have arisen through misunderstanding of some alteration in the original.

If there is an element of conjecture in the last three instances the next three are simple enough. At w 564 $D^1$ makes Townshead say of the Gipsies, 'they have scarce had the time to be lowsie yet', whereas H$f$ have 'theire time', which seems to me unidiomatic and senseless, though retained by Simpson. At w 716, 'As I am true Tom Clod' is the reading of $D^1$: HNF omit 'Tom', surely by accident, though Simpson is content to do without it. Their similar omission of 'of my Mothers' a few lines later (w 728) has been already mentioned (p. 34): it is clearly accidental, and even Simpson restores the reading of $D^1$.

I am tempted to add one further instance, in which the reading of $D^1$ is certainly original, though its relevance to our present inquiry is doubtful. At B 578–81 Puppy says, according to $D^1$:

> Yes, and Ile stand to't, that a wise Gypsie . . . is as politicke a piece of Flesh, as most Iustices in the County where he maunds.

For the last word HNF read 'stalkes', which Simpson retains. But 'maund' is a recognized canting term for begging, which fits the present passage perfectly, and was certainly not invented by a scribe. If, therefore, 'stalkes' was substituted out of ignorance, it is a clear case of corruption in HNF. It so happens, however, that at w 1001–2 (in a revisional passage) there occurs the phrase 'ye may stalke the Gypsies walke', where 'stalke', meaning to go stealthily, is used in a more or less technical sense. Can it be, then, that we have here to do with a case of revision? That Jonson sacrificed so excellent a word as 'maunds' through fear of misunderstanding, it is impossible to suppose in view of what he says at w 77–9, but he may have had another motive. It will be noticed that, except for an obscure and hypothetical allusion at w 561— 'Can they cant and mill?'—Jonson has nowhere else admitted that his aristocratic Gipsies were beggars, and he may have wished to avoid the imputation here.

This is the case for the independence of $D^1$, and though it may not be overwhelming, the evidence in favour of a com-

---

[1] Strictly, since $D^2$ is absent, we do not know whether 'w$^{th}$ a' or 'or a' is the earlier form of the error, but it is natural to assume that the latter, which makes sense of a sort, is an emendation of the former.

mon source for HNF[1] will have to be accepted unless rebutted by other evidence in favour of a different grouping. That there is at least prima facie evidence of a conflicting character cannot be denied.

Though not extensive, the most serious evidence is that which would associate D[1] and D[2]. There are two clear instances of common error where the other texts are correct. The first is at B 348 where H (followed by NF) reads:

> If yo[r] hand you hallowe
> Good fortune will followe

whereas for 'hallowe' D[1] and D[2] substitute 'hollowe'. There is no doubt that, in spite of the imperfect rime, 'hallowe' is correct, for the allusion is to 'crossing' the palm with silver. But unless the scribe or compositor were attending to the sense there would be a natural inclination to accommodate the rime, and this might even be done unconsciously.[2] The second is at B 439 in a difficult passage that runs in H (supported by NF at the point in question):

> you shall o[r] Queene be and see who
> importunes
> the hurt of either yo[rs] or you ...

The meaning appears to be 'see who dare intend you harm'. *O.E.D.*, without citing the present passage, records for 'importune' the sense of 'import or portend', characterizing it as 'A Spenserian misuse' imitated by Marston. Of this I take the meaning 'intend' here to be an easy extension.[3] But the force of 'see who' is by no means obvious, and 'he who', which is the reading of D[1] and D[2], would be a tempting substitute for anyone who did not notice that it left the lines without a principal verb.[4] In neither of these instances is coincidence out of the question. But in considering the possibilities we must not overlook the fact that D[1] and D[2] may have been set up by the same compositor, and that in setting up D[2] he is likely enough to have kept an eye on his earlier

---

[1] It happens that D[2] is absent in all the passages so far discussed, and nothing has therefore been proved about its relationship. But we shall find ample evidence that it, in fact, belongs to this general group.

[2] In this connexion it is interesting to note that the scribe of N first wrote 'hollowe' and then altered the first 'o' to an 'a'. There can, of course, be no dependence of N on D[1] or D[2], which were probably not printed till years later.

[3] The word is used in its ordinary sense at B 414.

[4] That at least one scribe was puzzled by them appears from the fact that D[2]NF substitute 'heart' for 'hurt', thus giving 'importune' its usual meaning at the cost of reducing the whole passage to nonsense.

## Evidence of the Scribal Variants

work whenever he had trouble with his copy. In fact there is little doubt that this is the explanation of several small similarities between the texts.[1] Two are in stage directions, where scribes and compositors are always prone to indulge their individualities. At B 309 $D^2$ prints 'Dance 3. 2 Straine' for 'Dance 2. 2 Straine' (as in HNF), an error that cannot be unconnected with the fact that $D^1$ here calls for 'Dance 3' (cf. p. 51). Again, in the direction for the entrance of the Clowns at w 505, $D^1$ and $D^2$ alone have 'to them Puppy' to indicate that he comes on after the rest.[2] In view, therefore, of the likelihood of contamination, we cannot regard occasional common errors in $D^1$ and $D^2$ as evidence of any close relationships between $d^1$ and $d^2$.

There are three readings common to $D^1$ and H that might be regarded as errors not shared with the other texts. The most interesting is in the conclusion, at w 1266. The whole speech, the last of the masque, had better be quoted as it stands in $D^1$:

> Love, love his fortune then, and vertues knowne,
> Who is the top of men,
> But make the happinesse our owne.
> Since where the Prince for goodnesse is renoun'd,
> The Subject with felicity is crown'd.[3]

With this H agrees; but for 'make' in the third line $D^2$ and F read 'makes',[4] thus substituting an indicative dependent on 'Who' for an imperative coordinate with 'Love'. Either reading is perfectly grammatical and the difference in meaning is not great. It might, however, be argued that after 'But' and in view of the last line the reading of $D^2F$ is slightly more natural.[5] At the same time a subjective argument such as this would be but insecure ground on which to base so far-reaching

---

[1] Some general typographical resemblance has already been noticed at p. 15.

[2] Other points of resemblance are at B 283, where $D^1$ and $D^2$ alone have the spelling 'errours' for 'errors', at B 484 where they alone have an exclamation mark after 'Tom', and at w 905 and 907 where $D^2$ may have borrowed the form ''hem' from the lost leaves of $D^a$, since $D^1$ shows a partiality for this Jonsonian spelling.

[3] The rimes show that the first line ought to be two, but this error is common to all the texts.

[4] N reverts to 'make', but this must be an individual peculiarity, since we are bound to conclude that 'makes' was the reading of $f$—unless we are prepared to assume that 'makes' was introduced independently into $D^2$ and F.

[5] Simpson, I suppose, thought so when he rather surprisingly altered the text of H in accordance with $D^2F$. But I doubt whether he would have departed from his copy-text had he not been under the erroneous impression that $D^1$ agreed with $D^2F$, whereas, in fact, it agrees with H.

a conclusion. What is undoubtedly a common mis-spelling in $D^1$ and H is found at w 339, 'Height Vesper', where $D^2NF$ (and also Con) have the correct spelling 'Hight'. But this, though curious, is too trivial to carry weight: it may even be original, though Simpson alters it.[1] The last agreement is at w 640. One of the satirical fortunes given to the Wenches mentions 'Dowcets', whereupon a Clown exclaims,

> Ha, Pru', has he hit you in the teeth with the sweet bit?

and another adds,

> Let it alone; she'll swallow it well enough...

So $D^1$, supported by H. But NF ($D^2$ being absent) have 'let her alone', which is certainly the more pertinent reading. However, 'Let it alone' may be used in the general sense of let the matter rest, don't interfere; and the variant may have been introduced by a scribe, even unconsciously—or else possibly in revision.[2] Clearly no great weight can be attached to any of these.

Lastly, there are eight readings in which it might appear that $D^1$ and $f$ were associated in error where H was correct.[3] Three are quite simple cases, and in each I believe H to be corrupt. I only include them here because Simpson takes the opposite view. The only one of any interest is at w 186-7. In H the passage stands as follows:

> Heres no Iustice Lippus
> will seeke for to nip vs
> in Cramp-ringe or Cippus
> and then for to stripp vs
> and after to whipp us
> while here we doe tary
> (his Iustice to vary)

This can only be made to yield reasonable sense by treating the last line as an afterthought, as H indicates by the parentheses that seem in the manuscript to have been added after the line had been written. $D^1$ and NF transpose the last two

---

[1] See, however, p. 73, note 2.

[2] That the scribe of $f$ (or of the source of $d^2f$) was given to emendation seems likely from two variants at the end of the Porter's speech at Burley. At B 21 the substitution of 'heape' for 'poure' avoids the awkwardness of 'poure on more' and at B 25 that of 'them' for the second 'him' is in concord with the plural subject. Since the speech was not repeated at Windsor there would be no call for Jonson to revise it.

[3] In the present connexion I do not consider agreements between $D^1$ and N significant, for reasons discussed at p. 65, where instances are recorded.

lines and so preserve the natural order of thought. These then, by critical standards, should be original. At w 656 H has it that Tom Clod 'lost all his hobnailes at post and at paire', but D¹, supported by NF, 'at post and pare'. Since 'post and pair' is the name of a card game, H is unidiomatic. Again at w 685 H makes Townshead say:

> I sweare Ile neuer marry for that and be but to giue fortune my foe the lie

where 'and' stands, of course, for 'if'; but idiom requires 'if it be', and D¹ and NF alike duly read 'an't be', for which 'and be' in H is apparently no more than a slip.[1]

Rather less obvious is a fourth instance at w 254. The Captain, reading James's fortune, and before he has recognized him for the King, speaks of his 'territories store',

> w^ch you like a Lord and a Prince of yo^r peace
> Content w^th yo^r hauinge despise to increase

So H, which in reading 'a Prince' has the support of Con alone, but is followed by Simpson (who seems not to have known of any variant). The meaning of 'a Prince of your peace', however, escapes me. D¹ and NF, on the other hand, read 'the Prince', and their meaning I take to be 'which you in lordly manner and as the ruler of your peaceful way of life . . .'. But at first sight it looks as though 'Lord' and 'Prince' should be parallel and equally connected with 'of your peace', in which case they would of course need the same article, and I conclude that assimilation occurred in H and Con independently.

The remaining four instances are more complicated. The most significant is at w 149. The passage runs in H as follows.

> what sayes Alchindus
> and Pharaotes Indus
> Iohn de Indagine
> w^th all theire paginæ
> treating of Palmistry
> and this is all mistry

but for the fifth line D¹ has

> Faces and Palmistry,

and ƒ(N)

> of faces and Palmistrye . . .

---

[1] It might be plausibly argued that 'and' would pass well enough for 'an't' in rustic speech; but while independent normalization in the two printed texts would not surprise us, it would be much less likely to occur in N or ƒ.

There is no doubt that H gives what at first sight appears to be the most satisfactory reading, and as such it was naturally retained by Simpson. It is also clear that if H is original there must exist some close relation between $f$ and $D^1$ that would be inconsistent with the independence of the latter. Now, I do not pretend to understand the text altogether or to say exactly what it was that Jonson wrote, but I think that closer consideration throws some doubt on the reading of H. To me at least 'treating of' looks very like sophistication, and it would certainly be no surprise to find Jonson coupling physiognomy with palmistry, as indeed he does at B 450. The reading of $f$ is not elegant but it makes sense of a sort, and may have arisen through an attempt to emend that of $D^1$. Whether this can possibly be original I hardly know: there may be some deep-seated corruption. In any case, I think that the position is too obscure to form the basis of any critical argument.

There is another difficult variant in the conclusion at W 1205. The whole speech runs in H:

> Glorie of o$^{rs}$ and Grace of all the earthe
> how well yo$^r$ figure dothe become yo$^r$ bir⟨the
> as in you forme and fortune equall stood
> and onelie vertue gott aboue yo$^r$ blood

In the third line $D^1$ reads 'As in your forme' and $D^2$, followed by NF, 'As if your forme'. The reading of $D^1$ makes no sense: that of $D^2$NF is no doubt possible, but there is some force in Dr. Simpson's privately expressed opinion that the reading of H is sufficiently superior to incline us to accept it as correct. If that be admitted, then the readings of $D^1$ and of $D^2$NF, though not identical, are sufficiently alike to raise a suspicion of relationship between the texts. The suspicion, however, is not a strong one, and there are several possible explanations, for which reference may be made to the notes.

Another reading that might be thought to impugn the independence of $D^1$ is at B 345, where H reads:

> Face of a Rose
> I pry'thee dispose
> some small peece of siluer it shalbe no losse
> but onelie to make the signe of the Crosse . . .

In place of 'dispose' $D^1D^2$F all have 'depose', but N has 'despose' and Con agrees with H. Here, of course, to dispose or to depose equally means no more than to provide. *O.E.D.*

cites the present passage under 'Depose' (vb., sense 1), for the meaning to lay or put down (to deposit), but it seems that the associated sense (1. b), to put in some one's charge, would be equally appropriate. Under 'Dispose' it also gives several senses, such as to deposit or assign, that fit the passage no less well: indeed, it is not easy to distinguish the meaning of the two words. Were it not for the support given to H by N and Con, one would not hesitate to pronounce it in error, although Simpson (without apparently knowing these texts) follows it. But the support may not be as significant as it looks. In N the spelling rather suggests a perversion of 'depose', and the authority of Con is not high. And when we consider that in the present sense 'depose' is at the best unusual, whereas the common phrase 'to dispose of' an object would naturally come to mind, we may perhaps allow that the chance of more or less unconscious substitution in several unrelated texts is not negligible. For my part I have little doubt that the reading of $D^1 D^2 F$ is, in fact, original.[1]

Lastly, there is a very complicated variant involving three readings in w 250–1. The couplet runs in H:

> To hunt the braue stag not so much for yo<sup>r</sup> food
> as the weale of yo<sup>r</sup> bodie and the healthe of yo<sup>r</sup> blood

Here 'your' appears three times and on each occasion it is replaced by 'the' in at least one text. The actual readings are:

$D^1$: the . . . the . . . the
Con: the . . . your . . . y<sup>r</sup>
H: yo<sup>r</sup> . . . yo<sup>r</sup> . . . yo<sup>r</sup>
N: y<sup>r</sup> . . . your . . . your
F: the . . . your . . . your

(Confusion between 'y<sup>e</sup>' and 'y<sup>r</sup>' is, of course, easy, and it may have occurred in N, but otherwise it is doubtful whether it enters into the problem.) So far as HNF are concerned there is agreement in the second and third places (and simple opposition to $D^1$); but as regards the first place they disagree (N following H, and F following $D^1$). Now if, as is possible, Con is an independent (if unreliable) witness, its evidence should decide in favour of HNF in the second and third places, and in favour of $D^1 F$ in the first. (It will be noticed that the second and third are truly parallel and must agree, but that the first

---

[1] Of course, the reading of $D^2$ might well be due to contamination by $D^1$ (see pp. 58–9), and contamination of F by $D^2$ is not out of the question (see p. 65). But such successive contamination is clearly most improbable.

is only apparently parallel and may differ.) I suggest, therefore, that the original had 'the ... your ... your' (as in F and Con); that in D¹ the second and third were wrongly attracted to the first; and that the first was wrongly attracted to the second and third independently in H and N (the latter suggesting that, in fact, the reading of *f* was 'yᵉ').

It seems, therefore, that the variants that conflict with the independence of D¹ are either doubtful, or of little weight, or capable of other explanation: moreover, they are mutually contradictory. This being so we may, I think, regard the group HD²NF as established, with source of its own independent of D¹. We have next to inquire whether the members of this group are each independently derived from this source, or whether they fall into subsidiary groups.

### (2) EVIDENCE FOR THE GROUP NF

That N and F form a group by themselves and are derived from a particular source, which we have called *f*, is almost too obvious to need formal demonstration. Where the evidence is so abundant I confine myself to those portions of the text in which D² is present, in order not to risk including readings that may, in fact, have been shared by *d*².[1] One of the most curious points and most indicative of common derivation, the arbitrary writing of phrases as separate lines at w 835, 847–8, has been already noted (p. 44). The speaker's name is omitted at w 838 and again at w 983. Verbal errors are common: w 216 'Vrands' ('urands') for 'viands', w 290 'Sallance' for 'ballance', B 454 'Cupid' for 'Cupid's', w 548 'pish' ('pish') for 'parish', w 677 'tri'mge' for 'tryeing', w 894 'perfumes' for 'perfumers' (corrected in some copies of F), w 938 'slirted' for 'flirted', w 1049 'they' for 'the', B 913 'since' for 'sine' (riming with 'wine'), w 1123 'an' for 'and', w 1150 'meane' for 'meant', w 1217 'and' omitted. These will suffice for the purpose.

In considering the relation of N and F there are two points to be borne in mind. N and H are both manuscripts written possibly as early as 1621: F and D² are texts printed in 1640 or 1641. It is therefore only natural that in many spellings and the like H and N should agree on the one hand and D² and F on the other. Such readings merely illustrate the habits of scribes and compositors separated by a couple of decades

[1] I give the readings in the exact form in which they appear in N, adding that of F in parentheses if materially different.

and have no bearing on textual relationships. Furthermore, the printer of F may have been acquainted with $D^b$, and although we were, in fact, unable to trace any definite typographical resemblance (see pp. 15–17), the possibility of conflation remains, and should we (as possibly at w 264–7 and 1243) find unexpected resemblances between F and $D^2$ (or $D^1$, according to the part of the text in question), we must not rashly infer any close relationship between $f$ and $d^2$ (or $d^1$).[1]

A feature that might at first sight throw some doubt on the close relation of N and F is a number of instances of anomalous agreement between N and other texts. Three have already come to notice. At w 1266 N has 'make' like $D^1$ and H, where $D^2$ and F have 'makes' (p. 59); at B 345 N has 'despose' where H has 'dispose' and $D^1D^2F$ 'depose' (p. 62); and at w 250 N and H read 'your' ($y^r$, '$yo^r$') where $D^1$ and F have 'the' (p. 63). We decided that these agreements were most likely due to accidental variation in N, as the form of the last two suggests. We know too that the scribe of N was given to conjectural emendation and showed considerable skill in that dangerous game (cf. p. 94). In the Windsor Prologue (w 16) he altered 'growe' to 'proue' because 'growe a disease' was ambiguous, and in the additional stanzas of Cock Lorel (w 942) he achieved a decided improvement by altering 'before, & behinde' to 'hee lefte=behinde'. These readings are found in no other text. On the other hand, when at B 408 he corrected 'know' ($D^2F$) to 'knewe', and when at w 899 he restored metrical smoothness by reading 'neuer had' for 'had never' ($D^2F$), he returned to the original reading of H; and when at B 456 he corrected 'told' ($D^2F$) to 'rob'd' he returned to the original reading preserved both in $D^1$ and H. At B 8 N agrees with $D^1$ in reading 'affects' where H has 'effecte̲' with the concurrence of F; but this is most likely because H and F independently substituted a more obvious word. There is then nothing in these readings to invalidate the group NF.

## (3) EVIDENCE FOR THE GROUP $D^2f$

Glancing through the textual variants one is struck by the frequency of the grouping ($D^1$) H : $D^2$NF.[2] Now if $D^1$ is independent, the agreement of $D^1$ and H should guarantee their

[1] Instances of resemblance between $D^1$ and F have already been examined (pp. 60–4), but we found no need either to infer a special relationship or to invoke conflation.

[2] The full form is comparatively rare owing to the restricted field for which $D^1$ and $D^2$ are both present.

readings as correct, from which it would follow that in the variants in question there was common corruption in D²NF. In the absence of D¹ the variant might, on the other hand, be due to error in H, and this is undoubtedly sometimes the cause; it follows that in these cases D²NF can only be condemned of error if such error is manifest.

Among instances of manifest error the most obvious is the omission of the last half-stanza of the Prince's fortune, w 367–9, for which H is thus our only authority.[1] Another glaring mistake is the printing or writing of w 873–4 as one line, owing apparently to a corruption that destroyed the rime. H reads:

>and chaunt out the farce
>of the grand devillſ arse

of which D²NF make nonsense (or at best a different and certainly not intended sense) by substituting 'fart' for 'farce'. Another pair of lines coalesce at w 1198–9, though here the rime (an identical rime) is preserved. A further case of misunderstanding is at w 464, where H has

>There's written Francke

(i.e. there is openly written) but where, owing it seems to mistaking 'Francke' for a proper name, D²NF read

>Thus written to Franke . . .[2]

We may further note that (D¹ being absent) w 862,

>like a chime in yo$^r$ eare

is preserved only in H; and since it is not a line we can reasonably suppose to have been either invented by the scribe or suppressed in revision, we can only infer an accidental omission common to D²NF.

A number of purely verbal variants points in the same direction. In w 925(H),

>w$^{th}$ a Clarcke like a gizard truss'd vnder each arme

the 'thrust' that D²NF substitute for 'truss'd' is no less clearly

---

[1] The most obvious, but not the most significant, for omissions are not, in fact, very good evidence of the exclusive derivation of the texts in which they occur. There is always the possibility that the texts in question were copied after accidental damage to an original that may have given rise to other texts before mutilation (cf. *The Play of Antichrist*, 1935, p. lii).

[2] N in the first instance omitted this line and the next, but later added them in the margin. It may be significant that Tan and Raw omit the couplet altogether, presumably as not intelligible.

an error for making quite good sense—it is, in fact, repeated from w 909. Other obvious errors in D²ƒ are: B 408 'know' for 'knew' (corrected in N), B 441 'heart' for 'hurt', B 456 'told' for 'robd' (corrected in N), B 475 'given you' for 'gi'n you' (destroying the rime), and w 915 'have choakt' for 'choake'. The last is a deliberate emendation for the sake of a better sequence of tenses, but overlooks the fact that it again destroys the rime: it might even be an alteration made by the author in a moment of aberration.

I should like to call attention to one further error, an error that occurs in a passage neither in D¹ nor H, and for which therefore D²NF are our only authorities. The last couplet of the Earl of Buccleuch's fortune (w 499–500) runs in D²:

> Pallas, shall be both your Sword, and your Gage;
> Truth, beare your Shield, and fortune your Page.

Now though Simpson introduces this into his text more or less as it stands, it is obvious nonsense: Fortune cannot be expected to go about carrying Buccleuch's page. We should have to read 'be your Page' did the metre allow it. Nor is it altogether clear why an abstract personification like Truth should be supposed to *bear* his shield, and the comparatively material Pallas *be* his sword. The only remedy is to alter 'beare' to 'be', and the former may be no more than an error in the source of D²NB. But I am by no means certain that it was not (like 'one' at B 413) a slip of the author's.[1]

A very interesting variant which, if with Simpson we were to rely on H, would imply a common error in D²NF, is found in the Cock Lorel ballad at w 938. D¹ is unfortunately defective. H reads:

> All wᶜʰ he blewe away with a fart

but instead of 'blewe' D² has 'flirted', of which 'slirted' in NF is an obvious corruption. This at first sight looks like an error, though a very strange one. The nearest sense recorded in *O.E.D.* under the verb 'flirt' is to flick with the finger. But under the substantive, which usually means a rap or quick movement of the hand,[2] there is recorded a rare use for a gust of air, with a quotation of 1699, 'some small flurts of a Westerly Wind'. Here, then, is exactly the meaning we want,

---

[1] Lord Buccleuch's fortune, like Lady Exeter's, appears to have been a last-minute addition, and in both cases Jonson's draft may have been hastily written.

[2] As in flirting a fan: cf. w 1021–3 in H, 'haue a licence to play at the hedg a flirt for a sheet or a shirt'.

and the reading is one that no scribe would have invented. In 'flirted', therefore, we undoubtedly have Jonson's original reading, altered in H to the synonymous 'blewe' by a scribe to whom the word was unfamiliar.[1]

There is thus ample evidence for the existence of the group $D^2NF$ implying a source for these texts of which H is independent. Against this I know of only one variant that might suggest a different grouping.[2] In H w 1042–4 run:

> mine owne is as ample
> and fruitfull a nose
> as a witt can suppose

and with this N and F agree. But $D^2$ reads 'As wit can suppose', and this certainly seems the preferable reading. At the same time the reading of H, which may be paraphrased 'as the understanding of any man can conceive', is perfectly possible and perhaps not un-Jonsonian, and it may have been the very plausibility of the alternative that led to the omission of 'a' in $D^2$. In any case so speculative a variant can carry no weight against the conclusion already reached.

We have now completed our inquiry and appear to have established the existence of a textual group $HD^2NF$ independent of $D^1$, of a group $D^2NF$ independent of H, and of a group NF independent of $D^2$. This can be summed up in the formula

$$D^1\{H[D^2(NF)]\}$$

and the genetic relationship of the texts may be displayed diagrammatically thus:

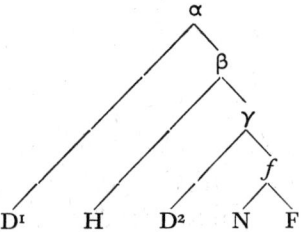

---

[1] We cannot argue that Jonson himself substituted 'blewe' in revision (a possibility we recognized in the somewhat similar case of 'maunds' at B 581: see p. 57) since there is no evidence of his having had anything to do with the production of H. It is theoretically possible that Jonson altered 'blewe' to 'flirted' in revision, but it is not a possibility that need be seriously considered. I am pleased to add that Dr. Simpson now accepts 'flirted', remarking that it makes a better line.

[2] That is in passages in which $D^1$ is absent. Anomalous agreements between $D^1$ and $f$ or N have already been considered at pp. 60–4.

The editorial implications of this scheme, in so far as the common text is concerned, are normally as follows:[1]

D¹ is the only text in which a reading opposed by a consensus of the other texts can be original;

Agreement between N and F establishes the reading of $f$: if N and F disagree, the reading of $f$ is established by the agreement of either with D² (or if D² is absent, with H);

Agreement between D² and $f$ establishes the reading of $\gamma$: if D² and $f$ disagree, the reading of $\gamma$ is established by the agreement of either with H (if D² is absent and H and $f$ disagree, the reading of $\gamma$ is indeterminate, unless the agreement of D¹ with $f$ proves the presence of individual error in H);

Agreement between H and $\gamma$ (or if D² is absent, between H and $f$) establishes the reading of $\beta$: if H and $\gamma$ (or $f$) disagree, the reading of $\beta$ is established by the agreement of either with D¹ (if D¹ is absent or divergent, H and $\gamma$ (or $f$) are of equal extrinsic authority);

Lastly, agreement between D¹ and $\beta$ establishes the reading of $\alpha$, and if they disagree they are of equal extrinsic authority.

For the bulk of the revisions $\beta$ is, of course, our ultimate authority; for certain specific additions and alterations, $\gamma$; for the final revisions, $f$. In the sections in question, for the text of $\beta$, H and $\gamma$ (or where D² is absent, H and $f$) are of equal authority; for the text of $\gamma$, D² and $f$; for the text of $f$, N and F.

The construction of a critical text is governed by these few rules. To say that apart from revision, revision is irrelevant, sounds like and is a truism. Nevertheless, it may not be superfluous to point out that, except where intentional alterations were made by the author, there is not an original version and a revised version, but a single text going back to one original: so far as the common text is concerned, D¹ is as much an authority as $\beta$ for what was spoken at Windsor, and $\beta$ is as much an authority as D¹ for what was spoken at Burley. In

---

[1] By 'normally' I mean apart from coincident error, conjectural emendation, and contamination. The only probable instances of contamination are a few readings of D² borrowed from D¹ (see pp. 58–9). There is a possibility of contamination of F by D² (see pp. 15–16, 65), but the only hints of it actually found are at w 264–7 and 1243 (see notes), and it would in general be indistinguishable from variation in N.

Textual inferences from the scheme, which should in theory be obvious, are in practice complicated by the partial absence of D¹ and D². I have disregarded the slight complications introduced by occasional deficiencies in other texts.

reconstructing the Burley and Windsor texts, when one discovers, as frequently happens, that $D^1$ and β have different but equally possible readings, it is tempting to keep one in one text and the other in the other, as representing Burley and Windsor traditions respectively. But it would be uncritical to yield to the temptation: there are not two textual traditions, but one.

When we look beyond the immediate editorial problem and try to form a complete picture of the textual history of the masque, we need to combine the data we have just acquired respecting scribal variation with what we have previously learned respecting revision. The simplest way to do so would be to suppose that the several stages of revision were carried out in the course of transcription, that is, in the actual process of writing the manuscripts β, γ, and ƒ. In that case the stemma printed above would represent at once the variational and revisional facts. It seems, however, inherently improbable that the masque should have been three times copied by the author and each time in some measure revised. There is, moreover, the difficulty that β, besides extensive revision, contains errors that it is difficult to suppose that Jonson would have made in copying his own work; this also applies to γ and even more strongly to ƒ. It thus becomes clear that we must regard revision and transcription as distinct operations, as it is on the face of it likely that in fact they were. We shall, therefore, have to combine the stemma on p. 68 with the diagram at the end of the previous section (p. 53). Such a composite diagram would take the following form:[1]

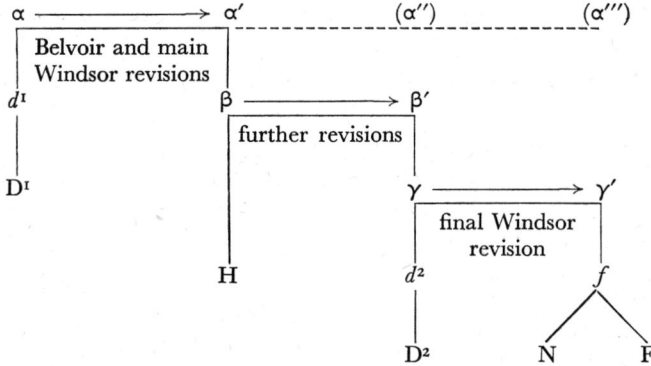

[1] In discussion I have, as a rule, avoided using the symbols α′, β′, γ′ as not strictly necessary and possibly confusing. Thus when I speak of revision in β, I mean revision that manifests itself in β, having actually been carried out in α′; and similarly in other cases.

# Evidence of the Scribal Variants

It is not without regret that one abandons the idea of 'continuous copy' upon which successive revisions were carried out (and I have allowed it to retain a sort of ghostly existence in the diagram), but the textual facts are inexorable. The only way to reconcile the textual evidence with the postulate of successive revision in a single manuscript would be to suppose that γ was copied substantially from an unaltered β with insertion of certain revisions from α″, and that ƒ was copied substantially from an unaltered γ with insertion of the final revisions from α‴. This is not theoretically impossible, though it has a factitious air; but in view of the detailed dovetailing, particularly of the final revisions in ƒ, I hardly think that the idea can be seriously entertained.[1]

### NOTE ON SOME SUBSIDIARY TEXTS

#### 1. *The Conway manuscript (see p. 9)*

This manuscript, which is endorsed 'The Gypsies Maaske at Burley', contains the fortunes of the original version, but it differs from D¹ in including the Countess of Exeter's, and from all the main texts in placing the Countess of Buckingham's immediately after that of her daughter-in-law, the Marchioness, instead of before Lady Purbeck's. The first may be taken as evidence that Lady Exeter was, in fact, present at Burley: the second is apparently a disarrangement of its own.

Its chief interest lies in the fact that it records the names of some of the speakers. The actual headings, in order, are as follows:

| | | |
|---|---|---|
| B 247 | The kings fortune spoken by my Lo: Marquesse Bu: [the song, B 276–86, is omitted, but in its place is the heading:] |
| 287 | Daunce and the fortune is persu'd by the same |
| 310–11 | The Princes by Lo: Feilding |
| 337–8 | the Lady Marquesses by Mʳ: Porter |
| 419–20 | the Countesse of Buckingham |
| 388–9 | the Countesse of Ruttland Mʳ: Porter |
| 406–7 | the Countesse of Exeter |
| 445–6 | The La Purbecks by my Lord Feilding |
| 469–70 | My Lady Hattons |

[1] A conceivable line of argument would be that while ƒ was in the main copied from an unaltered γ, the whole of the section containing the final revisions, namely w 570–837, with 978–83 as an appendix, was copied from α‴. In this section D² is absent as far as w 810, so that the D²ƒ variants that normally prove ƒ's derivation from γ are almost entirely absent. (There is, in fact, only one small D²ƒ variant, at w 836, and this could easily be explained.) But if in this section ƒ were indeed copied from α‴, we should expect to find specific agreements between it and D¹ (which is present down to w 810), whereas its affinities are clearly with H (e.g. in w 678–9, 690 ff., 716, 728; see pp. 55–7: for its agreement with D¹ at w 656 see p. 61).

## Introduction

Here 'my Lo: Marquesse Bu:' is, of course, Buckingham, who therefore took the part of the First Gipsy, always called the Captain. 'Lord Feilding' is Buckingham's brother-in-law, William, Baron Feilding, who became Earl of Denbigh the following year: he took the Second Gipsy. Endymion Porter, it seems, took the Third Gipsy. Further, we know from B 438, 'Two of your Sons are Gipsies too', that one of Buckingham's brothers was present,[1] almost certainly John Villiers, Viscount Purbeck, who therefore probably spoke his mother's fortune as Fourth Gipsy.[2] A Fifth Gipsy, to whose identity we have no clue, spoke Lady Hatton's fortune (she was Lady Purbeck's mother). There seem to have been seven Gipsies in all (as probably provided for in the original form of the directions at B 93–4 and W 86–7: see note), the other two being the Patrico and the Jackman, who were presumably played by professionals. (The Patrico is not 'metamorphosed': nothing is said of the Jackman.) The fortune of the late comer, Lady Exeter (the only Lady not connected with Buckingham), fell to the Patrico.

The endorsement itself illustrates the eccentric spelling of the scribe, and this is further seen in several peculiar readings of the text.[3]

| | | | |
|---|---|---|---|
| B 249 | straak *for* stroak | B 334 | Eeuen *for* evening |
| 255 | suine *for* swine | 353, 441 | eather *for* either |
| 273 | ragnes *for* raigne | 402 | reneiw *for* renew |
| 304 | amonke *for* Among | 461 | ether *for* either |

These almost suggest a scribe unfamiliar with English, and so does the miswriting of 'helpe' as 'heple' at B 447 and again at B 478. Manifest errors peculiar to this manuscript are:

| | | | |
|---|---|---|---|
| B 251 | the *omitted*. | B 359 | hee *for* He's |
| 265 | to *omitted*. | 361 | aske *for* ak's |
| 267 | Beanes *for* Barnes | 371 | cast *for* ras't |
| 268 | Mercurius *for* Mercuries | 375–6 | *as one line.* |
| 274–5 | *as one line.* | 393 | still *for* Stile |
| 290 | fall *for* fate | 412 | as *for* Is |
| 313 | ²the *omitted*. | 416 | For *omitted*. |
| 315 | fortunes *for* fortune | 454 | Cupitts *for* Cupid's |
| 343 | pine *for* Rime | 458 | murder *for* murther |
| 347 | ¹the *omitted* | 476 | persewe *for* preserve |
| 350 | this *for* these | 480 | selfe *for* Sexe |
| 354 | fallen *for* to fall | | |

[1] Unless 'Two of your Sons' means one son and one son-in-law.

[2] As Cole observes (p. 8), his younger brother Christopher and his half-brother Edward had lately been in trouble over monopolies and Buckingham had thrown them to the wolves. They are unlikely to have been present. Cole did not know of Con and supposed (p. 9) that Lord Purbeck spoke his wife's fortune, since this 'is cast, unlike all the others, in the vein of a lover'.

[3] In the writing 'a' and 'u' are generally indistinguishable. In the lists that follow corrections are from D¹, except for B 406–17 where they are from D².

## Evidence of the Scribal Variants

Some of these (e.g. B 393, 454, and even 350) may be no more than eccentric spellings. At B 354 'fallen' in place of 'to fall' looks at first sight like an emendation or even an original reading—Kate was already married to her Gipsy—but the phrase 'it will be your fate' at B 357 proves that Jonson really intended the future. The following readings, although not necessarily wrong in themselves are found in no other text, and may be assumed to be errors.

| | | | | |
|---|---|---|---|---|
| B 251 | know *for* troe | | B 358 | once *omitted*. |
| 262 | great *omitted*. | | 359 | hee *for* He's |
| 266 | quallityes *for* quality | | 371 | new *for* newly |
| 273 | ragnes *for* raigne | | 396, 397 | yee *for* you |
| 302 | state *for* states | | 401 | that *for* Who |
| 321 | fitter one *for* fitter | | | held *for* knowne |
| 325 | to *for* of | | 410 | already *for* ready |
| 334 | Eeuen *for* evening | | 423 | this *for* ²the |
| 340 | euer *for* e're | | 426 | stole *for* stolne |
| 342 | shall *omitted*. | | 448 | could *for* would |
| 346 | One *for* Some | | 466 | doe *for* may |
| 347 | But *omitted*. | | 476 | that *for* the |
| 357 | dare *for* doe | | | | |

The readings of Con acquire importance for us only when those of the main texts differ in such a way as to leave the original in doubt, that is, as a rule, only when there is a conflict between H and $D^1$, or if $D^1$ is absent between H and $D^2$. It then becomes important to establish, if possible, the precise position of Con in the textual scheme.[1]

One point we may notice at starting is that in B 270–2 Con shows no affinity either with the highly exclamatory punctuation of $D^1$ or with the almost complete absence of punctuation of H: it usually adopts an intermediate pointing more like that of $D^2NF$, though without any close similarity. These, however, are clearly peculiarities of the compositor of $D^1$ and the scribe of H, and all we can infer is that Con was not derived from either of these individual texts. Similar independence is shown by the fact that Con does not reproduce the individual errors or peculiarities of either $D^1$ or H. Thus it corrects the spelling of both at B 329 'Height'.[2] It corrects $D^1$ at B 254 'time', B 348 'hollow', B 363 omission of 'you', B 392 'O' (for 'and'), and B 439 'he' (for 'see'); to which we may, I think, add B 332 'Of'. It corrects H at B 339 'Horle' (but see note), and B 395 'will' (for 'shall'); and I think that at B 304 we may take 'amonke' as correcting H 'amongst'.[3] It also corrects $D^2$ at B 408 'know'.

---

[1] Since the detailed evidence will be found in the textual apparatus it need not be repeated here, and we can proceed directly to its analysis.

[2] Since spelling is certainly not a strong point with Con we may perhaps infer that 'Height' is due to independent error in $D^1$ and H rather than to their having reproduced a misspelling of the original.

[3] There is one seeming agreement with an error in $D^1$ and one with an error in

Some anomalous variants involving Con have already been discussed. In the curious case of 'the' and 'your' at B 256–7 we decided (pp. 63–4) that 'the' was original in B 256 and 'your' in B 257, and that Con merely agreed with the correct reading of D¹ in the first and of H in the second line. It has, therefore, no significance. More important are two other cases in which Con agrees with H. At B 260 H and Con alone read 'a Prince' for 'the Prince'. But we saw (p. 61) that the agreement of D¹NF proves the latter to be correct, and to have been the reading of β; and since Con cannot be directly dependent on H, their agreement must be a coincidence (due to assimilation with 'a Lord'). The same applies to B 345, where we decided (pp. 62–3) that 'depose' must be original and 'dispose' (or 'despose') due to coincident error in Con, H, and N. Significant too is the error 'one' at B 413, which is in all the available texts. If the error arose in β, then Con is descended from β; if Con is not descended from β, then the error was already in α—which is not unlikely. So far, then, the position of Con is not determined by any evidence that will bear examination.

There are half a dozen straight variants between D¹ and H in which the evidence of Con, if independent, would be decisive.

B 258 Y'are H: You are D¹ Con
    territories H Con: Territorie D¹
259 and H Con (&): but D¹
267 You'are H: You are D¹ Con

B 319 shall H Con: should D¹
322 offerd H Con (offer'd): offred D¹
443 besides H Con: beside D¹

To these we may add where D¹ is absent:

B 417 it H Con: *om.* D²N F

The two instances in which Con supports D¹ may be immediately dismissed. In B 267 H has preserved a Jonsonian 'apostrophus' that D¹ and Con have ignored, no doubt independently. In B 258 β probably had the same peculiarity, again ignored by D¹ and Con, but made the occasion of an elision in H.¹ In the four other cases, if Con is derived from β its evidence adds nothing to our knowledge: if, however, it is independent, it confirms the reading of H and convicts D¹ of error. In the additional case, B 417, the support of Con at least suggests that H represents β correctly, and if Con is independent

H, which therefore cancel out. At B 322 D¹ and Con have 'Than' where all other texts have the certainly original 'then': a case of independent modernization. At B 345 H has 'pry'thee' and Con 'prethee' where all the other texts have 'pray thee': another case probably of partially coincident variation. That accidental coincidence occurs is seen at B 254 where Con and N have 'lucke sake' and all other texts 'lucks sake', and at B 340 where Con and NF have 'euer' where D¹HD² have a contracted form.

¹ We may similarly dismiss two cases not included above, namely B 367 and 417, in which H and N have 'wilbe' and Con agrees with the printed texts in reading 'will be'.

## Evidence of the Scribal Variants

of β it further proves that β correctly represented the special original used for this fortune.

There remains one crucial reading in which D¹ and H and Con all differ. Presumably B 369 originally ran

> There is neuer a line in your hand but doth tell vs

but each text, confronted with this unexpectedly long line, has eliminated a syllable near the beginning, and done so in a way of its own; H reading 'there's neuer', D¹ 'There is not', and Con 'there is nere'. I do not see how any of these readings can be derived from any other, and I conclude that the three texts must be independently derived from α. This involves, of course, accepting the implications of this conclusion respecting the readings of D¹ when H is supported by Con. At the same time it must be admitted that a textual conclusion based on a single reading can only carry limited weight.[1]

### 2. *The Tanner and Rawlinson manuscripts (see p. 9)*

These two manuscripts are much less important than the Conway, and may be considered together as they are evidently closely related. They contain the same four Lords' fortunes out of the eight spoken, and give them in the same order: the Lord Keeper's, the Lord Steward's, the Lord Treasurer's, and the Lord Chamberlain's. Thus they agree with H against the other texts in wrongly placing the Lord Chamberlain's last instead of first, but differ from all in placing the Lord Steward's between, instead of after, those of the Lord Keeper and the Lord Treasurer, and in heading it 'The Lord Dukes [Tan 'the lo: Duks'] fortune'—the Lord Steward was Lodovick Stewart, Duke of Lenox and later of Richmond. They have a number of readings not found in any of the main texts, and some of these they share. In the following list I star those that are manifest errors.

w 376, 378  who *for* that Raw  
    382  the *for* theire Tan Raw  
    384  *have *omitted* Raw  
    388  yt is *for* tis Raw  
        he is *for* hee's Raw  
    389+finis *added* Raw  
    392  this *for* the Tan  
    396 this *for* that Tan Raw  
    400–1  **as one line* Raw  
    401  **for *for* of Raw  
    402–5  **as two lines* Raw  

w 406  Layd *for* too Raw  
    407  that *for* thats Raw  
    409  neuer *for* yet not Tan Raw  
    414  I am come *for* I come Raw  
        and *omitted* Tan  
    415  I pray *for* pray Tan  
    416  youl *for* you Raw  
        rech *for* stretch Raw  
    417  therrand *for* the errand Tan  
        bin *for* beene Tan  
    418  by *for* o' Tan  

---

[1] The notes on w 281–2 and B 369 should be consulted.

|   |   |
|---|---|
| w 421 ²the *omitted* Raw | w 460 \*good *omitted* Raw |
| 422 peticõns (t *altered from* n) *for* pensions Raw | 461 master is *for* masters Tan Raw |
| 423 the Exchequer *for* thExchequer Tan | 462 w^ch *for* that Tan Raw |
| \*office *for* creditt Raw | 464–5 \**omitted* Tan Raw |
| 455–6 \**as one line* Raw | 467 ²by *omitted* Raw |

Of these readings 19, including 7 errors, are peculiar to Raw; 7 are peculiar to Tan; and 6, including 1 error, are common. This is sufficient to establish their common origin and to prove that they are not immediately derived from either β or γ, though they might be derived from either through some other manuscript (not γ or *f*).

The reading 'peticõns' at w 422 in Raw appears to have been a deliberate alteration, for the scribe started to write 'pensions' but changed his mind when he got as far as 'pen'. It can hardly be said to make any real sense though I have not starred it as necessarily wrong. The common omission of w 464–5 is interesting, because the scribe of N also omitted the lines in the first instance, and only later added them in the margin in the corrupt form of γ (cf. p. 66). No doubt in each case the omission was due to the couplet being unintelligible in the form presented to the scribe, and the omission therefore serves to associate Tan and Raw with γ rather than with H. Of this we find further evidence in other variants recorded in the apparatus and now to be examined.

In eight cases the evidence of our two manuscripts is ambiguous or rather discrepant. At w 385 Raw agrees with H 'hath', and Tan with D²N F 'has', and alike in this line and w 389 HFRaw have 'beene' and D²NTan 'bin'. So again at w 417 HD²FRaw have 'beene' and NTan 'bin'. In the same line HNTan read 'errand' and D²FRaw 'Errant', mere variant spellings; and at w 420 HD²FTan have 'will be' and NRaw 'wilbe', a merely scribal trick. Lastly at w 402 and 404 (H being absent) D² and Tan spell 'venture' and NFRaw 'venter'. All these variants are clearly due to the individual predilections of the scribes and are without serious value as evidence.

We are left with nine straight variants between H on the one hand and D²NF on the other, with one or other of which both Tan and Raw agree. They support H in four readings: w 381 'euerie' against 'ev'ry', w 392, 457 'in' against 'i'', and w 408 'you'll' ('youle') against 'you will'. Little weight can be attached to any of these. On the other hand, they support D²NF in five readings: they include w 402–5, which are not in H; they omit H's redundant 'S^r' at w 414; in the next line they read 'Since' instead of 'sin'' and 'for no' instead of 'not for'; and at w 418 Raw has 'on' (Tan 'by') instead of 'o''. The last is again trivial, but the first four are significant. If, therefore, as is probable, the lines w 402–5 were added in γ rather than omitted in H, and if, as is almost certain, 'Since' at w 415 is an error in γ, it follows that it is from γ that Tan and Raw are derived. This conclusion, however, carries with it no textual consequences of any importance.[1]

### 3. *The Chilmead manuscript* (Add.: *see p.* 10)

This, which contains the duet of w 508–33 with a musical setting, is from the textual point of view negligible. It is headed 'The Gypsies, Patrico & Iackman'. At w 514 it agrees with D²NF in reading 'them' for ''em' as in H, and again at w 523 in reading 'on the' for 'o' the'. At w 524 it has the more explicit 'h'as' (i.e. he has) for the 'has' of the other texts. At 515 instead of 'do-do-downe' it has 'Downe // //', and it adds a 'Chorus' made up from the last two lines.

## V. ANALYSIS OF THE VARIANTS

I propose, as the final step in our examination, to group the variants according to the texts in which they arose, and to ascertain, so far as possible, which should, whether on intrinsic or extrinsic grounds, be regarded as errors.

My object is twofold. In the first place we desire to ascertain, from a study of their demonstrable errors, the relative reliability of the several texts. For example, D¹ and β contain, of course, many variants in which either reading might be correct, and in choosing between them it should be some sort of a guide to know the relative propensity to error in the two texts. In other words, we know that their external authority is equal; what we are now seeking is their relative intrinsic authority.

But there is another object. We have already seen that whereas D¹ contains (so far as it has survived, and but for one probable omission) the original Burley version of the masque, and H contains the bulk of the revisions made for the Windsor performance,[2] there were also further revisions that appear in D², and yet others that appear in NF. Most of

---

[1] If Tan and Raw are derived from γ independently of d² and f, they should settle differences between these manuscripts; but such differences are as a rule already settled by H. They would, therefore, only be important either where H, D², and f all differed (and no case seems to occur) or where H was absent, as in B 402–5 and 485–500. The second passage is not in Tan or Raw either: in the former Tan supports D² and Raw supports NF.

[2] Here and in what follows I ignore the alterations introduced at Belvoir. These are either recorded in H or else can only be surmised from allusions in the text. The former are substantial: the details of the latter are necessarily unknown to us, but they were probably mere excisions. There is no reason to suppose, and it is in the nature of the case unlikely, that the text underwent between Burley and Belvoir any detailed revision of the kind that is here in question.

these revisions are substantial and easily detected, but we cannot avoid the suspicion, which, in fact, we shall find justified, that some alterations may have been introduced involving no more than an isolated word or phrase, and therefore liable to be mistaken for scribal variations. We need to isolate those readings that appear to be either certainly, probably, or possibly due to revision, and to ascertain how they are distributed through the text. Should we find them widely distributed, and should we find that in practice the distinction between revision and scribal variation is impossible or at least difficult to draw—should we, for example, find the possible cases many and the relatively certain cases few—it will have important consequences for editorial practice in any attempt to establish the texts of the two versions. I have said before (pp. 69–70) that, *apart from deliberate revision*, there is only one textual tradition, a tradition to which *each* text is a witness. This must always remain true—in theory. But in practice, unless we can determine the limits of revision, we shall have to give up all attempt to distinguish between it and scribal variation, and be forced to act as though there were more than one textual tradition. In other words, so far as the portions of the masque common to the two versions are concerned, we shall have to allow $D^1$ to represent a Burley tradition, and the other texts to represent a Windsor tradition in all cases of variation not obviously due to corruption.[1] This, in my view, would be to admit a serious editorial defeat, and I trust that a critical review of the evidence may enable us to avoid it.

Meanwhile we cannot pursue our inquiry into the reliability of the several texts until we have cleared this matter of revision out of the way.

### REVISIONAL VARIATION

Here we are only concerned with revision by the author carried out with a view to fitting the text for the final performance at Windsor. There are also, it is true, some variants in extant texts that are clearly intentional alterations and will be considered later; but since there is no reason to suppose that Jonson was in any way concerned with any of the actual texts that have come down to us, these individual variants must be ascribed to the ingenuity of scribes or compositors, and there is nothing in their character to make such an as-

---

[1] And since revision manifests itself progressively through H, $D^2$, and NF, we should, in fact, be driven to take the highly aberrant NF text as the basis of our own.

sumption improbable.[1] Major revision, of a kind to imply intervention by the author took place exclusively in the three hypothetical manuscripts β, γ, and ƒ, and manifests itself in variation between D¹ and β, H and γ, and D² (or, in the absence of D², H) and ƒ respectively; and it is therefore the variants between these pairs that we must scrutinize for minor revisions that might be mistaken for scribal variants. The criterion to apply is obvious. The reading of the extant text (D¹, H, or D²) must itself be one that we can, on internal grounds, be reasonably sure is Jonson's and not a scribal error; and the variant in the hypothetical manuscript (β, γ, or ƒ) must also be one that we can reasonably suppose Jonson to have substituted for the other. When these conditions are fulfilled we are bound to hold the variant as at least possibly due to revision and to treat it accordingly. The reader may apply his own acumen to the lists that follow. My own opinions on the individual readings are given in the notes, and it is on my ability to make these opinions critically acceptable that any claim on my part to be able to distinguish between revision and scribal variation must rest.[2]

The revision we are discussing is that made in preparation for the Windsor performance. It follows that we are not concerned with any alterations that may be found in those portions of the text that were not repeated at Windsor, notably the entrance speech (B 1–27, only spoken at Burley) and the Ladies fortunes (B 337–480, only spoken at Burley and Belvoir). There are, it is true, a couple of variants in the former (B 21, 25) that satisfy the conditions of revision, and though they are not, perhaps, beyond the capacity of a scribe, it is conceivable that Jonson, on reading through the text, may have touched it up here and there even in the portions that were being discarded. We must allow for his having had eventual publication in mind.[3] But since the readings, sup-

---

[1] Hypothetical texts also appear to contain a few deliberate alterations, the nature of which preclude our ascribing them to the author.

[2] If I have treated as scribal errors any variants that are, in fact, due to revision, they will be found among the 'inferential' errors of γ and ƒ recorded on pp. 90 and 92, or among 'residual variants' on pp. 99–100 and 100–1. (The only reading I myself feel any doubt about is that at W 43.) Readers who wish to pursue the question of possible revision should scrutinize these lists. I trust that I have not dismissed as 'intrinsic' errors any variants that could conceivably be credited to Jonson.

[3] In this connexion it is significant that, so far as we know, the readings first appeared in ƒ, the manuscript that we must believe Jonson to have kept in his own hands.

posing them to be revisions, can never have been spoken in performance, they have no place in the present text.

*Apparent revision in* β.—The first and main revision ($\alpha > \alpha'$) shows itself in variation between $D^1$ and β. Yet of all the variants between these texts only eleven pass muster as revisions, and not all of these are certain—some might properly be queried, but doubt is always a matter of degree.[1] What is even more important is their distribution: with two exceptions they occur within a space of 130 lines in the earlier part of the antimasque, between the country dance and the Patrico's restitution speech. This is no doubt partly accidental, for the end of the antimasque is unfortunately missing in our only copy of $D^a$. But it is permissible to conclude that the β-variants possibly due to revision are practically confined to the antimasque, which is just that portion of the work in which major rewriting (as distinct from excision or substitution) is most in evidence. Here is the list:[2]

| | | | |
|---|---|---|---|
| w 52 | hoofe > hard hoofe | w 673 | not withstanding > *non vpstante* |
| 208 | strict > longe | | |
| 635 | maunds > stalkes | 674 | Tow. *inserted (fresh speech)*. |
| 643 | who's > who standes | 712 | man *added*. |
| 655 | in Christmas will > will in Christmas | 760 | a pair of > my fine |
| 657 | Hobnaile > right naile | 763 | gone *omitted*. |

*Apparent revision in* γ.—The second revision (β > β'), showing itself in variation between H and γ, was much less extensive. Its major features are three insertions and one transposition: to these may be added a passage of three lines near the end of the antimasque, w 979–81, that seems to have been partly rewritten since it contains five variants. This, which was further recast in *f*, has been already considered (p. 44) and need not concern us here. Of the three variants that remain, one comes from the conclusion (and might be queried) and two (which are certain) from the Cock Lorel ballad (which also supplies one of the major additions) in the antimasque, and again in the latter part of it. This may again be due to accident, for the beginning is not present in $D^2$. Thus if, in the second revision, any alterations were made in the earlier part, we should be unable to distinguish them

---

[1] I feel somewhat less certain of five than I do of the other six.

[2] The major revisions are of course self-evident; but the categories of major and minor naturally merge into one another, and I have included here one or two instances that have already been dealt with in Section III.

from alterations made in the third and final revision. The only three variants certainly belonging to the second revision are:

w 880    he came thither >      w 881    made > caus'd
            for comming their         1241    the estate > all the state

*Apparent revision in f.*—The third and final revision ($\gamma > \gamma'$) shows itself in variation between $D^2$ and $f$, or where $D^2$ is absent between H and $f$. There are ten instances of possible verbal revision (all but two, I think, more than possible) but all except the last two may be really cases of revision in $\gamma$, since we are unable to check them by the presence of $D^2$.

w 596   Chardge if I > charge,      w 737   daintye *added*.
         (*see note*).                         748   and *omitted* (cf. p. 43).
    598   if we can *omitted*.           750   I *omitted* (cf. p. 43).
    640   it > her                        835   a > his
    691   with > at                     836   and other Minstrells *added*
    736   Monie *added* (cf. p. 43).             (cf. p. 44).

The result of our inquiry is, I think, encouraging. Out of all variants only twenty-four can make out a prima facie claim to be regarded as due to authorial revision, and of these all but three come from the heavily revised antimasque. Not all are necessarily revisional, but they seem to constitute a fairly definite class, and several are closely connected with passages manifestly rewritten. There is no reason to suppose that doubtful cases are alarmingly frequent (about a third, I should say) or that it is generally beyond the skill of an editor to distinguish with reasonable confidence between the author's revisions and the scribes' variations. The course of an editor is therefore clear. The choice between readings of $D^1$ and $\beta$ depends inevitably upon intrinsic merit, and among the readings of $\beta$ preferred will naturally be those judged to be due to revision. The text chosen as copy for the Windsor version is H, modified as critical procedure may demand. Beyond this no variant from the copy-text will be admitted unless it can make out a plausible case to be due to revision (in the second or third stage): any variant whose claim, after careful scrutiny, is allowed, must be admitted even though its revisional nature may not be conclusively established.

### DISTRIBUTION OF ERRORS

We are here concerned with the distribution of errors as an indication of the relative reliability of the several texts.

For this the question of revision is irrelevant, and in what follows I therefore disregard not only the larger and more obvious cases of recasting, but likewise those particular instances of revisional variation that we have just been considering.[1]

Nor need we aim at a complete collection of all variants due to scribes and compositors: a record, complete I hope for all practical purposes, will be found in the textual apparatus. For our present investigation we are at liberty to ignore whatever scribes and compositors might regard as falling within their individual competence rather than governed by the authority of their copy.[2] I therefore exclude from the present survey (i) everything of the nature of a stage direction (except speakers' names) since in the form and even sometimes in the substance of these scribes were clearly inclined to indulge their own fancies; (ii) differences of spelling, giving the term a rather wide extension to include such variants as 'then' and 'than', 'venter' and 'venture', 'beside' and 'besides', 'among' and 'amongst', 'my' and 'mine', 'methink' and 'methinks', 'pray thee' and 'prethee', 'luck sake' and 'lucks sake', 'hether' and 'hither', 'farder' and 'farther', and even 'you' and 'ye' and 'hath' and 'has' (unless in any case the rime is affected);[3] (iii) the use of contracted forms like 'i'', 'o'', 'th'', 'ha'', ''hem', ''em', and so forth (unless they affect the rimes); and (iv) word-division (whether permissible or clearly erroneous).[4]

Our investigation is complicated and made to some extent uncertain by the fact that not one of our authorities contains an absolutely complete text. $D^1$ lacks, of course, everything peculiar to the Belvoir and Windsor performances; but besides this it omits one fortune (B 406–17) probably spoken at Burley, and wants, owing to the loss of four leaves from our only copy of $D^a$, an uncertain number of lines corresponding to W 811–1085 and B 908–12.[5] H lacks the later additions and has apparently two accidental omissions. $d^2$ contained what was presumably the fullest text of any, though it too had at

---

[1] Scribal variants in passages added or substituted in revision are, of course, included under the relevant texts.

[2] Under this heading I do not, however, intend to include conjectural emendation.

[3] Mere differences of spelling are not generally recorded in the apparatus; nevertheless, many variations have been thought worth including there that would only confuse our present inquiry.

[4] In the case of variation between different copies of a printed text, I adopt the corrected reading unless the error is known to be derived from the copy.

[5] Conjecturally reconstructed, these lines here form B 759–912.

## Analysis of the Variants

least two accidental omissions: but $d^2$ only survives in the two long sections printed in $D^2$, namely W 262–366, B 336–480, W 371–548 and W 811–1085, B 908–26, W 1086–1291. In NF three passages were cancelled in revision and again a few lines were accidentally lost. One consequence is that the amount of text preserved by our several authorities differs very considerably. The implication of this for our investigation we shall consider in a moment. Another consequence of the accidental mutilation of $D^1$ and the incompleteness of $D^2$ is a textual ambiguity with which we are already familiar. In the passage lost from $D^1$ we are left uncertain whether apparent errors in β arose in β or were inherited from α (supposing the lines to have been in α at all); and in passages not in $D^2$ we are left uncertain whether errors of $f$ arose in $f$ or were inherited from γ.[1]

The importance of the marked difference in length of the texts preserved in our several authorities lies in this. We propose to rate the reliability of each text according to the number of errors it contains. But a scribe will naturally make more mistakes in a long text than in a short one. What, therefore, really concerns us is not the total number of errors in a text, but the number of errors *per* hundred or thousand lines or the number of lines *per* error. We need, then, in the first place to know the number of lines in each text, and for the present purpose we want the number of lines of actual text apart from all directions, headings, and speakers' names (where these stand as separate lines).

A careful reckoning yields the figures given in the table on p. 84.[2] But no exact computation of length is possible. There are naturally as a rule more words to a line in prose than in verse, and different texts differ to some extent in the proportion of these: some prose lines are not full, and the printing of texts parallel sometimes leaves a gap in a line: minor revision sometimes affects the length to a small extent. For these reasons I do not think the units in the figures calculated can be regarded as significant, and I have therefore given, beside the actual figures, figures adjusted to the nearest ten. It is these approximate figures that I shall use in estimating the reliability of the texts: they have the further

[1] Similar uncertainties might, of course, arise in connexion with accidental omission in other texts, but no actual instances seem to occur.

[2] The lines in question are those of the present edition. It would have been less trouble to have counted the actual lines in the several prints and manuscripts, but that would not, in prose, have yielded a constant basis of comparison.

advantage of making calculation easier. There is, of course, the usual uncertainty over γ and *f* (due to the incompleteness of D²): it is possible, though not I think probable, that some of the lines known to be absent from *f* were in fact already absent from γ. The figures are as follows:

| Texts | D¹ | β | H | γ | D² | *f* | N | F |
|---|---|---|---|---|---|---|---|---|
| Lines | 781 | 1384 | 1382 | 1408 | 866 | 1388 | 1387 | 1382 |
| Approx. | 780 | 1380 | 1380 | 1410 | 870 | 1390 | 1390 | 1380 |

Two points should be made clear before we proceed. I have spoken of 'errors' in the several texts, and I shall continue to do so since I have been unable to find a more exact and at the same time an equally convenient term. But I use it here in the special sense of any reading (not a revision) in which a particular text departs from that of its immediate source.[1] These include, besides ordinary mistakes of transcription, deliberate departures such as would not ordinarily be called errors, especially as some of them are actually corrections. Thus, if D² and F agree in an error, that error must have been both in γ and *f*; and if N conjecturally restores the reading of β (as it occasionally does) it certainly departs from its immediate source (*f*), and its reading is therefore here classed as an error, although in fact it reverts to a more original reading previously corrupted. Such intentional variants I have tried to distinguish in the lists that follow, classifying as 'emendations' those intended to improve the text in a reading not apparently erroneous; as 'conjectures' those intended to restore the text where corrupted, but which are themselves mistaken (or doubtful); and as 'corrections' those that are (at least presumably) correct.

The other point is that errors (in the sense here used) may be determined in one of two ways. 'Intrinsic' errors (and these are all errors in the ordinary sense) are readings that in their nature cannot be correct.[2] Other readings (which may or may

---

[1] Or, more precisely, its latest source textually determinable. For example, the actual immediate source of D² is *d*² (the manuscript from which the cancels in the Duodecimo were printed), but of the text of *d*² we know nothing apart from those of D² and γ, with either of which, when they differ, *d*² may have agreed. (In other words, a variant in D² may have arisen in D² or in *d*².) Thus for textual purposes the 'immediate' source of D² is taken to be γ. This qualification is, of course, generally understood in the genealogical criticism of texts, consideration being confined to what may be called 'nodal' manuscripts, i.e. those that mark a branching of the scribal tradition.

[2] Intrinsic errors (unless they are also inferential) may nevertheless be original

not be errors in the ordinary sense) may be convicted of error (in our sense) through variation from those of certain other texts: these I call 'inferential' errors.[1] Normally (that is, apart from contamination, conjectural emendation, and coincidental error) agreement between $D^1$ and $\gamma$ (or $f$ when $\gamma$ is indeterminate) will convict a variant in H; agreement between $D^1$ and H, a variant in $\gamma$ (or $f$); agreement between H and $f$, a variant in $D^2$; agreement between H and $D^2$, a variant in $f$; and agreement between $D^2$ (or H) and N or F, a variant in F or N respectively.

In the lists that follow I have marked with a dagger (†) those errors whose point of origin is (at least theoretically) doubtful owing to the defection of some other text; and in the lists of intrinsic errors I have marked with a star (*) those readings that are also condemned on inferential grounds. I have not, as a rule, discussed the readings: the evidence for inferential errors will, of course, be found in the textual apparatus, and wherever that evidence is ambiguous it is discussed in the notes; my reasons for regarding other readings as intrinsic errors (unless self-evident) may likewise be sought in the notes.

*Errors in* $\alpha$.[2]—In the first place we may ask whether any intrinsic errors appear in all texts and must consequently be ascribed to $\alpha$. Four are, I think, reasonably certain. The clearest case is at w 1263–4, where the rimes prove that two lines have everywhere been written or printed as one. Scarcely less certain to my mind is the loss of the speaker's name at w 692. Another is 'Maudlin' at B 690. This, it is true, appears only in $D^1$, owing to the passage having been rewritten in β,

---

readings if they are either oversights of the author or else slips in the archetype, where this is distinct from the autograph. Possible examples are B 413 'one' and w 500 'bear'. But while this introduces an element of uncertainty into the discussion of individual readings, it is too remote a contingency to affect appreciably the general analysis, and may therefore be ignored.

A reading may only reveal its erroneous character when compared with one from another text. If revision be ruled out (as we do here) one or other reading must be unoriginal (i.e. an error), and in that case there may be no doubt which it is. A good instance is $\gamma$'s 'thrust' at w 925, which would pass unchallenged but for H's 'truss'd'. Thus not all intrinsic errors are immediately obvious.

[1] The categories are not, of course, mutually exclusive; many intrinsic errors are also inferential. For example, the true order of w 186–7 is evident on inspection, but the inversion in H is likewise proved by the agreement of $D^1$ and $f$.

[2] Of course, every hypothetical manuscript may have contained, and probably did contain, obvious slips that were independently corrected in its descendants. If one of those descendants failed to correct such a slip, it would inevitably appear as an individual error in that descendant.

but it can hardly be an error of the scribe or compositor, and is doubtless a slip of the author's for 'Meg'. I am also inclined, with Simpson, to accept at B 11 Cunningham's conjecture 'sillabes' for 'sillables', since not only is it (or 'syllabes') Jonson's recognized spelling, but it also makes a smoother line.[1]

*Errors in* $D^1$.—$D^1$, the only representative of $\alpha$ as distinct from $\alpha'$, is confined to the Burley version, and even of this version it lacks one of the Ladies' fortunes probably spoken there (B 406–17), a fortune that must have been incorporated in $\alpha$ after the transcription of $d^1$ but presumably before the revision that produced $\alpha'$. The field of $D^1$ is further restricted by the loss of four leaves of $D^a$ containing an uncertain but considerable number of lines (160 according to my reconstruction) that must have been in $\alpha$ but survive only in the revised version of $\alpha'$ represented by $\beta$. The length of $D^1$ as it survives is reckoned at 780 lines. Reconstruction of $\alpha$ depends, of course, on comparison of $D^1$ and $\beta$, but again the field is slightly restricted by the absence from $\beta$ of three lines (B 306–8) cancelled in revision and of a one-line speech (B 233–4) accidentally lost. For these four lines of text $D^1$ is our only authority. It is also our only authority for the original form of certain passages in the antimasque that were rewritten in the course of revision (notably B 530–46).

Errors in $D^1$ must, of course, be sought among the variants between $D^1$ and $\beta$, since no reading common to these two texts can be an error in the sense of being a departure from the reading of $\alpha$. There are 24 intrinsic errors in $D^1$ as follows:[2]

| | |
|---|---|
| B 11 to *omitted*. | B 54 Quinguinever *for* quinquennium |
| 35 Ammon *for* Aymon | |
| 44 same *inserted*. | 178 Tuns *for* Tun |

[1] Of course, 'sillables' may very well be a coincident error in $D^1$ and $\beta$: if it stood in $\alpha$, this can hardly have been autograph. I also strongly suspect an original error of some sort at w 149, though it is possible that either $D^1$ or *f* may preserve the correct reading conjecturally altered in H. Again, at w 1205 H's 'in you', while probably correct, may nevertheless be a conjectural emendation, though partially coincident error in $D^1$ and $\gamma$ seems on the whole the more likely explanation. I have further conjectured the omission of 'came' in w 912. Here $D^1$ is defective, so that it might be an error in $\beta$; I have not, however, included it among the errors of $\beta$, since, if I am right in supposing it to be an error, it is much more likely to be an original oversight. Simpson implies an original error in w 1123 when he prints 'And ⟨so⟩ to wishe away offences', but I believe the insertion to be not only unnecessary but definitely wrong.

[2] Errors in an extant text are of course given in the exact form (except for

## Analysis of the Variants 87

B 210 drops *for* droughtes
 211 thee *for* there
 233 †1 *for* 4(?)[1]
 254 time *for* line
 348 hollow *for* hallow (*conj.?*)
 363 you *omitted.*
 392 O *for* and
 394 it *omitted.*
 439 he *for* see (*conj.?*)
 511 They can *for* Can they

B 553 *omitted.*
 558 And *for* But
 592 must *inserted.*
 625 a *omitted.*
 659 ha *omitted.*
 710 left *for* lost
 926 May- *for* Mas
 945 your *for* you
 959 looke *for* lookes

D¹ cannot be convicted of error by any combination of readings in the other main texts, being itself of equal authority with β from which they are all derived. But if Con is an independent witness to the readings of α, as is possible, its agreement with β, where D¹ differs, would prove D¹ to be wrong. We have already seen (p. 73) that several such cases occur. Some are intrinsic errors; others concern only spellings and contracted forms, which we here leave out of account. There remain, however, six significant variants in which D¹ would appear to be condemned:

B 257 the ... the *for* your ... your
 258 Territorie *for* Territories
 259 but *for* and

B 319 should *for* shall
 332 Of *for* For
 369 not *for* never

The errors of D¹ include, of course, errors by the scribe of *d*¹ as well as those of the compositor. One whole line and half a dozen single words are omitted: on the other hand, two words are wantonly inserted. The errors are often ignorant and careless, several are probably graphic in origin, and a few like 'drops' for 'droughts' are surprising. Conjecture is rare, doubtful, and unhappy.

*Errors in* β.—β contains a complete text but for the accidental omission of w 227–8 and the absence of three later additions, namely the Earl of Buccleuch's fortune (w 485–500), probably four lines of the Lord Keeper's (w 402–5), and the concluding three stanzas of the Cock Lorel ballad (w 940–51). It contains, according to our reckoning, 1380

distinctions of type or script) in which they occur. The precise form of the readings of which they are corruptions is naturally conjectural: it may sometimes be inferred from the nature of the corruption, sometimes from the reading of the main extant text used for comparison. No particular authority attaches to the form in which the assumed original readings are here given.

[1] The speech is only in D¹ and the error may therefore have been in α, though this is unlikely. The correction is not certain.

lines. Where β and D¹ are both present they are of equal authority; where D¹ is (for whatever reason) absent, β is our ultimate authority, though not, of course, itself original. There are 8 intrinsic errors in β, but only one (marked with a dagger) in a passage not in D¹. This may, therefore, have been in α, and it is, indeed, very likely a slip of the author's. The errors are:[1]

| | |
|---|---|
| B 189 knackes *for* knackets (*conj.*) | W 678 with a *or* or a *inserted.* |
| W 227–8 *omitted.* | 690 Patr. *for* 4 Gypsie. (*conj.*) |
| | 716 Tom *omitted.* |
| B 413 †one *for* ones | 728 of my Mothers *omitted.* |
| W 564 theire *for* the | |

β cannot, any more than D¹, be convicted of error by any combination of readings in the main texts. If Con is independent it may convict it, as it appears to convict D¹: it probably does condemn β's 'there's' at B 369, but this is only a contracted form, with which we are not here concerned.

It will be seen that the known errors of β comprise the omission of a one-line speech, of one phrase, and of one odd word, one rather inexplicable insertion (perhaps due to alteration in the copy), a couple of reasonable but erroneous conjectures, and practically nothing else.

*Errors in* H.—H contains the same text as β except for the accidental omission of W 1149–50. Its approximate length is reckoned as the same. It has 16 intrinsic errors:

| | |
|---|---|
| W 186–7 **reversed.* | W 890 spies *for* spied |
| B 203 **and *omitted.* | 938 blewe *for* flirted (*conj.*) |
| W 656 **at *inserted.* | 955 vnderstood *for* vnderstand |
| 685 **and *for* an't | |
| 695 **Beckarman *for* Beckharman | 1122 Soveraingne *for* Soveraigne |
| 751–2 **handkercheiḟe *for* handkercheife | 1149–50 *omitted.* |
| | 1156 them *for* then |
| 839 *as part of previous speech.* | 1169 an *for* and |
| 852 it *omitted.* | 1179 i'th the *for* i'the |

From W 839 to 955 D¹ is defective, and W 1122 to 1179 are in a revisional passage, which is therefore not in D¹. None of the readings in these lines can be inferentially condemned.

[1] In the case of hypothetical manuscripts the exact form of an erroneous reading is, of course, conjectural. It is given in the form it takes in the leading extant representative, unless this is suspected of individual variation.

# Analysis of the Variants 89

The variant at w 938 is, of course, a deliberate alteration of a reading that was not understood. Being found only in H, it cannot however, like the similar alteration at w 635, be suspected of being due to the author.

Unlike D¹ and β, H may be proved wrong by agreement between other main texts, namely D¹ and γ. There are 17 such purely inferential errors:

| | | | |
|---|---|---|---|
| B | 8 effecte *for* affecte (*conj.?*) | w 627 | that *for* this |
| | 15 as *for* which (*emend.?*) | 710–11 | first for mee . . . a goe *for* first . . . agoe for mee (*emend.*) |
| w | 106 yoʳ *for* the (*? corrected*) | | |
| | 149 treating of *for* faces and(?) (*conj.*) | 722 | them *for* those (*emend.?*) |
| | 250 yoʳ *for* the | 735 | Masters *omitted*. |
| | 254 a *for* the | 777 | here *omitted*. |
| B | 345 dispose *for* depose (*conj.?*) | 791 | yee *or* you *omitted*. |
| | 373 dares *for* dare | B 926 | Mas̃ *omitted*. |
| | 395 will *for* shall | w 1218 | sum̃ers for sum̃er |

The scribe of H was not notably accurate, but his errors are not as a rule very serious. He omitted one couplet and half a dozen single words, and he misassigned one line. Two others he accidentally transposed, and he appears to have tinkered with the result rather than admit his mistake. On four occasions he seems to have conjecturally altered what he did not understand or thought wrong, and he occasionally tried to improve the text, without much success.

H has 33 readings here claimed as errors: to these must be added 8 inherited from β, making 41 in all.

*Errors in* γ.—The approximate length of γ is 1410 lines. But our specific knowledge of its text depends on D², and D² consists only of two sections totalling approximately 870 lines; in the other 540 lines we are unable to distinguish between γ and *f*. Here attention is concentrated upon those readings that can with certainty be assigned to γ: doubtful readings are treated under *f*. There are 27 intrinsic errors in γ; but in the case of w 500, where D¹ and H are both absent, γ is our ultimate authority, and the error is very likely due to the author:

| | | |
|---|---|---|
| w 306 | fortunes *for* fortune | w 442 the *for* they |
| 367–9 | *omitted*. | 464 Thus written to *for* There's written (*conj.*) |
| B 408 | know *for* knew | |
| 441 | *heart *for* hurt (*conj.?*) | 500 †bear *for* be |
| 456 | *told *for* robd | 837 Gipsies *for* Gipsie |
| 475 | *giuen *for* gi'n | 862 *omitted*. |

90    *Introduction*

w 864 sing *for* sing't
865–6 *omitted, together with the prefix at* 867.
    872 those *for* these
    873 fart *for* farce
873–4 *as one line.*
    899 had neuer *for* neuer had
    915 haue choakt *for* choake (*emend.*)
    920 a *inserted.*

w 923 And *for* Was (*emend.?*)
    925 thrust *for* trust
    1119 Clow. *for* Clo[d].
    1134 which *for* and (*emend.?*)
    1135 the *for* that (*emend.?*)
1198–9 \*as one line.
    1205 \*if your *for* in you *or* in your (*conj.?*)
    1286 a *omitted.*

Readings of γ can, of course, be inferentially condemned by the agreement of D¹ and H, but owing to the very restricted field for which D¹ and D² are both present (hence the very few starred readings in the above list) there is in fact only one inferential error that is not also intrinsic, namely:[1]

w 1266  makes *for* make

The errors of γ, so far as they can be ascertained, show a great lack of care and intelligence. Three lines, two lines, and one line are at different points omitted, though only one odd word. Twice two lines are written as one. There is a good deal of conjecture and attempted emendation, nearly all unfortunate and on occasion betraying gross misunderstanding or disregard of rime.

Of course, like H, γ inherited the 8 errors of β. But only one of these (B 413) falls within the limits of D²; the addition of this brings the total number of errors in γ, as we know it, up to 29. Considering the comparative shortness of the text the number is rather large.

*Errors in* D².—D² has, of course, the same field as we have been obliged to accept for γ. It has 10 intrinsic errors (all inferential as well):

w 298 \*fortunes *for* fortune
    302 \*unto *for* to
    305 \*Forrune *for* Fortune
B 348 \*hollow *for* hallow (*conj.?*)
    366 \*you *for* he
    439 \*he *for* see

w 841 \*Ninglington *for* Niglington
    1015 \*or *omitted.*
B 908⁷ \*hither *for* hether
w 1110 \*heart *for* art

There are also 17 purely inferential errors proved by the agreement of H and *f*.

w 328 Starres *for* States
    833 and *omitted.*

w 908 a *for* the
    956 now *omitted.*

[1] One reading of γ, B 417 'will be' for 'it will be', is probably condemned by the agreement of Con with H.

| | | | |
|---|---|---|---|
| w 966 | at *omitted.* | w 1075 | For *prefixed.* (*conj. possibly cor.*) |
| 971 | for *inserted.* | | |
| 1005 | left *inserted.* (*emend.?*) | 1082 | And *for* With |
| 1032 | to *omitted.* | b 909 | tell *for* tell't |
| 1044 | a *omitted.* (*conj.?*) | 911 | As *omitted.* (*conj.?*) |
| 1062 | fleshy *for* fleshly | 912 | Beere and his *for* bread, beere, and (*emend.*) |
| 1063 | Clod. *for* Pup. | | |
| 1064 | Pup. *for* Clod. | | |

D² is to a slight extent contaminated by D¹, namely at B 348 and 439. Otherwise its errors though rather frequent are not usually important, except for the remarkable substitution of 'Starres' for 'States'. It interchanges two speakers' names. Seven small words are omitted, and the fact that all but one are inessential suggests possible intention. But conjecture does not otherwise appear to play any important part, though there is one unnecessary but not unreasonable attempt at improvement and one conjecture that may be correct but is at best only partial.

Besides its own 27 errors D² has, of course, the 28 original errors of γ which it inherited, and the solitary error that (in this portion of the text) γ inherited from β; making 56 errors in all. In *d²*, which presumably contained a complete text, the number of errors was probably considerably larger, even allowing for the compositor's misprints in D².

*Errors in f.*—This is a complete text but for three passages of the antimasque cancelled in revision; it is reckoned at 1390 lines, twenty less than γ. In assessing the reliability of *f* we have to remember that in two sections (see pp. 82–3) it is inevitably debited with a number of errors that probably belong to γ. To this question I shall return. Meanwhile, the ostensible number of intrinsic errors in *f* is 44:

| | | | |
|---|---|---|---|
| w 42 | †*wretchcock *for* wretchock | w 210 | †*royall *for* loyall |
| 47 | †*Guinquennium *for* Quinquennium | 216 | †*vrands *for* viands |
| | | 219 | †*feaste *for* feasts |
| | | 248 | †*shall *for* should |
| 52 | †*Starling *for* Stauling | 261 | †*haue *omitted.* |
| 53 | †*Iacke *for* Iarke | 290 | *Sallance *for* ballance |
| 133 | †*or *for* our | b 454 | *Cupid *for* Cupid's |
| 141 | †*omitted.* | w 549 | †*come *for* ²couie |
| 162 | †*myne *for* minte | 630 | †*the *for* they |
| 164 | †*towne *for* tonne | 633 | †*pollique *for* pollitique |
| b 192 | †*trinkets *for* trickets | 640 | †*swallow'e *for* swallow't |
| w 192 | †further *for* farder | 644 | †*2 Gip. *omitted.* |
| 204 | †*drought *for* droughts | 655 | †*1 *for* 4 |

| | | | |
|---|---|---|---|
| w 671 | †*1 *for* 4 | w 847–8 | *the Deuills-Arse? *as separate line.* |
| 674 | †*forget *for* forgot | 894 | *perfumes *for* perfumers |
| 677 | †*tri'mge *for* try'inge | 938 | slirted *for* flirted |
| 686 | †*Com Pan *for* Come Paul | 983 | *Coc. *omitted.* |
| 767 | †*omitted.* | 1040 | *and *for* for |
| 781 | †*Disceptio *for* Deceptio | 1049 | *they *for* the |
| 796–7 | †*as one line.* | B 913 | *since *for* sine |
| 800–1 | †*as one line.* | w 1123 | *an *for* and |
| 835 | *aske him *as separate line.* | 1150 | meane *for* meant |
| 838 | *omitted.* | 1217 | *and *omitted.* |

The number of purely inferential errors is 24, proved by the agreement of H with $D^1$ or $D^2$ or both. Either $D^1$ or $D^2$ is almost always present.

| | | | |
|---|---|---|---|
| w 37 | †each of *for* of each | w 627 | †rimes *for* rime |
| 43 | †verye *inserted.* | 638 | †a *for* the |
| 63 | †out *for* forth | 673 | †a *inserted.* |
| 77 | †we here *for* here we | | †thei'le *for* they |
| 83 | †Gypsyes *for* Gypsye | 717 | †with *for* of |
| 88 | †1 *omitted.* | 729 | †a *inserted.* |
| 102 | †slight *for* slightes | 765 | †Towne- *for* Townes |
| 118 | †the *for* your | 1007 | or *for* and |
| B 189 | †our *inserted (conj.)* | 1021 | a *omitted.* |
| w 208 | †shrinke *for* wincke *(conj.)* | 1034 | hath *for* haue |
| B 450 | hands *for* hand | 1039 | theire *for* your |
| w 561 | of *for* in | 1067 | were *for* are |

In *f* the errors are many and careless. One line is omitted, though only a couple of odd words: on the other hand, four speakers' names are absent. Twice it writes two lines as one: contrariwise it twice writes a few odd words as a separate line for no apparent reason. It makes two conjectures: the first seeks to restore the metre injured by an error in β; the second seems due to a misunderstanding. They resemble those found in γ, where indeed they may have originated.

There are 68 errors that, so far as we can tell, originated in *f*; to these must be added 36 inherited errors, 28 originating in γ and 8 in β: a total of 104.

I return to the question of the total errors probably originating in γ, of which, on the information we now have, some estimate should be possible. There are two courses. (1) Either we may proceed on the assumption, which is certainly not generally true, that in any particular text the incidence of error is constant throughout, and we may apply this either (*a*)

## Analysis of the Variants

to γ or (b) to f. (2) Or else we may proceed on the assumption, which may or may not be true, that in various parts of the text the incidence of error will vary uniformly in different texts. Since the estimates can in any case be no more than rough approximations, we may neglect the slight difference in length between γ and f and reckon each as 1410 lines.

Now f is credited with 68 errors in 1410 lines; 21 in the 870 lines for which $D^2$ is present, and 47 in the 540 lines for which $D^2$ is absent: whereas γ is credited with 28 errors in the 870 lines for which $D^2$ is present. On assumption (1) and basis (a) we find that if γ has 28 errors in 870 lines, in 540 lines it should have 17 errors. In other words, we should expect γ to show 17 errors in the part of the text where $D^2$ is absent, and a total of 45. On assumption (1) and basis (b) we find that if f has 21 errors in 870 lines, in 540 lines it should have 13 errors. In fact it has 47, of which, therefore, we should expect 34 to belong to γ. Between 17 and 34, the estimates arrived at on the two bases, there is a wide discrepancy, in fact one is exactly double the other. I am afraid this throws some doubt on our alternative assumption, for if the incidence of error in the several parts varied uniformly in the two texts, we should expect calculations on the two bases to yield consonant results. Be this as it may, the estimate on assumption (2) is as follows. In 870 lines where $D^2$ is present γ has 28 errors and f 21, a total of 49: in 540 lines where $D^2$ is absent γ and f together have 47 errors. But if out of 49 errors 28 belong to γ, then out of 47 errors 27 should belong to the same. This estimate has at least the merit of lying between the other two. Perhaps the most we can say is that the number of errors in γ in the 540 lines for which $D^2$ is absent was probably between 20 and 30, and that the mean of 25 is as likely a number as any other. Where an estimate has to be made I shall therefore adopt this figure of 25.

*Errors in* N.—N omits one line of f, but its approximate length is taken as the same, 1390. It has 14 intrinsic errors (all of them also inferential):[1]

| | | | |
|---|---|---|---|
| w 45 | *and *repeated*. | b 433 | *the *for* they |
| | *feede *for* fed | w 494 | *fo *or* fr *for* for |
| 268 | *teell *for* tell | 697 | *o *for* a |
| b 347 | *sighne *for* signe | 839 | *written as a heading*. |
| 373 | *w$^{te}$ for w$^{th}$ | 852 | *if *for* it |

[1] We should perhaps add w 811 'ye' inserted; but an attempt seems to have been made to erase the word.

## 94 Introduction

w 989 *Mistorye *for* Misterye    w 1114 *knigt *for* knight
   990 *Worthis *for* Worthie      1122 *y *for* y$^e$ (the)

Of these two or three may be no more than eccentric spellings. The rest, except w 839 (due to confusion in the copy), may pass as mere slips of the pen. There are also 9 purely inferential errors, proved by the agreement of D² or H with F:

w 16 proue *for* growe (*emend.*)    w 935 vntill *for* till
   250 yo$^r$ *for* the            942 hee left=behinde *for* before,
B 345 despose *for* depose (*conj.*)           and behinde (*emend.*)
   408 knewe *for* know (*cor.*)    1266 make *for* makes (*cor.*)
   456 rob'd *for* told (*cor.*)
w 899 neuer had *for* had neuer
       (*cor.*)

The outstanding feature of N is its readiness to alter the text conjecturally and its success in doing so. Its two emendations are real improvements, which one would not hesitate to ascribe to the author if they occurred in a hypothetical manuscript. Of its five conjectures four are actually correct and restore the original reading. And for the two other alterations in the above list the scribe may also have had his reason.

N might have been expected to reproduce all the 104 errors of *f*, but in fact, since it corrects 4 of them, it cannot be said to inherit more than 100. With its own 23 errors (in our sense) its total errors are therefore 123.

*Errors in* F.—F is shorter by 6 lines than *f* and its length is reckoned at 1380. It has 24 intrinsic errors of its own (all of them also inferential):

B 14 *favovrs *for* favours    w 548 *pish *for* parish (pish)
w 4 *an *omitted.*               606 *Knells *for* Nells
  28 *the *for* one              710 *y'em *for* them (y$^{em}$)
  31 *Countries *for* Counties    715 *So. *for* Tow.
  35 *Marshes *for* Marches    732 *Tom. *for* Tow.
  48 *to *for* or                 740 *Tom. *for* Tow.
  52 *or *for* to                 803 *hither *for* hether
  74 *To *for* Or               902 *Yeamans *for* Yeomans
165 *wring *for* ring          1000 *arowse *for* avowes
300 *and *omitted.*            B 908$^7$ *hither *for* hether
B 460 *troches *for* torches    w 1203 *Eath *for* Earth
461 *cheeks *for* cheeke        1229 *lore *for* love

F is also condemned in 4 further readings by the agreement of D² or H with N:

B 8 effects *for* affects (*conj.?*)    w 557–8 of one *omitted.*
472 not *for* noe                 813 the *inserted.*

## Analysis of the Variants

These errors of F, though not many more than those of N, are very different in character, being mostly careless and unintelligent. Literal misprints are conspicuous: several errors are due to the misunderstanding of contractions (w 547, 710) or abbreviated names (w 715, 732, 740), some manifest complete disregard of the context (w 31, 35). One possible conjecture is mistaken.

F has 28 individual errors and it inherited 104 from $f$, making a total of 132. [See additional note on p. 231.]

We are now in a position to assess the reliability and character of the several texts both hypothetical and actual. The known errors they contain are set out in the accompanying table. Since, however, the texts differ greatly in length, the crude figures afford a poor basis for comparison. I have therefore calculated the corresponding figures for a uniform length of 1000 lines, which is conveniently near the mean of the several texts, and these figures are added in parentheses. Further, for the manuscripts $\gamma$ and $f$, I give both the actual figures and also the figures as conjecturally adjusted in the manner described on pp. 92–3. Lastly, the texts $D^1$ and $\beta$ cannot be inferentially convicted of error, which makes comparison with the others rather uncertain. I have tried to overcome this difficulty by assigning to them conjecturally and in brackets a number of inferential errors based on the proportion of total intrinsic to inferential errors found in the other texts, actually 135 : 72, though it must be admitted that no very reliable result can be expected from such a method.

For purposes of comparison we shall, of course, adopt the finally adjusted figures, while recognizing that they are to some extent conjectural. As regards individual accuracy—that is, the fidelity with which the immediate source is reproduced—the order of merit and relative reliability of the several texts is as follows:[1]

| $\beta$ | N | F | H | $f$ | $D^2$ | $\gamma$ | $D^1$ |
|---|---|---|---|---|---|---|---|
| 9 | 17 | 20 | 24 | 31 | 31 | 36 | 47 |

Here it is surprising to find that the despised N and F attain greater individual accuracy than any other extant text. When, however, we turn our attention from the individual fidelity to the general reliability of the text, we naturally get a very

---

[1] The low position of $D^1$ and $D^2$ is doubtless due to their being credited both with the scribal errors of $d^1$ and $d^2$ and the misprints of the actual texts.

## Distribution of Errors

| Texts | D¹ | β | H | Y | Y adjust. | D² | f | f adjust. | N | F |
|---|---|---|---|---|---|---|---|---|---|---|
| No. of lines; approx. | 780 | 1380 | 1380 | 870 | 1410 | 870 | 1390 | 1390 | 1390 | 1380 |
| Individual errors — intrinsic | 24 (31) [13] [(16)] | 8 (6) [5] [(3)] | 16 (12) | 27 (31) | .. | 10 (11) | 44 (31) | .. | 14 (10) | 24 (17) |
| Individual errors — inferential | | 8 (6) | 17 (13) | 1 (1) | .. | 17 (20) | 24 (17) | .. | 9 (6) | 4 (3) |
| Individual errors — total | 24 (31) [37] [(47)] | 8 (6) [13] [(9)] | 33 (24) | 28 (32) | 53 (36) | 27 (31) | 68 (49) | 43 (31) | 23 (17) | 28 (20) |
| (adjust.) | | | .. | .. | .. | .. | .. | .. | .. | .. |
| Inherited errors | .. | .. | .. | 1 | 8 | 29 | 36 | 36 | 100 | 104 |
| Total errors | 24 (31) [37] [(47)] | 8 (6) [13] [(9)] | 41 (30) | 29 (33) | 61 (43) | 56 (64) | 104 (74) | 79 (57) | 123 (88) | 132 (96) |
| (adjust.) | | | .. | .. | .. | .. | .. | .. | .. | .. |

different picture, owing to the accumulation of errors in the course of repeated transcription. The order and figures now appear as follows:

| β | H | γ | $D^1$ | $f$ | $D^2$ | N | F |
|---|---|---|---|---|---|---|---|
| 9 | 30 | 43 | 47 | 57 | 64 | 88 | 96 |

It is these figures that concern the editor. For instance, it has already been observed that the external authority of $D^1$ is the same as that of β and therefore higher than that of β's derivative H: we now learn that the intrinsic authority of $D^1$ is much inferior to that of H, and that the authority of β (the readings of which, where $D^1$ is present, are generally determinable) is considerably higher than either, since it has less than a third of the demonstrable errors of H, and less than a fifth of those of $D^1$. Again, where $D^1$ is absent and $D^2$ is present, the external authority of H is the same as that of γ and therefore higher than that of γ's derivative $D^2$: but the intrinsic authority of H is appreciably higher than that of γ (adjusted) and far higher than that of $D^2$, which has more than twice its errors. Where $D^2$ (as well as $D^1$) is absent (and the readings of γ are therefore indeterminate) the intrinsic superiority of H over $f$ and $f$'s derivatives N and F is, of course, even more marked (but this is not a very common occurrence). Lastly, where $D^1$ and H are both absent the intrinsic authority of $D^2$ is slightly lower than that of $f$ (adjusted) but higher than that of either N or F. These are facts that an editor should bear in mind when weighing the claims of equally plausible variants.

Although for an editor the questions of the external and internal authority of the several texts are those of chief importance, it will nevertheless be of interest to examine briefly the individual characters of the texts, since these have, of course, their own importance for the final result.

$D^1$ is characterized by considerable carelessness and a liability to omission and misreading.

β, evidently a very reliable text, shows some tendency to omission and to incorrect though not unintelligent conjecture.

H is characterized by rather frequent but generally unimportant errors; it makes some omissions, one misassignment, and one transposition. Its treatment of the text is a little high-handed and perhaps not entirely ingenuous.

γ is characterized by carelessness and incompetence, a tendency to omit groups of lines, and considerable interference with the text, generally uncalled-for and sometimes disastrous.

Errors in $D^2$, though frequent, are with one exception of no great importance. A number of small omissions may not all be accidental, and there is one attempt to improve the text.

*f* is marked by many careless errors. One line is omitted, and a peculiar feature is the repeated omission of the speakers' names. Conjectures are few and may properly belong to γ.

N is remarkable for the fact that almost all its so-called errors, of which there are not very many, are either small slips of the pen or else conjectures and emendations that are always reasonable and generally correct.

The errors of F, though not excessive in number and some of them mere slips of the compositor's, reveal great carelessness and complete lack of intelligence.

N is individually by far the most careful and most intelligent of the extant texts, and it is interesting to compare its achievement with the rather poor showing of H. Had Lord Newcastle's secretary had access to the independent information and the admirable manuscript available to the scribe of H, he would have produced a text much superior to any we now possess. Nor was it his fault that his exemplar was so inferior, seeing that he appears to have borrowed it from the author himself.

### RESIDUAL VARIANTS

We have now disposed of what appear to be verbal revisions and what must be regarded as scribal errors and conjectures good or bad, and it only remains to collect those variants that have equal external authority and cannot be condemned on internal grounds—those readings, namely, between which an editor will have to exercise his discrimination.

It will, of course, be understood that the classes that I have called Residual Variants (or Alternative Readings) and Intrinsic Errors are in fact contiguous and that the boundary between them may be a matter of opinion. In many cases the choice between alternative readings is fairly obvious: on the other hand, the nature of an error may not be immediately apparent or may even be questioned. I have endeavoured to draw a distinction between those variants in which one reading is all but certainly wrong and those in which one has, at

## Analysis of the Variants

most, a strong claim to preference. The difference will be appreciated if we compare the reading of D¹ at B 211 'thee', the inconsistency of which generates conviction in a small scribal error, with the reading of the same at B 87 'doe doubt', the only reason for rejecting which is the ease with which the error might arise. All doubtful cases have, I hope, been adequately discussed in the notes, but I cannot expect that the reader will in every case approve my decision. The most I can hope for is that if another critic might raise some of my intrinsic errors to the status of alternative readings, he would still in the end agree with me in rejecting them. In the case of readings here classed as alternative it would naturally be vain to look for even this measure of agreement.

*Variants between* D¹ *and* β.—For the bulk of the text, substantially what constituted the Burley version, our ultimate authority is α, and the text of α has to be reconstructed from a comparison of D¹ (so far as it is extant) and β.[1] There are 33 variants, but we have already seen (p. 87) that in 6 instances the reading of D¹ is probably condemned as unoriginal by the agreement of Con with β: these are starred in the following list.[2] In cases where H fails us the reading of β is indeterminate and has to be replaced by that of γ, or, if D² is absent, by that of *f*. The latter happens in one instance, marked in the list by '(*f*)'.

B 13 built: *hath built*
   42 pursuing: *pursuing her*
   43 she: *she greate*
   45 the last: *last*
   48 in the: *of the*
   50 was: *were*
   60 or: *and*
   64 the: *theire*
   87 doe doubt: *doubt*
 105 or: *and*
 133 amongst: *among*
 143 jolly: *theire iolly*
 163 *Faces*: Of faces (*f*)[3]

B 217 did yet: *yett did*
 257 *the . . . the: *your . . . your*
 258 *Territorie: *territories*
 259 *but: *and*
 319 *should: *shall*
 332 *Of: *for*
 369 There is: *There's*
    *not: *neuer*
 470 4. Gypsie.: *5. Gypsie.*
 506 Clod.: *Town*
 511 and: *or*
 520 Bag-pipes: *bagpipe*
 556 Ptolomy: *Ptolomęes*

[1] For the original version of w 811–1085 and for B 908–12, accidentally lost from Dᵃ, we have no direct authority at all: it has to be conjecturally restored (see B 759–912) from the revised version, for which our ultimate authority is β.

[2] The variants 'among' : 'amongst' and 'has' : 'hath', which were treated as a mere difference of spelling in considering errors (p. 82), are here included as substantive. I have also found it necessary to include one case of contraction (B 369).

[3] Here H has substituted a conjectural emendation and, D² being absent, D¹ and *f* are equal authorities for the reading of α.

B 565 Meg: *Peg*
579 i'th: at    o'th: o'
590 *find it*: finde (H)¹
B 597 *escapes*: scapes
629 2 Gypsie.: *3. Gip.*
754 here: *here's*

I have italicized the readings adopted in the text, and it will be seen that in 8 instances I have preferred the reading of D¹ and in 25 that of β. Thus D¹ has been judged to be in error in three-quarters and β in one-quarter of the cases. Our previous investigation led us to believe that the number of errors in D¹ and β were 47 and 9 respectively, a proportion of over five to one (p. 97). To this the three-to-one ratio now appearing is as near as could reasonably be expected. It perhaps points to the conclusion that the errors of β are on the whole more specious than those of D¹.

*Variants between* H *and* γ.—For the Countess of Exeter's fortune (B 406–17, presumably added to α after *d*¹ was transcribed) and for the Belvoir alterations and the main Windsor additions and substitutions (derived from α′ presumably in different states of revision) our ultimate authority is β, the text of which has to be reconstructed from a comparison of H and γ, so far as γ is known. But where D² is absent the readings of γ are indeterminate and have to be replaced by those of *f*. This happens in four instances, which are marked in the list by '(*f*)'. There are 35 variants, but in one instance (starred) the reading of γ is probably condemned as unoriginal by the agreement of Con with H.

w 305 *fortunes*: fortune
309 *would*: could
B 417 **it wilbe*: will be
w 385 *hath*: has
414 Come Sʳ: *come*
415 sin': Since
not for: for no
429 *health*: your health
440 Nurse: *a Nurse*
471 hand Sʳ: hand
yᵒʳ wellcome: *welcome*
593 mirthes: *Mirth* (*f*)
678 with a: or a (*f*)²
726 *whimpering*: whining (*f*)
747 *Turnups*: Turners (*f*)
835–6 as: *as of*
w 839 flagonfleakean: *Flagon-feakian*
846 aske: *aske on*
877 him: *him once*
884 recouered to: *recouer'd vnto*
886 his: *the*
899 neuer had: *had neuer*
908 next: *very next*
963 me: *vs*
976 *purse*: pocket
993 *a brother*: brother
B 908⁷ *hath*: Has
w 1099 *by*: With
1154 *and*: Or
1166 Anie: *From any*

¹ The couplet was rewritten in γ or *f*, and H is the only witness to the reading of β.
² The words are in any case an error; the only question is which form of the error was in β. I assume that *f*'s reading is an attempted emendation.

w 1175 *of*: in
1177 from: Or
1281 *Courtſ*: Court

w 1284 *was*: is
1289 *poesie*: Poetry

It will be seen that in 21 instances I have preferred the reading of H and in 14 that of γ (or *f*), judging H to be in error in two-fifths and γ (or *f*) is three-fifths of the cases. Our previous investigations led us to believe that the number of errors in H and γ were 30 and 43 respectively a proportion of just under three to four. With this the two-to-three ratio now appearing is again reasonably consonant.

*Variants between* D² *and f*.—For the second Windsor revision (made in β') as well as for any passages (derived from β) accidentally missing in H, our ultimate authority is γ, the text of which has to be reconstructed from a comparison of D² and *f*. (Fortunately D² is present for all the passages concerned.) Four passages claim attention: Lord Buccleuch's fortune (w 485–500), the last three stanzas of the Cock Lorel song (w 940–51), both of which are certainly additions, four lines of the Lord Keeper's fortune (w 402–5), which are also probably additional, and a couplet in the blessing of the senses (w 1149–50), which was clearly omitted in H. The total number of lines in question is only 32, and the only variants are in w 402 and 404, where D² has 'venture' and *f* 'venter', and this we decided (p. 82) not to regard as substantive.

*Variants between* N *and* F.—For the final revision (carried out in γ') our ultimate authority is *f*, the text of which has to be reconstructed from a comparison of N and F. But the main alterations made were excisions, and the few lines added or rewritten in the process (see w 572, 644–5, 670, 979–81) contain no substantive variants.

This concludes our analysis. It may, however, be well to recall that at the outset we deliberately excluded from consideration certain classes of variants. It follows that there are many differences of spelling, contraction, and the like, as well as in the form of stage directions, to which an editor will have to devote attention, but which find no record in the above lists. In all these, however, critical judgement is complicated by considerations other than those of the genetic relation of the texts. The main difficulties that arise are discussed at the end of the note on the present edition.

# THE PRESENT EDITION

This is an attempt to exhibit side by side two texts of Jonson's masque representing respectively the version performed at Burley-on-the-Hill (supplemented by the alterations made at Belvoir) and the version performed at Windsor. Unfortunately in respect of neither version is our knowledge complete. Owing to the loss of four leaves from the unique copy of the original issue of the Duodecimo, we possess only the revised version of a substantial portion of the anti-masque, and how much of this appeared in the earlier version is uncertain: on the other hand, the composite version found in all our other authorities includes, often without warning, lines and passages that obviously can have formed no part of the Windsor performance. It follows that the content of both texts as here presented is in some measure conjectural.

The Duodecimo as originally printed contained the whole of the Burley version (with the probable exception of the fortune of one of the Ladies, who arrived unexpectedly) and nothing more. The Windsor version is contained, but not alone, in the composite texts, and of these much the most reliable is the Heber-Huntington manuscript. (The Belvoir alterations have also to be sought in the composite texts.) It seemed obvious, therefore, to take the original state of the Duodecimo ($D^1$) as my copy-text for the Burley version (so far, that is, as it was available) and the Heber-Huntington manuscript (H) as my copy-text for the Windsor version, eliminating in the latter case what presumably belonged only to the earlier versions and supplementing what remained with further additions and alterations preserved in the other composite texts. But I have made these my copy-texts only in the sense that I have taken them as the basis of my own in spelling and some other accidental features, and have not in either case necessarily accepted their substantive readings.[1] This procedure follows upon the recognition of the fact that, apart from the revision that distinguishes the later from the earlier version, the extant texts are all witnesses to a single tradition. The composite texts are as much authorities for the wording of the Burley version as $D^1$ is for that of the Windsor version.[2] Consequently, except where revision is acknowledged or assumed, my texts, so far as they are parallel, do not differ in any significant readings, but only in spellings and other accidentals, which owing to the individual habits of

---

[1] By the substantive readings of a text I understand the verbal variants, which normally group themselves according to the genetic relationship of the authorities, and by the accidental features the formal details of presentation, such as spelling, which are normally to a large extent determined by the individual habits of the scribe or compositor.

[2] For example, it happens that for one speech undoubtedly spoken at Windsor (w 227–8) $D^1$ is our only authority.

scribes and compositors cannot be subjected to the ordinary methods of critical reconstruction.

In determining the content of the Windsor version on the basis of the composite texts I have, of course, been guided by the internal evidence they afford, and have simply excluded on the one hand whatever is stated in those texts (usually in H) to have formed no part of that version, and on the other hand whatever it is clear from the text itself cannot have been spoken there. This, though involving an element of conjecture, was a comparatively simple matter. It was much more difficult to determine the content of the Burley version in that section for which $D^1$ is not available. It has been done in the manner explained on pp. 36–8, and in order to draw attention to the conjectural character of this portion of the text I have divided it off from the rest by rules and printed it (for the most part) in italics. For this section I have adopted $D^2$ as my copy-text, being the one that resembles $D^1$ most closely in accidentals. At the end of it there is a slight complication. It so happens that six lines, B 897, 908–12, were presumably omitted in the Windsor performance, and they therefore do not appear on the opposite page. If they formed no part of the Windsor version they cannot, of course, have been revised, and there is consequently nothing conjectural about them as part of the Burley version, even though we lack in their case the authority of $D^1$. They have, of course, been reconstructed like the rest on the basis of $D^2$, but in recognition of their special status they have not been italicized.

The establishment of the form and wording of the texts involved, as it always does in cases of the sort, two distinct problems: first the distinguishing between significant readings and mere differences of spelling and so forth, and next the choice between significant variants. As regards the latter, the majority of variants are, of course, eliminated either by their intrinsically erroneous nature or by the relation of the texts in which they occur. The residue are those the choice between which constitutes the normal task of the editor (unless he is content to follow one of several authorities blindfold) and must ultimately depend on his individual judgement. Every case has been discussed in the notes: there are less than seventy in all. Much more troublesome, though of minor importance, is the problem of distinguishing substantive readings from accidentals: the copy-text rules the latter but not the former. Any hard-and-fast rules that one could lay down would be to some extent arbitrary, and to seek to do so would, I think, be uncritical. Although between different forms the choice of a scribe or compositor will usually be guided by his own habits or fancy, enough evidence may yet survive to make one form or another likely as that prevalent in the original. We may do well to bear in mind, for example, that our manuscript authorities (H, N) are possibly some twenty years older than the printed ones (D¹, D², F) and that as regards accidentals scribes are on the whole more conservative than compositors. It follows that the manuscripts may well have kept closer to the spelling and graphic form of the original than have the prints; and in my view it would be uncritical to refuse any help they can afford in an attempt to approach as near as may be to the accidental features of the original, even if this means restricting to some extent the guidance of the copy-text. On the other hand, a particular authority, whether manuscript or print, may have idiosyncrasies of its own that are manifestly not derived from the original, and which it would therefore seem wanton to preserve. I shall return at the end of this note to the discussion of the actual procedure I have adopted.[1]

Thus I have not thought myself bound to follow the chosen copy-texts in any slavish manner. My aim has been to produce critical editions of Jonson's successive versions of his masque, not editions of the particular documents in which they happen to have come down to us. I have, of course, adopted whatever substantive readings were vouched for by the textual evidence, or where this was ambiguous, were approved by my own choice. But in accidentals as well there are several particulars in which I have departed from the copy-texts. H commonly begins verse lines with minuscule letters; but since there is a general convention (which, incidentally, Jonson usually followed both in manuscript and print) in favour of capitals, I have supplied them; and I have done the same silently in the few exceptional cases in D¹. More important is the matter of italics. H uses two scripts, one for the body of the text, the other for distinction in headings and in particular words. But, so far as the text is concerned, the distinction is made in so arbitrary and inconsistent a manner as to become almost meaningless. Moreover, the difference of script, though usually clear enough, is not always so, and it is at times impossible to say what the scribe's intention really was.[2] I therefore decided to disregard the distinction of script altogether. That being so, there seemed no reason to retain the corresponding

---

[1] After what I have said above it may seem surprising that I should have chosen different copy-texts for my two versions. But to have printed throughout most of the work an identical text would have been vain repetition; and after all, D¹ does alone represent the Burley version and H is the best authority for the Windsor version, and there is some interest in having the work in more or less the exact form in which it appears in the earliest printed edition on the one hand and in a contemporary manuscript on the other. Moreover, each has its own features and merits and failings. The print is fairly carefully punctuated, and even if its punctuation be of no particular authority, it is generally reasonable: the manuscript is almost devoid of punctuation, and in this respect at any rate can hardly represent the original.

[2] Cole and Simpson both seek to preserve the distinction, but they often disagree, and at times I should differ from both. I may mention that the other composite texts (D², N, F) are in some respects even more arbitrary in their use of 'italics', though they are more sparing of it.

distinction of type in D¹, for though roman and italic are there used in a perfectly normal manner, the distinction does not appear to me to serve any important purpose. This has left me free to make distinctions of type serve my own ends: I have used italics for headings and stage directions and for the few Latin words and phrases and one or two book-titles occurring in the text, and small capitals for speakers' names, and have thereby, I hope, made the text at once clearer and more sightly.[1]

Furthermore, I have regularized the erratic use of capitals within the line, frequent in H, less so in D¹. Many capitals, both in prose and verse, are without significance, but I have considered each case and have retained any for which sufficient reason could be found. Generally I have reserved capitals for proper names and for words that could be regarded as titles or personifications. To be consistent I have occasionally had to introduce capitals in similar cases: both changes have been made silently.[2] I have also expanded all contractions in the originals, and have only recorded those of whose significance there could be any doubt. In general, the prints follow the modern convention with regard to Uu–Vv and Ii–Jj, and the manuscripts the old convention, and I have naturally followed the copy-texts in this. But no text is altogether consistent in its use, and I have taken the liberty of altering unconventional forms without notice.[3] The irregular measures found in the Lords' and Ladies' fortunes and in the conclusion are marked by varying indentation of the lines. This differs appreciably in the several texts, and in none is it very consistent. I have followed the copy-texts in a general way, but have felt free to alter the arrangement whenever it seemed desirable to do so. The freakish indentation occasionally found in the long speeches in octosyllabic verse I have disregarded.[4] On the other hand, the paragraphing in the first of these speeches appears to be original and intentional, and I have followed the copy-text. Similar division occasionally found elsewhere is more uncertain, and I have ignored it.

[1] The copy-texts are not always consistent in the abbreviation of speakers' names. I have silently adopted a uniform style, without, however, normalizing the spelling. Long ſ has been discarded. H has several different forms of final -(e)s, and the scribe himself may not have been very clear about the distinction between them (see p. 19, note 2). Two of them, ę and ſ (both of which Simpson renders by ę) I have treated as contractions and replaced by -es.

[2] There is a tendency, more marked in D² than in H, to capitalize the dishes of the Devil's banquet. This I have made consistent. It would have been very difficult to determine which stood for titles of office and which not.

[3] Where a manuscript reading is introduced into a printed copy-text or vice versa it has, of course, been made to conform to the convention of the copy-text. Whenever either copy-text has to be supplemented from another source (normally D¹ from D² and H from N) this source is naturally treated with the same degree of freedom as the main copy-text.

[4] Simpson apparently tried to reproduce the indentation of H more or less exactly, but in fact he often misrepresents it.

In the matter of punctuation I have not treated the two copy-texts alike. $D^1$ is on the whole well punctuated, if somewhat heavily by modern standards: I have followed it except where it seemed misleading, and I have recorded all departures from it along with other departures from the copy-text. H, on the other hand, contains hardly any punctuation, and what there is I have felt at liberty to disregard, including its not uninteresting use of full stops in connexion with numerals. In its place I have introduced a punctuation of my own designed to bring out what I conceive to be the sense of the original. I have, of course, given due consideration to such points as appear whenever there could be any question about the interpretation, and have recorded any that seemed to imply an interpretation different from my own, or to be of any intrinsic interest, but I have done so only in the collations. I have preserved the word-division of the copy-texts unless manifestly erroneous.[1]

There are three ranges of footnotes. In the first are recorded (in heavier type) alternative readings that have the same claim to originality as those admitted into the text; that is to say readings of equal extrinsic authority and not intrinsically condemned. We are here concerned with the class of variants between which an editor has to make his choice, as explained on pp. 99–101. In this range I have eschewed lemmas, and I have given no sigils since the variants reappear in the collations. In the second range are recorded all peculiarities and points of doubt in the readings of the copy-text (including certain marginal mutilations in H), all obvious errors of the same, and any other readings that I have felt bound to reject. (There follows in brackets the rejected punctuation of $D^1$, or of $D^2$ where this replaces $D^1$ as copy-text.) Here I have given lemmas, but not, of course, sigils since all readings are those of the copy-text. The third range consists of the collations and gives a complete record of variations in the several texts. I do not, of course, record all differences of spelling or punctuation, but only those that appear to me to possess some interest or significance. The sigils used are explained in the first section of the Introduction (pp. 11–12), but I have introduced one additional convention. It is for critical purposes so important, and at the same time it is so difficult, to keep in mind the exact limitations of $D^1$ and $D^2$, that I have adopted the modified symbol $*D^1$ where $D^2$ is absent, and the modified symbol $*D^2$ where $D^1$ is absent. There are, of course, similar though minor limitations in the case of other texts, but since they are of less critical importance I have not thought it worth while complicating the record further.

---

[1] Simpson, printing from H, also introduced his own (and to my mind rather heavy) punctuation, but he appears to have endeavoured to retain whatever points there were in the original, with occasionally rather inconsistent results. And along with punctuation proper he introduced a good many hyphens, and a great many apostrophes to indicate contracted forms. In both these respects I have been content to follow the original.

Wherever both versions appear, the first two ranges of notes (if called for) appear likewise; and where the two versions are different, each has, of course, its own range of collations. Where, however, the two versions are parallel, the collations are substantially identical:[1] to duplicate them would be absurd, and to place the whole below one or other text would still be a waste of space. In this case therefore the collations have been divided between the two pages as happened to be convenient, line-references and lemmas being, however, always to and from the Windsor text. In cases of partial revision it has been possible to avoid duplication by giving below the Burley text those collations peculiar to that version and referring to the Windsor text for the rest. Where one version is absent and a whole page free of text, advantage has been taken of the blank space to print in it the whole of the notes belonging to the other text.

Lemmas are of course drawn from the text to which the collations refer; but in view of the fact that the copy-texts have been to some degree normalized (as described above) I have tried the experiment of giving each lemma, not necessarily in the exact form in which the reading appears in my text (which would be the normal procedure), but in the form (as regards capitals and contractions, but not as regards type or script) in which it appears in the original, unless this form is erroneous or the reading has been rejected in my text, in which case the lemma is of course taken from my own text and the reading of the copy-text appears among the variants. Variants are given in the exact form (except as regards type or script) in which they appear in the first text cited.[2]

In a case like the present it is important to bear in mind the ultimate authority[3] upon which the various sections of the text rest, and

[1] So, too, of course, is the first range of notes, but since these are few and of prime importance they have been duplicated. As regards the collations, even where the versions, owing to revision, have ceased to be strictly parallel, the minutiae of the text are often preserved and may afford evidence respecting the original reading. When such a reading from a non-parallel passage is recorded it is placed within parentheses.

[2] Where a variant involves the presence or absence of punctuation I have adopted the device (proposed by McKerrow in his *Prolegomena to the Oxford Shakespeare*, p. 76) of placing a small caret-mark after a reading to indicate the absence of any stop. In the collations to the Windsor text lemmas followed by a caret are fairly frequent, and the reader should remember that (in accordance with my practice explained above) such lemmas (unless H is cited among the variants) record the absence of a stop in the copy-text and not in my own text. One other convention needs to be mentioned: when a word occurs more than once in a line (or a letter more than once in a word) the occurrences are distinguished in reference by superior numerals prefixed.

[3] Strictly speaking the phrase 'ultimate authority' is ambiguous. It should properly mean the hypothetical manuscript in which the passage first appeared, but owing to the imperfection of the record it may not be possible to trace the tradition back so far. As I use the phrase it means the earliest authority textually ascertainable. For instance, w 227–8 were doubtless in α, but owing to accidental omission in β, the textual tradition cannot be traced back farther than $D^I$ (and

it may be worth while recapitulating the facts and explaining the measures taken to make them apparent in the text. $D^1$ contains the whole of the Burley version with the exception of Lady Exeter's fortune (assuming that this was really spoken at Burley and was not a Belvoir addition) and the section of the antimasque lost from $D^a$. These have been supplied (the second conjecturally) from $D^2$. But almost the whole of the matter in $D^1$ is also present in the composite texts, and where this is so the ultimate authority is α. The exceptions are: one speech accidentally omitted in β (B 233–4), three lines suppressed in revision (B 306–8), and a few passages in the antimasque rewritten (of which the most important is B 529–46): for these $D^1$ is our only authority. For Lady Exeter's fortune (B 406–17) and for the lost section of the antimasque (B 759–912) the ultimate authority is β.

Wherever the Windsor version retained the Burley text unaltered, H (except for the one speech accidentally omitted) runs parallel with $D^1$, and the ultimate authority is α. The passages peculiar to Windsor are more complex. The text here printed on the right-hand pages aims at representing the final state of that version (except in one respect to be explained shortly), but that state was only reached in stages. The bulk of the revision appears in H, and for this main revision the ultimate authority is generally β. The exceptions are two passages (W 367–9 and 865–6) which disappeared in γ, and for which H is our only authority, and two lines (W 1149–50) accidentally omitted in H, and for which therefore our ultimate authority is γ. But later on further alterations were made; these appear in $D^2$NF, and for them the ultimate authority is γ. They are the shifting of the Lord Chamberlain's fortune (W 371–89), which, however, involved no alteration of the text, the insertion (probably) of four lines (W 402–5) in the Lord Keeper's, the addition of one for the Earl of Buccleuch (W 485–500), and the appending of three new verses (W 940–51) to the Cock Lorel ballad. Some textual changes were also made in the antimasque. The final adjustments, all in the antimasque, appear in N F, and their ultimate authority is $f$. One passage already modified in γ (and so preserved in $D^2$) was further revised (W 978–82), one couplet was replaced by another completely different (W 644–5), and three passages were omitted (W 573–81, 664–70, 829–32), the first two with some modification of the context. Since, however, there is reason to suspect that two of the omissions were made in deference to censorship, and being reluctant to sacrifice any part of Jonson's work, I have retained all three passages in the text, but as a warning I have enclosed them in brackets. Wherever it has been necessary to supplement or to depart from the text of H

consequently we do not know when the speech was first misassigned to '1 Gypsie'): again W 1149–50 were doubtless in β, but owing to accidental omission in H, the textual tradition cannot be traced beyond γ.

(except in the case of w 227–8, for which $D^1$ is our only source) I have adopted N as copy-text, this being the one that is nearest to H in formal presentation. All passages of H belonging to the Windsor version that have been displaced from the text I have printed at the foot of the page between rules (in the same way as I have printed the Belvoir alterations below the Burley text) and I have done the same with the intermediate version of $D^2$ at one point and the alterations that accompany the omissions in $f$.

From this it will be seen that in respect of ultimate authority the Windsor version is much less uniform than the Burley version. In order to make apparent the textual facts of both I have placed in the margin opposite the beginning of each section the sigil of the hypothetical or other text that is the ultimate authority for the same.[1] Whenever a sigil so appears, that authority is understood to continue until another is indicated. The revisions in the Windsor text, when substantial, are referred to their proper authorities, and in the case of the later revisions the change of authority serves also to indicate a change of copy-text, this being more explicitly recorded in the notes. Minor revisions, however, though of course admitted into the text, do not involve any change in basic authority or copy-text. Attention is called to each such minor alteration by the prefixing to it of a star in the text, and against the line in which it occurs I place, in brackets, the sigil of the authority that introduced it.[2] Thus, if in a passage for which the general authority is $\beta$ there appears the marginal note '[$f$]', it is to be interpreted as meaning '$\beta$ modified by $f$'. Wherever revision or substitution has resulted in the versions being no longer parallel, the lack of correspondence is indicated by heavy rules down the inner margin of each page. The lines of the Burley and Windsor versions, that is the typographical lines of the present edition, have been numbered, and in reference the two versions are distinguished by the letters 'B' and 'W'.

I now return to consider more in detail certain aspects of my treatment of the text. And first something must be said respecting a licence I have allowed myself in dealing with the stage directions. So far as the text itself is concerned my aim has been to get as close as possible to the form in which each version left the author's hands. But it is clear that the form in which he wrote the directions was to some extent inadequate, and that successive scribes and compositors exercised their ingenuity in rendering them more explicit. I have not

---

[1] That is, the ultimate ascertainable authority. Owing to the limitations of $D^2$ our knowledge of $\gamma$ is imperfect, and some readings that are demonstrable only in $f$ may in fact already have appeared in $\gamma$. Where this ambiguity is present I have replaced the marginal symbol $f$ by $*f$.

[2] Such a bracketed sigil applies only to the single line to which it is affixed. In parentheses at the head of each page is the sigil of the authority carried over from the page before.

refused their help. I conceive the aim of a critical edition to be to make both text and action as intelligible as possible, always subject to the guidance of authority. Thus where our authorities have succeeded in making more intelligible or complete those apanages of the text that the author left imperfect, I have followed them. The precise textual facts will always be found recorded in the apparatus. Thus it will be observed that in my text the first heading of all (B 1) is drawn substantially from F; it was H that first reduced to order the entrance of the Clowns (w 501–6); $f$ (or possibly $\gamma$) supplied the full direction for the Country Dance (w 600–1); and $D^2$ and F independently added a finis to the Epilogue.[1] It ought not to be necessary to add that I should by no means countenance such scribal interference with the text itself.

But the principal matter to explain is my practice in regard to the spellings of the copy-text, which is intimately connected with the vexed question of the distinction between spellings and substantive readings. There will always, of course, be an intermediate class of word-forms over the assignment of which editors may disagree. I think that in drawing the distinction we should have regard to the evidence of the authorities as a whole. If the word-forms appear to be governed by the same genetic laws as the significant variants, then it is reasonable to treat them as such: if on the contrary their distribution is arbitrary, it may be presumed due to scribal preference, and the forms will naturally come under the designation of accidentals. At the same time the evidence is likely to vary alike in respect to different authorities and in respect to particular word-forms. An editor is therefore driven to consider each instance, or class of instances, very much on its own merits. And if an editor is prepared, as I am, to alter the spelling of the copy-text if he sees a reasonable prospect of thereby approaching nearer to that of the original, the distinction between spellings and more significant variants, while it will become even more difficult to draw, will at the same time lose much of its critical importance.

Having no respect for the copy-text as such, I have thought myself at liberty to remove what I take to be occasional eccentricities of the scribe or compositor. These are particularly common in H. Thus at w 129 I have replaced its mistaken spelling 'ioylly' by the normal 'iolly' as in the other texts; at w 409 I have removed its eccentric but not uncommon 'mutch'; at w 423 its 'Exchequer' may imply an intended 'Exchequeur', but I have printed 'Exchequer'; at w 536 I have, with some hesitation, replaced 'sprites' by 'spirites', which is the reading of the other texts; at w 921 I have altered 'could' to 'cold'; and at w 1228 I have replaced 'ayerie' by 'ayrie'.[2] I have

[1] The headings to the fortunes are particularly inconsistent, and I have not attempted to follow any particular text, selecting rather those that could be combined to yield a more or less uniform result.

[2] 'aëry', as in $D^1$, and 'airy' are the only legitimate alternatives: 'ayerie' is a

*The Present Edition* 111

also twice altered H's 'ben' to 'bene' in the compound 'bene-bowze' (good drink), the length being correctly indicated in D¹ and D² at w 52 and 996 respectively. At w 815 the spelling 'mell'ꞅ' for 'mell's' is hardly more than a slip and has, of course, been corrected; and although 'lettę' at w 598 is not altogether impossible for 'lette vs', it too is most likely a slip, and I have replaced it by 'letts'.

D¹ is habitually normal in spelling, but at B 703 I have altered 'Ballad' to 'ballet' as almost certainly due to the compositor.¹ D² happens to be the copy-text at B 853, and I have substituted 'Maior' for its 'Major', a not uncommon but quite indefensible form.²

The difficulty of distinguishing between substantive variants and differences of spelling is well illustrated by the alternation of 'you' and 'ye'. One would naturally regard it as significant, but scribes and compositors appear to have been of another opinion. Variation occurs in thirteen instances (w 105, 123, 705, 785, 791, 813, 989, 992, 1001, 1078, B 909, 911, 915) and is very erratic. There is, as a rule, no ground of choice, though the first instance is decided by the rime in favour of 'yee', as in D¹, where H, perhaps following β, has 'you'. This scribal change from 'ye' to 'you' is perhaps rather more likely than the reverse, but one cannot rely much on probabilities of the sort. Jonson doubtless wrote sometimes one and sometimes the other, and scribes and compositors seem to have followed their fancy rather than their copy. This is exactly what we expect to find in the case of accidentals, and the logical course is therefore to treat the variant, not as substantive, but as one of form only, and to follow the copy-text in each instance, unless it is known to be in error.³

There is persistent variation between the spellings 'been(e)' and 'bin': I have noted nine instances, w 385, 389, 417, 479, 480, 487, 537, 905, 965. Only eight are in H: always 'beene' except 'bin' at 965. All are in N: always 'bin' except 'bene' at 905. F always has 'beene'; D² five times 'bin' and four times 'beene'; only one instance is in D¹, 'bin' at 537. We seem to be dealing with individual preference on the part of scribes and compositors. In the holograph of Jonson's *Masque of Queens* the only spelling seems to be 'bene', and the same in the autograph letters: this, as we have seen, is once found in N. If this was the spelling of the original and survived in some hypothetical manuscripts, it would be liable to replacement by 'beene' or 'bin' according to the fancy of scribe or compositor. The hybrid, which may, however, have stood in β, since γ appears to have had the equally erroneous 'ay'rye.'

¹ HNF have 'ballett' or 'ballet', and at B 760, where D¹ is absent, the same spelling is found in H D² N F.
² N sometimes has 'their' for 'there' as a scribal idiosyncrasy: I have corrected it at w 880, where N is the copy-text for a revisional phrase. At B 361 D¹ prints 'ak's' (i.e. ask): I alter it to 'aks'.
³ One might have expected scribes and compositors to have reacted similarly to the difference between 'hath' and 'has'. There are, however, only three instances of variation (w 385, 835, B 908⁷) and there is nothing abnormal about them.

evidence, however, is perhaps hardly strong enough to warrant introducing the spelling 'bene' throughout; but I think it favours 'beene' rather than 'bin', and since 'beene' is the only spelling I have noticed in *Sejanus*, I conclude that Jonson was willing to accept it in print, and have therefore adopted it throughout.

The seventeenth century saw the introduction, or at any rate the general recognition, of the distinction between the spellings 'than' and 'then' for the conjunctive and adverbial (temporal demonstrative) uses respectively of what was originally one word. Here we are only concerned with the conjunction. There are ten instances: w 78, b 140, w 332, 637, b 670, w 971, 978, 1104, 1156, 1235. The spelling 'than' is confined to $D^1$ and $D^2$ (except for a single case in F at w 78) and in these it is constant (except for 'then' in $D^2$ at w 332 and 1235). Clearly 'than' is a compositor's modernization. The original must have had 'then' throughout, and I have consequently introduced this spelling even at b 670 where $D^1$ is our only authority.

There are a few other words of the original spelling of which we can be reasonably certain. Thus 'hether', which appears in w 535 (twice), 739, 803, and b 908[7], is the invariable spelling in H and N, and the last two instances are guaranteed by the rime: 'hither' is only found in $D^1D^2F$ at w 535, in $D^1$ at w 739, in F at w 803, and in $D^2F$ at b 908[7], in all cases evidently as a compositor's modernization.[1]

Again 'venter' and not 'venture' seems to have been the spelling of the original. The word occurs seven times: w 402, 404, b 532, w 680, 774, 797, 966. The spelling 'venter' is constant in H (four instances) and NF (six instances): 'venture' is constant in $D^1$ (four instances) and $D^2$ (three instances). I think we may trust the manuscripts, especially with the support of F, and dismiss 'venture' as a modernization by the $D^1D^2$ compositor. The instance at b 532 is only found in $D^1$, but even here I print 'venter'.

In the additative senses of the adverb 'beside' or 'besides', the latter spelling has now replaced the other, and the process was apparently already beginning in the sixteenth century. In cases of variation there is, therefore, some presumption that 'beside' is original. There are five instances: b 443, w 730, 746, 758, 1134. $D^1$ has 'beside' in the four where it is present; H has 'besides' twice and 'beside' three times; $D^2NF$ have only 'besides', which looks like modernization in γ. I think we shall be safe to adopt 'beside' throughout even at w 749 where 'besides' appears in a phrase only preserved in NF.

Etymologically analogous is the doublet 'among' and 'amongst', though in this case no distinction of usage has arisen. There are five instances: b 133, w 299, 543, 556, 762. In the third and last all available texts agree on 'amongst' and in the fourth the agreement of

---

[1] We find 'thither', rather inconsistently, at w 880 in a phrase only preserved in H, and I keep the spelling since H shows itself reliable in the case of 'hether'.

D¹ and H should guarantee 'amongst' against the 'among' of NF. These three are in prose. The first two are in verse and the evidence is curiously different. In the second the agreement of D¹D²NF (supported in a manner by 'amonke' in Con) should guarantee 'among' against 'amongst' in H: in the first it is D¹ that reads 'amongst' where HNF have 'among', so that here external authority is equally divided. I do not know whether the distinction between verse and prose is relevant, but I think we may fairly decide in favour of 'among' in the first two passages and 'amongst' in the others, which means treating the variant as substantive.

Then there are words in *in-*, *im-*, *en-*, *em-*. There are nine cases of variation: W 18, 103, 255, B 400, W 433, 473, 557, 1051, 1209. The *i*-forms are invariable in H; in N the two are about equally divided; D¹, D², and F are also inconsistent. This suggests individual habit or vagary. Jonson is likely to have been influenced by Latin in favour of the *i*-forms; and these I have adopted throughout, even at B 400 where the copy-text happens to have the *e*-form.[1]

In the earlier seventeenth century the modern distinction between the spellings 'of', 'off' and 'to', 'too' was already generally recognized, though not always followed. In particular 'too't' or 'toot' was common for 'to it', and indeed 'too' was not unusual for 'to' when emphatic. We have 'stand too' for 'stand to' in all texts at B 391; but this is for the sake of the rime. On the other hand, at W 75 H has 'to' for 'too' in the other texts; but I do not know that Jonson ever wrote it so, and I have treated it as an error. The spelling 'off' for 'of', if it occurred, might also be regarded as a mistake. On the other hand, 'of' is found for 'off' in HN at W 180, 1098, and 1283, where F in the first case and D²F in the others have 'off'. This looks authoritative, and since Jonson is known to have used this spelling (e.g. *Masque of Queens*, l. 181), I have of course retained it.

There are eight instances of the fused forms 'wilbe' and 'shalbe', at B 346, 357, 367, 417, W 420, 446, 965, and 1046. In each of these passages except W 420 H has the fused form; N has it only in four out of the eight. All the printed texts have the full form. Fusion was a habit with some scribes and it need not be original: I do not know that it was a Jonsonian habit. I have treated it as a scribal vagary and have printed the words in full.

Lastly we come to the troublesome question of elided and contracted forms, marked in many cases by the use of the apostrophe. Of these the most interesting is ''hem' for 'them', which appears in fourteen passages: W 69, B 193, W 559, 703, 705, 706, 710, B 672, W 745, 905, 907, 980, 1060, 1085. In the first nine instances it is in D¹ only, in the last five in D², which H joins on a single occasion at

---

[1] The word 'enough' (W 688, 719) hardly belongs to this class. N alone has the *i*-spelling (in both instances). I keep the prevalent and more normal form in spite of the fact that Jonson has 'inough' in *Sejanus* (III. 318).

w 1060. Since it is a distinctive (though not invariable) Jonsonian spelling, which it is most unlikely that any scribe or compositor would have introduced, I admit it to the text whenever it is preserved in *any* authority.

Generally speaking in the matter of contracted and elided forms the texts show marked and irregular variation. We may recognize two partially distinct uses, metrical and colloquial. In strict verse metre will of course decide whether a particular elision is or is not required, but in the present work the verse is as a rule too free to afford much guidance. We may note, however, that at w 252 metre demands the contracted 'Y'are' or 'your' of H and *f* rather than the full 'You are' of D¹; at w 261 'You'are' or 'your' as in H and N rather than 'You are' as in D¹ and F; and at w 408 the 'you'll' of H and not the 'you will' of γ. Colloquial elision often takes the form of the omission of consonants only, and so does not affect the verse: examples are 'o'' for 'of' or 'on', 'i'' for 'in', 'ha'' for 'have', ''em' for 'them'. The tendency of scribes and compositors would probably be towards expansion rather than contraction (as in the instances cited above) so that in cases of variation there is some a priori probability that the contracted form is the original. There are, indeed, a few instances that show that this is not always the case. If at w 771 'oth'r' in D¹ is intended to indicate a monosyllabic pronunciation, it seems to be mistaken; but the form is unusual and may be a mere blunder. More significant is w 1241 where γ clearly had the unmetrical 'he's'[1] in place of the correct 'he is' retained in D¹ and H; but this appears to have been a clumsy attempt to shorten an unexpectedly long line. In general the presumption in favour of the contracted form seems to hold good.

Before proceeding a word may be said about the use of the apostrophe as a mark of elision. The termination of the past tense and past participle (of weak verbs) is not as a rule syllabic and is written *-ed* or *-'d* or *-d* indifferently,[2] and the apostrophe is also sometimes absent in other cases, particularly in 'th' for 'the' and 'ha' for 'have'. In the chapter 'Of Apostrophus', with which Jonson rather unexpectedly opens the discussion 'of Syntaxe' in his *English Grammar*, he writes: '*Apostrophus* is the rejecting of a Vowell from the beginning, or ending of a Word. The note whereof, though it many times, through the negligence of Writers and Printers, is quite omitted, yet by right should, and of the learneder sort hath his signe and marke, which is such a *Semicircle*' placed in the top.' On the strength of this we might feel tempted to insist on the apostrophe being printed in all cases of elision.[3] But in spite of what he says Jonson's own practice is

---
[1] In N 'hees' was altered to 'heeis'.

[2] When the termination *is* syllabic we naturally expect the full form, and any other would be regarded as erroneous.

[3] No doubt Simpson would point to it as justifying his wholesale introduction of apostrophes: see p. 106, note.

not consistent. As a rule, indeed, he is meticulous in writing -'d in the past tense and participle; yet in the autograph *Masque of Queens* we find 'aduauncd' and 'auers'd' in consecutive lines (372–3). It will be safer to follow the copy-text in this rather trivial matter.

Contraction and elision are points on which we should in any case expect to find much scribal variation and individual licence. But there is a special reason to expect confusion in a work of Jonson's. For he had the peculiarity of sometimes indicating elision by an apostrophe while at the same time retaining the vowel elided. After the definition of 'Apostrophus' already quoted Jonson gives the following examples: 'Th'outward', 'Th'inward', 'ye'utter', 'ye'once', 'thou'art', 'to'awake', 'to'have'. In only two out of the seven instances is the vowel actually suppressed; in the other five both vowel and apostrophe appear. It is true that in two cases complete elision would be awkward both in speech and print, and the apostrophe merely warns the reader that the vowel is not to count metrically. But the last three cases are perfectly normal and there is no reason why the elision should not be made complete alike in speech and writing. We find just the same practice in Jonson's own works. There are six examples of incomplete elision in the holograph *Masque of Queens* and twenty-eight in Simpson's text of *Sejanus*. Many, indeed, are cases in which complete elision would be difficult in speech and misleading to the eye, such as 'Glory'of *Asia*' (*MQ*, 404) and 'borrow'a man' (*S*, V. 157); but there are plenty of others like 'now she'is growne' (*MQ*, 378) and 'to'vndoe' and 'They'are' (*S*, I. 257, II. 405). Now of such Jonsonian elisions[1] there are in fact eleven examples in the *Gipsies*, preserved either in H or N (and one also in F): B 17 N 'eu'erye', B 20 N 'ne'uer' (for 'neu'er' or 'neue'r'), W 195 H 'I'haue', W 261 H 'You'are', W 287 N 'heau'en', B 475 N 'giue'n', W 452 NF 'To'extinguish', W 520 H 'He'is', W 1055 N 'bee'it', W 1186 N 'heau'en', W 1189 H 'hee'is' (probably).[2]

The point I am aiming at is this. Since incomplete elisions would

---

[1] The usage, though never common, was not, it is true, confined to Jonson. There are some fifty instances in Ralph Crane's transcript of Middleton's play *The Witch* (see *The Library*, Mar. 1942, xx. 217, and the Malone Society's edition, 1949). Moreover, it lingered into the second half of the seventeenth century. Professor Nichol Smith has drawn my attention to instances in Cowley's *Miscellanies* as printed in the folio of 1668: thus in the verses 'On the Death of Mr. Jordan' (p. 6), 'A *Debter* more to *Him*, then *He* to'his *Own*' (ed. 1681 reads 't'his'), and 'The Epilogue' to *The Guardian* (p. 16), 'It may offend your *Highness*, and we'have now' (retained in 1681).

[2] At B 475 N is in fact incorrect: the rime requires 'gi'n' not 'giv'n', and the form of the elision cannot be original. Several of the elisions quoted are internal, and are therefore strictly excluded by the wording of Jonson's definition of 'Apostrophus'. Actually I have found no example of internal incomplete elision in either *The Masque of Queens* or *Sejanus*, but since complete internal elision is frequent, there seems to be no reason why the Jonsonian variety should not occur. The same remarks apply to initial elision after a consonant, but of this the *Gipsies* provides no instance either.

be unfamiliar to scribes and compositors, there would be a strong temptation to omit either the vowel or the apostrophe, and thus to produce just that confusion of fully elided and unelided forms that we find in the text of the *Gipsies*. That a compositor, even a compositor used to Jonson's habits, would be likely to omit the apostrophe in such cases, is proved by the fact that of the twenty-eight instances of Jonsonian elision in Simpson's text of *Sejanus*, only fourteen appear in the folio of 1616, in the other fourteen cases the apostrophe has been supplied by the editor on the authority of the quarto of 1605.[1] It therefore seems legitimate to assume that in our text many of the variants involving elision arose from a misunderstanding of Jonson's 'Apostrophus'. I have made bold to restore the Jonsonian form, and so to reconcile the evidence, in all variant cases (in the main texts) of the elision of internal or initial vowels and of final vowels before another vowel or initial *h*—unless, of course, the elision is erroneous as at B 475 and W 1241.[2] Since, however, I know of no instance of Jonsonian 'Apostrophus' where a consonant is in question,[3] I have not extended my practice to such cases, but I have made it my rule to prefer the contracted form, in whatever text it appeared,[4] unless there was some particular objection to it. All departures from my usual practice are, of course, discussed in the notes. Where, in the matter of contracted forms, I have departed from the copy-texts, I have not thought it necessary to record the fact (any more than changes in capitalization) along with the more important departures in the second range of footnotes, but all variants of the sort appear in the collations.

I have no doubt that an editor who was more familiar with Jonson's habits as a writer than I can claim to be, would be able to approach closer to the original text in spelling and other accidentals, but I have gone as far as, in view of my ignorance, I thought prudent.

[1] On three occasions Simpson creates a Jonsonian elision by himself supplying the vowel: III. 421 'worthi'⟨e⟩st', V. 807 'th⟨e⟩'vnfortunate', V. 898 'th⟨e⟩'insolent'. But for these readings he has no authority in the quarto, and I am sceptical of their authenticity. Indeed, I doubt whether Simpson intended the result he has produced.

[2] I do not, of course, imagine that all variants involving elision actually originated in the same way, or that my procedure results in every case in the restoration of the original reading; but I believe that this uniform procedure, besides being practically convenient, has the merit of producing a text generally closer to the original than would be produced by following the arbitrary guidance of the copy-texts.

[3] Jonson evidently recognized consonantal 'Apostrophus', for he wrote: 'This rejecting therefore, is both of Vowells, and Consonants, going before,

'Gower, lib. 4. *There is no fire, there is no sparke,*
　　　　　　　　*There is no dore, which may charke.*'

Unfortunately the point of this is, to me at least, obscure.

[4] On the ground that expansion would be more likely than contraction to occur in the course of transmission, as observed on p. 114. But the qualification given above in note 2 is perhaps even more pertinent here.

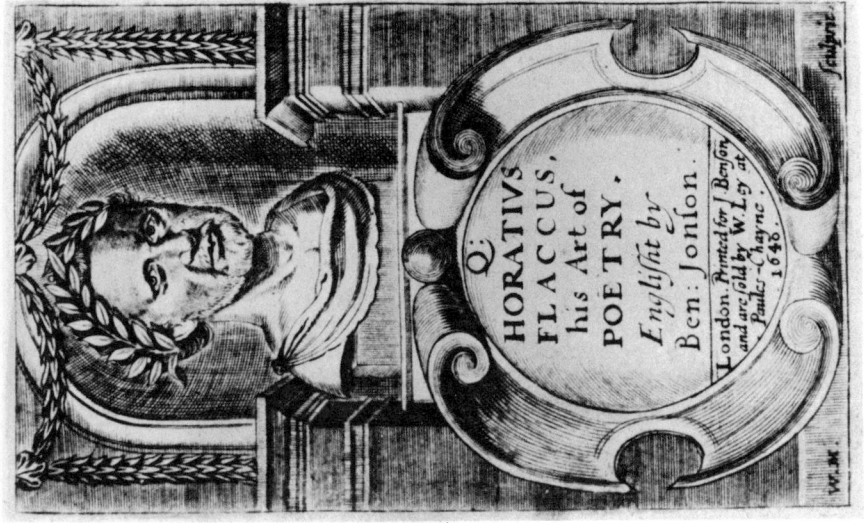

Duodecimo of 1640: Engraved title; (*left*) earlier state, from a copy in the Huntington Library; (*right*) later state, from the copy in the Cambridge University Library

## Q. Horatius
Flaccus:
*His Art of Poetry.*

ENGLISHED By
Ben: Jonſon.

With other Workes of the
Author, never Printed
before.

*LONDON:*
Printed by J. Okes, for John
Benſon. 1640.

## The Maſque
OF THE
GYPSIES.

Written by BEN: JONSON.

*LONDON:*
Printed by J. Okes, for
J. Benſon, and are to bee
ſold at his ſhop in St. Dun-
ſtans Church-yard in Fleet-
ſtreet. 1640.

(59)

Your *Mercuries* Hill too, a wit doth betoken,
Some Book-craft you have, & are pretty well spoken.
But stay! in your *Jupiters* mount, what's here?
A *King*! a *Monarch*! what wonders appeare!
*High*, *Bountifull*! *Just*! a *Jove* for your parts,
A Master of men, and that Reigne in their hearts
 Ile tell it my traine,
 And come to you againe.

### Song 3.

To the old, long life and treasure,
 To the young, all health and pleasure.
  To the faire their face
  With eternall grace,
And the foule to be lov'd at leisure.

To the witty all cleare mirrours,
To the foolish their darke errours;
 To the loving sprite,
 A secure delight,
To the jealous his owne false terrours.

After which the Kings fortune is pursued by the Captaine.

Could any doubt that saw this hand,
Or who you are, or what command

You

Duodecimo of 1640: Page 59 in the original setting (sig. D6) and in the cancel (sig. d1)

47

# A MASQUE OF THE METAMORPHOS'D GYPSIES.

## AS IT WAS THRICE PRESENTED TO KING IAMES.

FIRST,
AT BVRLEIGH
on the Hill.

NEXT,
AT BELVOYR.

AND LASTLY,
AT WINDSOR.

AVGVST,
1621.

Folio of 1641: Special title to the Masque
*(reduced)*

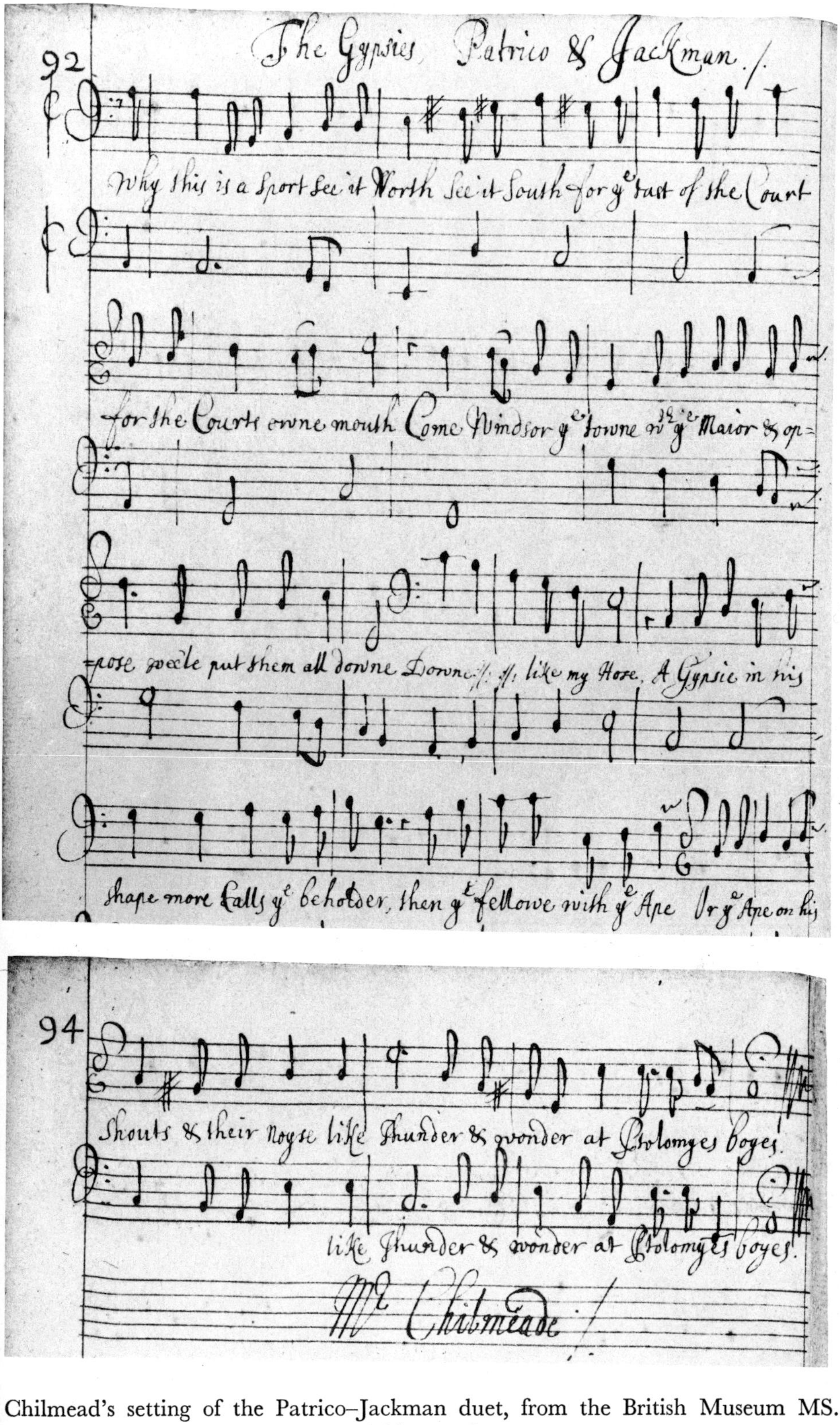

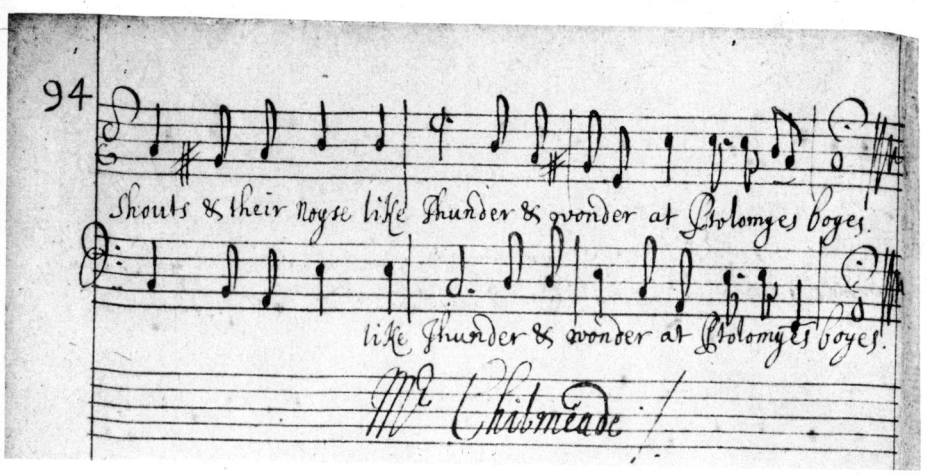

Chilmead's setting of the Patrico–Jackman duet, from the British Museum MS. Add. 29396
(fols. 71b, 72b: reduced)

# The GYPSIES metamorph'os'd

Enter

A Gipsie leading a horse laden w^th five little
children bound in a trace of scarfes vpon him
A second leading another horse laden w^th stolne
poultrie &c. The first leading Gipsie speakes
beeing the

## JACKMAN

Roome for the fiue Princes of Ægipt mounted all
vpon one horse like the fower sonnes of Aymon, to make
the miracle the more by a head, if it may bee. Gaze
vpon them as on the offspringe of Ptolomee begotten
vpon seuall Cleopatra's in their seuerall Countries
'Specially on this braue sparke strooke out of
Flintshire vppon Justice Jugge daughter then
Sheriffe of the countie: who running away with a
kinsman of Captaines, and her father pursuinge h[im]
to the marches, where geeate with Justice shee greate
with Iuggg Linage, they were both for the time turn'd
stone vpon the sight of eache other in Chester till
at last (for the wonder) a Iudge of the Crowe
ordayning there the memoriall of bothe theire
grauities, hee in beard, and hers in belly hath
remaind ded since ostentide in picture vpon the
most stone gate of the kingdome. The famous

that wth time would haue depart
youth without the helpe of Art
You doe keepe still kind the Glorie
of yor sexe is but yor storye

At Windsor in place of the Ladies
fortunes were spoken theise followinge
of the Lords

Dance. 2.

3. straine.

The Lo: Keepers
by the
Patrico.

As happie a palme   o{r} as most in the land
It should be a pure and an innocent hand
and worthy the trust
for it sayes you'll be iust
and carrie that purse
without any curse
of the publique weale
when you take out the seale
you doe not appeare
A Iudge of a yeare

At Beuer.

The fifte of August
will not let sawdust
lie in yo:r throates
or Cobwebs or oates
but help to scour ye:m
That if no Counsell
hath drawne James hether
but the good man of Beuer
our Buckinghams father
then so much the rather
make it a iolly night
for tis a holie night
&c.

All. A Gall a Gall a Gall.

quier you: all yo:r fill
earle Jack w:th his Gill
and shewie yee the King
the Prince &c and bring
the Guessers none haud
like Lords to appeare
w:th such theire Attenders
as you thought offenders
who nowe become nowe men
you'll know 'em for trade men
… his nowe Gall Reife
… more in bonifie
is so farr from a theife
as he giues y:e releife
w:th his bread, beare, and beife
And tis not long sine
you drancke of his wine
and it made yee fine
both Claret and sherie
then let vs be merrie
and helpe with y:e Gall
for a Gall a Gall
stand vp to the wall
both good men and tall
welcome one made all
make it a iolly night
if not a holie night
spight o' the Constable
or deane of Dunstable.

## The Gypsyes chang'd.

### Dance.

#### Patrico

*Phillipps MS 10100*

[8.2.]

This should have beene bound at y<sup>e</sup> end of y<sup>e</sup> Gypsies Metamorposed

Why now yu behould
 was truth that I tould
 and no demur
 they're changed in a trice
 and so will I
 be my selfe by and by
 I onelie now
 must studie how
 to take of w<sup>th</sup> grace
 by my Patricoes place
 some short kinde of blessing
 it selfe addressing
 unto my good Master
 with sighs in him fast
 then w<sup>th</sup> this faire flie
 And you that stand by
 be discovered he I
 Eache man w<sup>th</sup> his voice
 giue his heart to reioyce
 w<sup>th</sup> y<sup>e</sup> requite
 if my Lord hit right

Heber–Huntington Manuscript, page 49

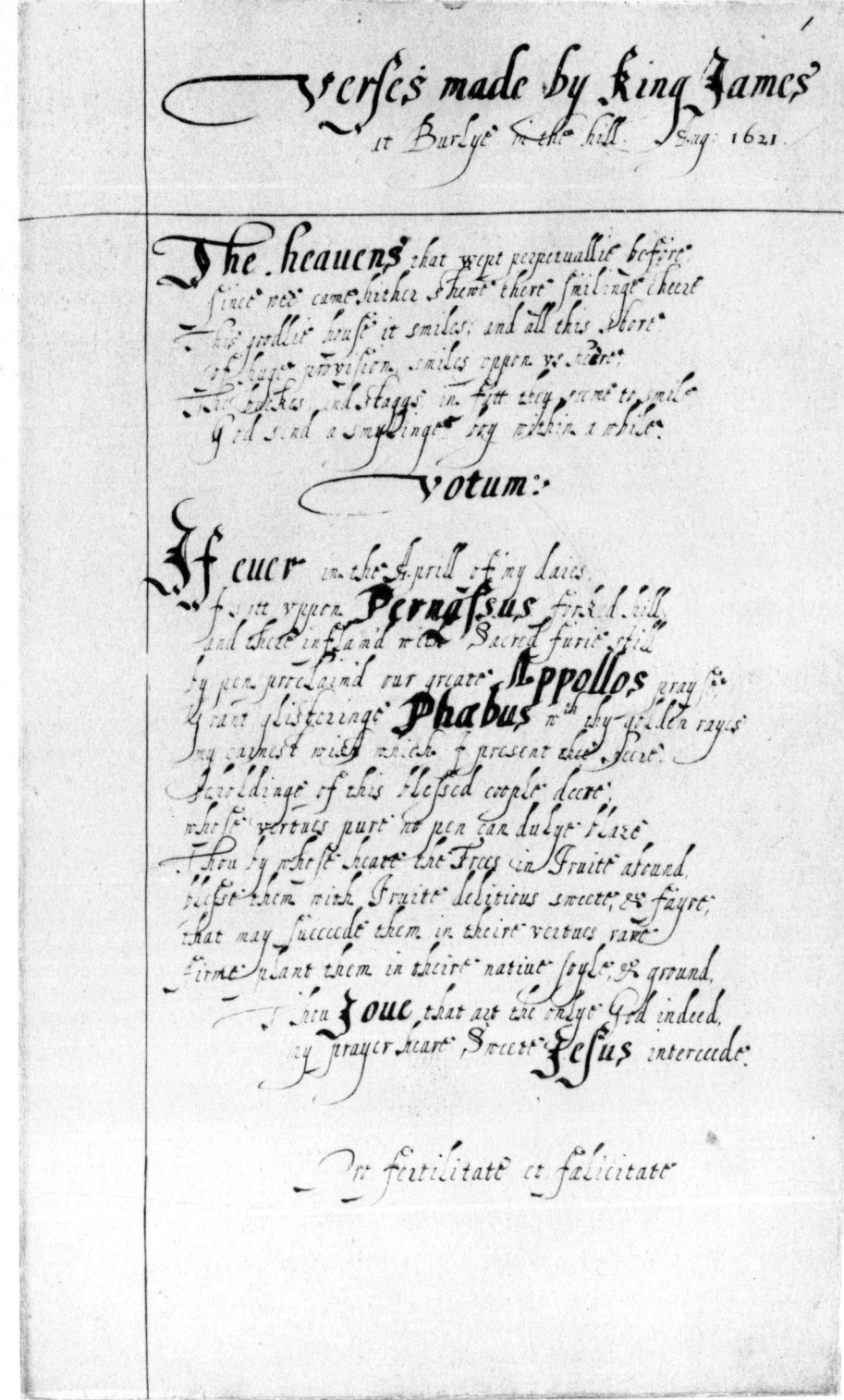

Verses by James I, from the Newcastle Manuscript (fol. 1): British Museum MS. Harley 4955
(reduced)

## Benjamin Johnson

Our knackes, and our dances,
we worke on the fancies,
of some of these Nancies,
these trinketts, and Tripsies
and make 'em turne Gipsies.
Heers no Justice Lippus,
will seeke for to nipp vs.

In Crampringe, or Cippus,
and then for to stripp vs.
and after to whipp vs.

his iustice to rant,
while these we decarye
but be wise and warye
and wee maye both carye,

y Kate, and the Marye
and all the bright acrye
a may ... Marye
If our braue Ptolomee
will but saye follow mee.

y George, and the Garter,
Intt our owne quarter,
or durst goe further,
in methods and order,
heer's a purse and a seale
I haue a greate mynde to steale.

That when our grickes are don
we might seeke our owne plan.
all this we maye doe,
and a greate deale more too,
if our braue Ptolomee
will but say follow mee.

### 3. Gipsie:

Captaine if euer at y bowzinge ken,
you haue in draught of Darbye fill'd your men,
and we haue seru'd there Armed all in ale,
wth the browne bowle, and charg'd in braggett stale.
of Mustard thus, and disciplin'd in drinke
in our longe watches, we did neuer shrinke

an old mans wife
as the light of his life
a younge one is but his shade
you will not importune
the change of your fortune
if you dare trust to my ~~budding~~ forecasting
tis presently good, and it will be Lasting

Dom
3 Aug 1621

1619 —   The Lee Purbecks by my Lord ffielding

Hyde yor wonder seemes a sparke
when I could for sure looke
neuer yet did Cypris trace
~~Smoother~~ lines in hand or face
Venus from cloth Saturne Mone
that you should bee Queene of soñe
And the other starres consent
Only Cupids not content
for though you the Theftes disguise
you haue rob'd him of his eyes
And to shew his envy further
in his church with you wth murder
Sayes although that all your light
hee must call his torches lighted
though your other cheekes disclose
mingled bathes of milke and roses
though Clearer eyes hee burnes of glasses
when hee stands and gathers kisses
And your selfe the reason why
wisest men for loue doe dye
hee will turne all hurts to tinder
and shall make the world one Cinder

My Lady Hattons

Mistris of a fayrer table
hath not history nor fable
others fortunes may bee showne
you are builders of your owne
And what euer heauen hath giu'n you
you preserue that state still in you
That which time would haue departe
youth without the helpe of arte
you doe keepe still and the glore
of your selfe, is but your store

The Gypsies Masque
att Burleigh

part of Ben Iusons
Maiesties Progresse
Iames: vol. 8. &c
II

# PARALLEL TEXTS
OF THE BURLEY—BELVOIR
AND THE WINDSOR
VERSIONS

α        *Speech at the Kings Entrance at Burly.*

If for our thoughts there could but speech be found,
And all that speech be uttred in one sound,
So that some power above us would afford
The meanes to make a language of a word,            5
It should be Welcome; in that onely voyce
We would receive, reteine, enjoy, rejoyce,
And all affects of love, and life, dispence,
Till it were cald a copious eloquence;
For should we vent our spirits, now you are come,   10
In other sillabes, were as to be dumbe.
Welcome, O welcome then, and enter here
The house your bounty'hath built, and still doth reare,
With those high favours, and those heap't increases,
Which shews a hand not griev'd, but when it ceases. 15
The Master is your creature; as the place;
And eve'ry good about him is your grace;
Whom, though he stand by silent, think not rude,
But as a man turn'd all to gratitude
For what he neve'r can hope how to restore,         20
Since while he meditates one, you poure on more.
Vouchsafe to thinke he onely is opprest
With their abundance, not that in his brest
His powe'rs are stupid grown; for please you enter
Him, and his house, and search him to the center,  25
    You'l find within, no thanks, or vowes, there shorter,
    For having trusted thus much to his Porter.

---

*This speech was presumably omitted at Belvoir.*

13 bounty built

*Head-title* The Masque of the Gypsies.        1] At the Kings
Entrance.        11 sillabes] sillables        to *omitted.*        13 hath
*omitted.*        [10 come,] come₍ₐ₎        19 gratitude₍ₐ₎] gratitude,]

B 1–27 *after* W 1–20 *in* NF.        1 Speech at] At *D¹ HN: The Speech
at F        at Burly] *om.* *D¹N        Burly] Burleigh F        3 uttred] vttered
HNF        8 affects] effectę HF        10 spirits] sperrittę H        11 sillabes]
Cunningham *conj.*: sillables *D¹ HNF        to] *om.* *D¹        13 bounty'hath]
*apostrophe in* N *only.*        hath] *om.* *D¹        14 favours] favovrs F        15 Which]
as H        16 Master] Maister N        17 eve'ry] every *D¹ HF : eu'erye N
20 neve'r] ne're *D¹ : neu'r H : ne'uer N : never F        21 poure] heape NF
24 powe'rs] powers *D¹ H : pow'res NF        25 ²him] them NF        26 there
shorter,] there( H

# Windsor Version

### Prologue at Windsor.

As many blessinges as there be bones
In Ptolomęes fingers, and all at ones
Held vp in an Andrews crosse for the nones,
    Light on you good Master!          5
    I dare be no waster
    Of time or of speeche
      Where you are in place;
    I onelie beseeche
      You take in good grace        10
    Our following the Court,
    Since tis for your sport,
    To haue you still merry
    And not make you wery.
    Wee may striue to please       15
So longe, some will say, till we growe a disease:
    But you Sir, that twice
Haue gracd vs alreadie, incourage to thrice;
  Wherein if our bouldnes your patience inuade,
  Forgiue vs the fault that your fauour hath made. 20

---

19 o$^r$] yo$^r$ (y *erased*)
w 1–20 *before* B 1–27 *in* NF    1 Prologue] The Prologue NF    3 Ptolomęes] Ptolomes N : Ptolome's F    4 an] *om.* F    5 Master] Maister N    16 growe] proue N    18 incourage] encourage NF

α         ## The Gypsies Metamorphos'd.

*Enter a Gypsie, leading a horse laden with five little children, bound in a trace of scarffes upon him: a second leading another horse, laden with stolne poultry, &c.*

*The first leading Gypsy speaks, being the*

### JACKMAN.

Roome for the five Princes of Ægypt, mounted all upon one horse, like the four sons of Aymon, to make the miracle the more by a head, if it may be: gaze upon them, as on the off-spring of Ptolomy, begotten upon severall Cleopatra's in their severall countyes; especially on this brave sparke, strook out of Flint-shire, upon Justice Juggs daughter, then Sheriffe of the county, who running away with a kinsman of our Captains, and her father pursuing her to the marches, he great with justice, she great with juggling, they were both for the time turn'd stone, upon the sight of each other in Chester, till at the last (see the wonder) a jugg of the towne ale reconciling them, the memoriall of both their gravities, his in beard, and hers in belly, hath remained ever since preserv'd in picture, upon the most stone juggs of the kingdome. The famous impe yet grew a wretchocke, and though for seven yeares together he were carefully carried at his mothers back, rock'd in a cradle of Welch cheese, like a maggot, and there fed with broken beer, and blown wine o' the best, daily, yet lookes he as if he never saw his *quinquennium*: 'tis true, he can thred needles o' horse-backe, or draw a yard of inkle through his nose; but what'is that to a growne Gypsie, one o' the blood, and of his time, if he had thriv'd? Therefore

42 pursuing to     43 she with     45 at last
     48–9 juggs in     50 was

35 Aymon] Ammon     37 Ptolomy] Ptolemy     42 her *omitted.*     43 great *omitted.*     44 time] same time     49 of] in     50 were] was     54 quinquennium] Quinguinever

w (*cont.*) 43 were] was *D1     carefullie] verye carefully NF     45 ¹and] and and N     fed] feede N     46 o'] of H*D¹     47 quinquennium] Quinguinever *D¹ : Guinquennium NF     48 o'] on H*D¹ : o N     or] to F     49 what'is] what is H : what's *D¹NF     o'] of *D¹NF

α ## The Gypsies Metamorphos'd.

*Enter a Gipsie leading a horse laden with fiue little children bound in a trace of scarfes vpon him, a second leading another horse laden with stolne poultrie &c.*

*The first leading Gipsie speakes, being the*

### IACKMAN.

Roome for the fiue Princes of Ægipt mounted all vpon one horse, like the fower sonnes of Aymon, to make the miracle the more by a head if it may bee. Gaze vppon them as on the ofspringe of Ptolomęe begotten vppon seuerall Cleopatra's in theire seuerall counties; especiallie on this braue sparke strooke out of Flinteshire vppon Iustice Iugges daughter, then Sheriffe of the countie; who running away with a kinsman of our Captaines, and her father pursueing her to the marches, hee greate with iustice, she greate with iugglinge, they were both for the time turnd stone vpon the sight of eache other in Chester, till at the last (see the wonder) a iugg of the towne ale reconciling them, the memoriall of bothe theire grauities, his in beard and hers in belly, hath remaind euer since preseru'de in picture vpon the most stone iuges of the kingdome. The famous impe yet grewe a wretchock, and though for seauen yeares together he were carefullie carried at his mothers backe, rockd in a cradle of Welche cheese like a maggott, and there fed with broken beare and blowne wine o' the best daylie, yet lookes he as if he neuer sawe his *quinquennium*. Tis true he can thred needles o' horse backe or drawe a yard of yncle through his nose, but what'is that to a growen Gipsie, one o' the blood and of his time, if he had thriu'd? Therefore

    35 pursueing to    36 she with    38 at last
        41–2 iuges in    43 was

    29 a *interlined.*    32 strooke] strucke    38 ¹the *omitted.*

w 24 &c.] *om.* NF    28 one] the F    Aymon] Ammon *D¹
30 Ptolomęe] Ptolemy *D¹ : Ptolome N : Ptolomie F    31 Counties] Countries F    32 strooke] strook *D¹NF : strucke H    35 ²her] *om.* *D¹    marches] Marshes F    36 greate] *om.* *D¹    37 time] same time *D¹    of eache] each of NF    38 ¹the] *so* *D¹ : *om.* HNF    41 preseru'de] pseru'd N    42 of] in *D¹    wretchock] wretchcocke NF

(α) (till with his painfull progenitors, he be able to beate
it on the    hoofe to the bene bouse, or the stauling
ken, to nip a jan, or clye the jarke) 'tis thought fit he 60
march in the infants equipage,

> With the convoy, cheats, and peckage,
> Out of clutch of Harman-beckage,
> To their libkins at the crackmans,
> Or some skipper of the black-mans. 65

### 2 GYPSIE.

> Where the cacklers, but no grunters,
> Shall uncas'd be for the hunters;
> Those we still must keep alive,
> I, and put them forth to thrive, 70
> In the parkes and in the chases,
> And the finer walled places,
> As Saint Jamses, Greenwitch, Tibals,
> Where the akorns, plumpe as chiballs,
> Soone shall change both kind and name, 75
> And proclaime 'hem the Kings game;
> So the act no harme may be
> Unto their keeper Barnabee:
> It will prove as good a service
> As did ever Gypsie Gervice, 80
> Or our Captaine Charles, the tall man,
> And a part too of our salmon.

### JACKMAN.

If here we be a little obscure, it is our pleasure, for
rather then we will offer to be our owne interpreters, 85
we are resolv'd not to bee understood: yet if any man
doubt of the significancy of the language, we referre
him to the third volume of reports, set forth by the
learned in the lawes of canting, and published in

---

60 and clye    64 To the    86–7 man doe doubt
64 their] the    85 then] than    87 doubt] doe doubt
[67 grunters,] Grunters∧    74 akorns,] Akorns∧    88 reports,]
reports:]

w (cont.) 69 game∧] game; *D¹: game: N: game. F    71 Barnabee∧]
Barnabee: *D¹: barnabee, N: Barnabee; F    73 Gervice] Jervice F
74 or] To F    75 too] so *D¹NF: to H    77 here we] wee heare N:
we here F    78 then] than *D¹F    80 doubt] doe doubt *D¹

# Windsor Version

(α) (till with his painefull progenitours he be able to beate
[β] it on the *hard hoofe to the bene bowse or the stauling
ken, to nip a ian or cly the iarke) tis thought fitt he
marche in the infantes equipage,

    With the conuoy, cheates, and peckage,    55
    Out of clutch of Harman-beckage,
    To theire libkens at the crackmans
    Or some skipper of the blackmans.

### 2 GYPSYE.

Where the cacklers, but no grunters,       60
Shall vncasd be for the hunters,
Those we still must keepe aliue,
I, and put them forthe to thriue
In the parkes and in the chases
And the finer walled places,          65
As Saint Iameses, Greenewich, Tiballs,
Where the akorns, plumpe as chiballes,
Soone shall chaunge bothe kinde and name,
And proclaime 'hem the Kings game;
So the act no harme may bee         70
Vnto theire keeper Barnabee:
It will proue as good a seruice
As did euer Gypsie Geruice,
Or our Captaine, Charles the tall man,
And a part too of our salmon.         75

### IACKMAN.

If here we be a little obscure, it is our pleasure, for
rather then wee will offer to be our owne interpreters,
we are resolued not to be vnderstood: yet if any man
doubt of the significancie of the language, wee refer 80
him to the third volume of reports sett forthe by the
learned in the lawes of cantinge, and published in

  53 and cly   57 To the   79–80 man doe doubt

  52 bene] ben   53 or] and   69 'hem] them   75 too] to

w 52 to] or F   bene] *so* *D¹NF : ben H   bowse] bouse *D¹ : bawse
NF   52–3 stauling Ken] Starlinge: Ken N : Starling, Ken F   53 or] *so*
*D¹ : and HNF   iarke] Iacke NF   56 Harman-beckage] Harman
Beckage NF   57 theire] the *D¹ : 'ther N   Libkens] Libkins *D¹NF
63 forthe] out NF   66 Saint] *so* F : St. *D¹ : Sᵗ HN   Iameses] Jamses
*D¹ : Iames'es H : Iames-es NF   69 'hem] *so* *D¹ : them H : 'em NF

(α) the Gypsie tongue. Give me my guittara: and roome for our Chiefe.

*Dance* 1.

*The Captaine danceth forth with six more to a stand.*
*After which the Jackman sings.*

*Song* 1.

From the famous Peak of Darby,
And the Devills-Arse there hard by,
Where we yearely keep our musters,
Thus the'Ægyptians throng in clusters.

Be not frighted with our fashion,
Though we seeme a tatter'd nation;
We account our ragges our riches,
So our tricks exceed our stitches.

Give us bacon, rinds of walnuts,
Shells of cockles, and of small-nuts,
Ribbands, bells, and saffron'd linnen,
All the world is ours to winne in.

Knacks we have that will delight you,
Slights of hand that will invite you
To indure our tawny faces,
And not cause you cut your laces.

All your fortunes we can tell yee,
Be they for the backe, or belly:
In the moods too, and the tenses,
That may fit your fine five sences.

Draw but then your gloves we pray you,
And sit still, we will not fray you,
For though we be here at Burly,
We'd be loath to make a hurly.

---

At Belvoir 118–19, *or possibly* 116–19, *were presumably omitted.*

---

105 or of

105 and] or      110 indure] endure      111 your] you r      [95 Song<sub>Λ</sub>]
Song.      109 you<sub>Λ</sub>] you,]

B 118 here] heere (*altered from* heare) N : here (*some copies* heare) F (*For other variants see* W.)

## Windsor Version

(α) the Gypsie tounge. Giue me my guittara, and roome for our Cheife.

### Dance 1, 85

*being the entrance of the Captaine with sixe more to a stand. After which the Iackman singes.*

### Songe 1.

    From the famous Peake of Darby
        And the Deuills Arse there hard by,      90
        Where we yearelie keepe our musters,
        Thus the'Ægiptians throng in clusters.

    Be not frighted with our fashion,
        Though wee seeme a tatterd nation;
        Wee account our ragges our riches,      95
        So our trickes exceed our stiches.

    Giue vs bacon, rindes of wallnutts,
        Shelles of cockles and of small-nuttes,
        Ribandes, belles, and saffrond linnen,
        All the world is ours to winne in.      100

    Knackes we haue that will delight you,
        Slightes of hand that will inuite you
        To indure our tawney faces
[β]         And not cause you *quit your places.

    All your fortunes we can tell yee,      105
        Be they for the backe or bellye,
        In the moodes too and the tenses
        That may fitt your fine fiue sences.

    Drawe but then your gloues, we pray you,
        And sitt still, we will not fray you.      110

    98 or of
    105 yee] you      106 the] yo$^r$ (*probably altered to* y$^e$).

w 83 Gypsie] Gypsyes NF    85 1] *om*. NF    86 being . . . Captaine] The Captaine danceth forth *D$^1$    being] which is NF    to a stand] attendant NF    88 1] *om.* NF    89 Peake] peacke N : Peacke F    90 hard by] hardbye N : hard-by F    92 the'] th' *D$^1$N : th H : the F    Ægiptians] Ægyptians *D$^1$ : Egiptians N    94 tatterd] totterd N    98 and] or *D$^1$    102 slight*e*] slyght NF    103 indure] endure *D$^1$NF    105 yee] *so* *D$^1$F : you H : yee (*altered from* you) N    106 the] *so* *D$^1$NF : yo$^r$ (*altered to* y$^e$ ?) H

(α)

PATRICO.

Stay, my sweet singer,
The touch of thy finger
A little, and linger
For me, that am bringer
Of bound to the border,
The rule, and recorder,
And mouth of your order:
As Priest of the game,
And Prelate of the same.

There's a Gentry Cove here,
Is the top of the shire
Of the Beaver-ken,
A man among men:
Yee neede not to feare,
I'have an eye, and an eare,
That turnes here and there,
To looke to our geere:
Some say that there be
One or two, if not three,
That are greater then he.

And for the Room-Morts,
I know by their ports,
And their jolly resorts
They are of the sorts
That love the true sports
Of King Ptolomæus,
Our great coryphæus,
And Queen Cleopatra,
The Gypsies grand-matra;
Then if we shall sharke it,
Here faire is, and market.

---

*At Belvoir* 130–3 (*presumably*) *were replaced by the two lines* (*copy-text* H, *typographically adjusted*):
        There be Gentry Coves here
        Are the cheife of the shire:
*and* 138–40 *were presumably omitted.*

---

133 amongst     143 And jolly

133 among] amongst    140 then] than    143 their] *omitted.*
[121 Stay,] Stay,    125 border,] border,    131 shire,] shire,
145 sports,] sports,    149 -matra;] -matra,]

## Windsor Version 127

(α)        PATRICO.

Stay, my sweete singer,
  The touch of thy finger
  A little, and linger
  For me, that am bringer           115
Of bound to the border,
  The rule and recorder
  And mouth of your order,
  As Preist of the game
  And Prelate of the same.          120

β    There be Gentry Coues here
     Are the cheife of the shire:

α    You need not to feare,
     I'haue an eye and an eare
     That turnes here and there     125
     To looke to our geare.

And for the Roome Mortes,
  I knowe by theire portes
  And theire iolly resortes,
  They are of the sorts             130
  That loue the true sports
Of King Ptolomæus,
  Our greate coryphæus,
  And Queene Cleopatra,
  The Gipsyes grand-matra:          135
Then if we shall sharke it
Here faire is and markett.

129 And iolly

121] *see note.*   129 iolly] ioylly   133 coryphæus] Coriphæus

w 118 yoʳ] the NF   121–2] *Windsor alternative not in* F.   122 shire] sheere N   123 You] Yee \*Dᴵ   124 I'haue] I've \*Dᴵ : I haue HNF   128 theire] ther'e N   129 theire] *om.* \*Dᴵ   iolly] *so* \*DᴵNF : ioylly H   133 our] or NF   coryphæus] Coryphæus \*Dᴵ : Coriphæus HNF   135 grand-matra] grande Matra NF

---

B 131 shire‚] shire, \*Dᴵ : shire, H : sheere, N : Shiere, F   132 Beaver-Ken] Beauer ken H : beuer ken N : Bever Ken F   133 among] *so* HNF : amongst \*Dᴵ   140 then] *so* HNF : than \*Dᴵ   (*For other variants see* w.)

(α)
>Leave pig by, and goose,
And play fast, and loose,
A short cut, and long,
With (ever and among) 155
Some inch of a song,
Pythagoras lot,
Drawne out of a pot;
With what sayes Alchindus,
And Pharaotes Indus, 160
John de Indagine,
With all their *paginæ*,
Faces and palmistry;
And this is all myste'ry.

Lay by your wimbles, 165
Your boring for thimbles,
Or using your nimbles
In diving the pockets,
And sounding the sockets
Of simper-the-cockets, 170
Or angling the purses
Of such as will curse us.
But in the strict duell
Be merry, and cruell,
Strike faire at some jewell, 175
That mint may accrue well,
For that is the fuell
To make the tun brew'ell,
And the pot ring well,
And the braine sing well, 180
Which we may bring well
About, by a string well,
And doe the thing well.
It is but a straine
Of true legerdemaine, 185
Once, twice, and againe.

163 Of faces

170 simper-] semper-    178 tun] Tuns    [160 Indus,] Indus.
163 palmistry;] Palmistry,    181 bring,] bring,]

---

w (*cont.*) 164 Tonne] Tuns *D¹ : towne NF        brew well] brew'ell *D¹
165 ringe] wring F

## Windsor Version

(α)
    Leaue pig by and goose
      And play fast and loose,
      A short cutt and longe,       140
    With (euer and among)
    Some inche of a song,
    Pythagoras lott
    Drawne out of a pott,
    With what sayes Alchindus       145
    And Pharaotes Indus,
    Iohn de Indagine,
    With all theire *paginæ*,
    Faces and palmistry;
    And this is all miste'ry.       150

    Lay by your wimbles,
      Your boringe for thimbles,
      Or vsing your nimbles
    In diuing the pockettes
    And sounding the sockettes       155
    Of simper the cocketts,
    Or angling the purses
    Of such as will curse vs;
    But in the stricte duell
    Be merrie and cruell,       160
    Strike faire at some iewell
    That minte may accrue well,
    For that is the fuell
    To make the tonne brew well,
    And the pott ringe well,       165
    And the braine singe well,
    Which wee may bringe well
    About by a stringe well,
    And doe the thinge well:
    It is but a straine       170
    Of true legier-demaine,
    Once, twice, and againe.

        149 Of faces

      149 Faces and] treating of

w 141] *om.* NF      148 paginæ] Pagine NF      149 Faces and] *so*
*D¹ : treating of H : of faces and NF      150 all miste'ry] all mystery
*D¹ : all mistry H : Almistrye NF      156 simper the Cocketts] semper-
the-Cockets *D¹ : Simper-the Cockets NF      162 minte] myne NF

(α)   Or what will you say now,
      If with our fine play now,
      Our knackets, and dances,
      We worke on the fancies                    190
      Of some o' these Nancies,
      These trickets, and tripsies,
      And make 'hem turn Gipsies?

      Here's no Justice Lippus
      Will seeke for to nip us                    195
      In crampringe, or *cippus*,
      And then for to strip us,
      And after to whip us,
      His justice to varry,
      While here we doe tarry.                    200

      But be wise and wary
      And we may both carry
      The Kate, and the Mary,
      And all the bright aery
      Away to the quarry,                         205

      If our brave Ptolomee
      Will but say Follow me.

### 3 GYPSIE

Captaine, if ever at the bouzing ken,
You have in droughtes of Darby drill'd your men;   210

    210 droughtes] drops    [193 Gipsies?] Gipsies.    198 us,] us.]

B 187 now,] nowe‸ HN : now? F        189 Knackets, and] knackes and
H : knackes, and our NF      191 o'] of HNF       192 Trickets] trinckits
N : trinckets F       193 'hem] 'em HF : e'm N        203 and] om. H
204 Aery] aerÿ H : a'erye N : ae'ry F      205 Quarry] Quary H      206
Ptolomee] Ptolomẹe H (*couplet not duplicated in* F). (*For other variants
see* W.)

## Windsor Version

(α)     Or what will you say nowe,
       If with our fine play nowe,
β       Our feates and our fingering,     175
       Here without lingering,
       Cousening the sightes
       Of the lords and the knightes,
       Some one of theire Georges
       Come of to saue charges?     180

α     Heres no Iustice Lippus
       Will seeke for to nip vs
       In crampe-ringe or *cippus*,
       And then for to stripp vs
       And after to whipp vs,     185
       His iustice to vary,
       While here we doe tary.

    But be wise and wary
       And we may both cary
β       The George and the Garter     190
       Into our owne quarter:
       Or durst I goe farder
       In methode and order,
       Theres a purse and a seale
       I'haue a great minde to steale,     195
       That when our trickes are done
       Wee might seale our owne pardon.
       All this we may doe
       And a greate deale more too
α       If our braue Ptolomęe     200
       Will but say Followe me.

          3 GYPSIE.

Captaine, if euer at the bowsing ken
You haue in draughtes of Darby drilld your men,

    173 nowe,] now⟨     178 knightes,] knigh⟨     186–7 *reversed*
    (186 *in parentheses*).     188 be *interlined*.     195 steale *cramped*
    *and reading doubtful.*     197 pardon] pd⟨

w 173 nowe ] now? F     175 fingering] fingringe NF     176 linger-
ing] lingringe NF     180 of] off F     charges?] charges , H : Charges. NF
186–7] *so* *D¹ NF : *reversed in* H     192 farder] further NF     195 I'haue]
I haue NF     200 Ptolomęe] Ptolomee *D¹ NF     203 bowsing]
bouzing *D¹ N : Bozing F     204 droughtę] drops *D¹ : draught NF

(α) And we have serv'd there armed all in ale,
    With the brown bowle, and charged in bragot stale:
    If muster'd thus, and disciplin'd in drink,
    In our strict watches we did never wink,
    But, so commanded by you, kept our station,             215
    As we preserv'd our selves a loyall nation:
    And never yet did branch of statute break,
    Made in your famous Palace of the Peak:
    If we have deem'd that mutton, lamb, or veale,
    Chick, capon, turkey, sweetest we did steale,           220
    As being by our *Magna Charta* taught,
    To judge no viands wholsome that are bought:
    If for our linnen we still us'd the lift,
    And with the hedge, (our trades-increase) made shift,
    And ever at your solemne feasts and calls,              225
    We have beene ready with the' Ægyptian brawles,
    To set Kit Callot forth in prose or rime,
    Or who was Cleopatra for the time:
        If we have done this, that, more, such, or so;
        Now lend your eare but to the Patrico.              230

### CAPTAINE.

Well, dance another straine, and we'le think how.

Dᴵ                4 GYPSIE.

Meane time in song doe you conceive some vow.

α           Dance 2.      Straine 1.                        235

### Song 2.

        The faiery beame upon you,
        The starres to glister on you,
            A moone of light
            In the noone of night,                          240
        Till the fire-drake hath o're-gone you.

                217 did yet

211 there] thee      217 yet did] did yet      233 4] 1      235
Straine 1.] *om.*    [239 light‸] light,]

---

w (*cont.*) Ægyptian *Dᴵ F : Egiptian N          221 ryme] Rhime F
227–8] *from* *Dᴵ : *om.* HNF      227 4] *ed. conj.* : 2 *Simpson conj.* : 1 *Dᴵ
229 1. straine] *om.* *Dᴵ

(α) And we haue seru'd there armed all in ale 205
With the browne bowle and chargd in braggatt stale;
If musterd thus and disciplind in drincke
[β] In our *longe watches wee did neuer wincke,
But so, commaunded by you, kept our station
As we preserud our selues a loyall nation, 210
And neuer yett did braunche of statute breake
Made in your famous Pallace of the Peake;
If we haue deemd that mutton, lambe, or veale,
Chick, capon, turky sweetest wee did steale,
As being by our *Magna Carta* taught 215
To iudge no viandes wholsome that are bought;
If for our linnen we still vsd the lifte
And with the hedge (our trades increase) made shifte,
And euer at your solemne feasts and calles
We haue beene readie, with the' Ægiptian bralles, 220
To sett Kitt-Callot forthe in prose or ryme,
Or who was Cleopatra for the time:
   If we haue done this, that, more, such, or so,
   Nowe lend your eare but to the Patrico.

CAPTAINE. 225

Well, dance another straine, and wee'll thincke howe.

D¹            4 GYPSIE.

Meane time in song doe you conceiue some vow.

α          Dance 2. 1 *straine.*

*Song 2.* 230

The faery beame vppon you,
The starres to glister on you,
  A moone of light
  In the noone of night,
Till the firedrake hath oregon you. 235

211 did yett

227-8 *omitted.*

w 205 there] thee *D¹     206 braggatt] Bragot *D¹ : braggett NF
208 wincke] shrinke NF     209 But, so,] But, so, D¹ : but, so, HNF
210 preserud] pseru'd N    Loyall] royall NF    211 yett did] did yet
*D¹    212 Pallace] Pallas NF    213 deemd,] deem'd, F    215
Carta] Charta *D¹NF    216 viande] Vrands N : urands F    219
feasts] feaste NF    220 the'] th' *D¹N : th H : the F    Ægiptian]

(α)
    The Wheele of Fortune guide you,
    The Boy with the Bow beside you
      Runne aye in the way
      Till the bird of day                        245
    And the luckyer lot betide you.

*Captaine goes up to the King.*

Blesse my sweet Masters, the old and the yong,
From the gall of the heart, and the stroak of the tongue.
With you, lucky bird, I begin; let me see,        250
I aime at the best, and I troe you are hee.
Here's some luck already; if I understand
The grounds of my art, here's a gentlemans hand;
Ile kisse it for lucks sake; you should by this line
Love a horse, and a hound, but no part of a swine,    255
To hunt the brave stagge, not so much for the food,
As the weale of your body, and the health of your blood.
You'are a man of good means, and have territories store,
Both by sea, and by land, and were born Sir to more,
Which you like a lord, and the prince of your peace,    260
Content with your havings, despise to increase.
You are no great wencher, I see by your table,
Although your *mons Veneris* sayes you are able.
You live chast, and single, and have buried your wife,
And meane not to marry, by the line of your life;    265
Whence he that conjectures your quality, learns,
You'are an honest good man, and have care of your barnes.
Your Mercuries hill too, a wit doth betoken,
Some book-craft you have, and are pretty well spoken.
But stay! in your Jupiters mount, what's here!        270
A king! a monarch! what wonders appeare!

    257 the body ... the blood    258 territorie    259 but were

    254 line] time    257 your ... your] the ... the    258
territories] Territorie    259 ²and] but    261 increase] encrease
[243 you∧] you,    245 day∧] day,    248 yong,] yong∧
253 hand;] hand,    259 more,] more.    265 marry,] marry∧]

---

w (*cont.*) teritoryes Con    253 ²and] but *D¹: & Con    254 the] *so*
*D¹NF : a H Con    255 increase] encrease *D¹N Con    261 You'are]
You are *D¹F Con : your N    haue] *om.* NF    264 stay∧] stay! D¹ : stay,
F    here∧] here! D¹ : here? D²F : here, N    265 kinge∧] King! D¹ :
King, F Con    Monarch∧] Monarch! D¹ : Monarch; D²NF : Monarch,
Con    appeare∧] appeare! D¹ D²F

(α)
    The Wheele of Fortune guide you,
    The Boy with the Bowe beside you
        Runne ay in the way
        Till the birde of day
    And the luckier lott betide you.       240

### CAPTAINE.

Blesse my sweete Masters, the ould and the younge,
From the gall of the hart and the stroake of the tounge!
With you, lucky bird, I begin: lett mee see,
I aime at the best, and I trowe you are hee.    245
Heres some lucke alreadie; if I vnderstand
The groundes of my art, heres a gentlemans hand.
Ile kisse it for luckes sake: you should by this line
Loue a horse and a hound, but no part of a swine,
To hunt the braue stag, not so much for the food,    250
As the weale of your bodie and the healthe of your blood.
You'are a man of good meanes and haue territories store,
Both by sea and by land, and were borne Sir to more,
Which you, like a lord, and the prince of your peace,
Content with your hauinges, despise to increase.    255
You are no greate wencher, I see by your table,
Although your *mons Veneris* sayes you are able;
You liue chaste and single, and haue buried your wife,
And meane not to marrie, by the line of your life.
Whence he that coniectures your qualitie learnes    260
You'are an honest good man and haue care of your barnes.
Your Mercuries hill too a witt doth betoken;
Some booke crafte you haue and are prettie well spoken.
But stay, in your Iupiters mount what's here?
A kinge? a monarch? what wonders appeare!    265

    251 the bodie ... the blood    252 territorie    253 but were

    243 tounge] tou⟨ *but the* u *might be an* n (cf. w 83).    250 ²the]
    yoʳ    254 the] a

    w 241 &c. *The King's and Prince's fortunes, in the Burley version, are present in*
Con.    241 Captaine] Captaine goes up to the King *D¹ : The kings
fortune spoken by my Lo. Marquesse Bu: Con    242 Masters] Maisters
N    younge] yong *D¹ N    243 tounge] tongue *D¹ F : tou⟨ H :
tonge N    247 my] myne NF    248 luckʃ] lucke N Con    should]
shall NF    line] time *D¹    250 ²the] *so* *D¹ F Con : yoʳ HN    251
yoʳ ... yoʳ] the ... the *D¹    ²of] ô N : o' F    252 You'are] You
are *D¹ Con: Y'are H : yʳ N : Your F    territories] Territorie *D¹ :

(α) High! bountifull! just! a Jove for your parts!
A master of men, and that raigne in their hearts.
  Ile tell it my traine,
   And come to you againe.    275

   *Song* 3.

To the old, long life and treasure,
To the young, all health and pleasure,
  To the faire their face
   With eternall grace,    280
And the foule to be lov'd at leisure.

To the witty all cleare mirrours,
To the foolish their darke errours,
  To the loving sprite
   A secure delight,    285
To the jealous his owne false terrours.

   *Captaine goes up againe.*

Could any doubt, that saw this hand,
Or who you are, or what command
  You have upon the fate of things,    290
Or would not say you were let downe
From Heave'n on earth to be the crowne,
  And top of all your neighbour kings?

To see the wayes of truth you take
To ballance businesse, and to make    295
  All Christian differences cease:
Or till the quarrell and the cause
You can compose, to give them lawes,
  As arbiter of warre and peace.

For this, of all the world you shall    300
Be stiled James the just, and all

[288 doubt,] doubt,   291 downe,] downe,   293 kings?] Kings.   294 take,] take,]

---

w (*cont.*) 288 kinge,] Kings. D¹ D² : kinges; N : Kings? F   290 ballance] Sallance NF

## Windsor Version

(α) Highe, bountifull, iust, a Ioue for your partes,
  A master of men and that raigne in theire hartes.
    Ile tell it my traine
    And come to you againe.

### Song 3. 270

  To the old longe life and treasure,
  To the young all healthe and pleasure,
    To the faire theire face
    With eternall grace,
  And the foule to be lou'd at leasure. 275

  To the wittie all cleare mirrors,
  To the foolishe theire darke errors,
    To the louinge sprite
    A secure delight,
  To the iealous his owne false terrors. 280

  *After which the Kings fortune is pursued by the*

### CAPTAINE.

  Could any doubt that sawe this hand
  Or who you are or what commaund
    You haue vpon the fate of things, 285
  Or would not say you were let downe
  From Heaue'n on earthe to be the crowne
    And top of all your neighbour kinges?

  To see the wayes of truthe you take
  To ballance business, and to make 290
    All Christian differences cease,
  Or till the quarrell and the cause
  You can compose, to giue them lawes
    As arbiter of warre and peace.

    For this of all the world you shall 295
    Be stiled Iames the iust, and all

---

w 266 highe,] High! D¹ : High, D²NFCon    bountifull,] bountifull!
D¹ : Bountifull, D² : bountifull, NF    iust,] just! D¹ : Just: D²NF : Iust,
Con    part ͜ ,] parts! D¹ : parts, D²F    268 tell] teell N    277 errors]
errours D¹D²    281–2] Captaine goes up againe. D¹ : Daunce and the
fortune is pursu'd by the same (*omitting* 270–80) Con    284 commaund]
command D¹D²F    287 Heaue'n] Heaven D¹HD²F Con : heau'en N

(α)         Their states dispose, their sons, and daughters,
            And for your fortune, you alone,
            Among them all, shall work your owne
                By peace, and not by humane slaughters.          305

D¹              This little, from so short a view,
                    I tell, and as a teller true
            Of fortunes, but their maker, Sir, are you.

α               Dance 2.    Straine 2.
            After which the Princes fortune is offered at by the   310

                        2 GYPSIE.

                As my Captaine hath begunne
                With the sire, I take the sonne.
                    Your hand Sir.
                Of your fortune be secure,                         315
                Love and she are both at your
                    Command Sir.

    309 Dance 2.] Dance 3.    Straine 2.] *omit*.    310 After] In
    [304 all,] all<sub>∧</sub>    306 little,] little<sub>∧</sub>]

---

w (*cont.*) 315 desart] desert *D²NF          319 2 Dance] Dance 3 D¹D²
2 straine.] *om*. D¹        320–1] The Princes by Lo. Feilding Con    320
After] In D¹      offerd] offered D¹D²F : offre'd N        327 Comaund]
Command D¹D²F

## Windsor Version

(α)  Theire states dispose, theire sonnes and daughters:
And for your fortune, you alone
Among them all shall worke your owne
    By peace and not by humaine slaughters      300

β  But why doe I presume, though true,
To tell a fortune, Sir, to you,
    Who are the maker here of all?
Where none doe stand or sitt in veiwe
But owe theire fortunes vnto you,      305
    At least what they good fortune call.

My selfe a Gypsye here doe shine,
Yet are you maker, Sir, of mine:
    Ô that confession would content
So highe a bountie, that doth knowe      310
No part of motion but to flowe,
    And giuinge, neuer to repent!

May still the matter wayte your hand,
That it not feele or stay or stand,
    But all desart still ouerchardge:      315
And may your goodnes euer finde
In mee, whome you haue made, a minde
    As thanckfull as your owne is large.

α      *2 Dance. 2 straine.*

*After which the Princes fortune is offerd at by the*      320

### 2 GYPSYE.

As my Captaine hath begunne
With the sire, I take the sonne:
    Your hand Sir!
Of your fortune be secure,      325
Loue and shee are both at your
    Commaund Sir.

    305 fortune      309 could

297 daughters:] daug⟨      299 Among] amongst

w 298 fortune] fortunes D²      299 among] *so* D¹ D² NF : amongst H : amonke Con      300 and] *om.* F      302 to] unto *D²      305 fortunes] Forrune *D² : fortune NF      306 fortune] fortunes *D²F : fortunes (s *perhaps altered*) N      309 would] could *D²NF      311 part] pʳᵗ N

(α)
See what states are here at strife
Who shall tender you a wife,
   A brave one,                          320
And a fitter for a man,
Then is offred here, you can-
   Not have one.

She is sister of a starre,
One the noblest now that are,      325
   Bright Hesper;
Whom the Indians in the east
Phosphore call, and in the west
   Height Vesper.

Courses, even with the sunne,     330
Doth her mighty brother runne
   For splendor:
What can to the marriage night
More then morne, and eve'ning light
   Attend her?                          335

---

319 should     332 Of

319 shall] should    329 Then] Than    332 For] Of    [318 strife$_\wedge$] strife,    325 are,] are$_\wedge$    326 Hesper;] Hesper.]

w (cont.) 345 her$_\wedge$] her? D$^1$ D$^2$ F : her, N    346 promise] pmise N
349 Grandsires] Grandsers N: Grandsiers F    351 laughter$_\wedge$] laughter
*D$^2$ F : laughter, N    354 labors] labours *D$^2$ N F

## Windsor Version

(α)
    See what states are here at strife
    Who shall tender you a wife,
      A braue one!                 330
    And a fitter for a man
    Then is offerd here you can⸗
      Not haue one.

    Shee is sister of a starre,
    One the noblest nowe that are,       335
      Bright Hesper,
    Whome the Indians in the east
    Phosphore call, and in the west
      Height Vesper.

    Courses euen with the sunne         340
    Dothe her mightie brother runne
      For splendor:
    What can to the marriage night
    More then morne and eue'ning light
      Attend her,                 345

β
    Saue the promise before day
    Of a little Iames to play
      Hereafter
    Twixt his grandsires knees, and moue
    All the prettie waies of loue         350
      And laughter?

    Whilst with care you striue to please
    In your giuing his cares ease,
      And labors,
    And by being longe the ayde
    Of the empire, make afraide         355
      Ill neighbours;

    Till your selfe shall come to see
    What wee wishe yet far to bee
      Attending,                 360
    For it skilles not when or where
    That beginnes which cannot feare
      An endinge;

      329 should     342 Of

w 328 states] Starres D²     329 shall] should D¹     332 Then] Than
D¹ Con     offerd] offred D¹ : offer'd D²NFCon     339 Height] Hight
D²NFCon     342 for] Of D¹     344 eue'ning] evening D¹ D²HF : Eu'ning N

β       2 *Dance. Straine* 3.

α       *After which the Lady Marquesse Buckingham's by the*

### 3 GYPSIE.

Hurle after an old shooe,
Ile be merry what eve'r I doe:                    340
Though I keep no time,
My words shall chime,
Ile overtake the sence with a rime.
Face of a rose,
I pray thee depose                    345
Some small piece of silver; it shall be no losse,
But onely to make the signe of the crosse:
If your hand you hallow,
Good fortune will follow;
I sweare by these ten,                    350
You shall have it agen,
I doe not say when.
But Lady, either I am typsie,
Or you are to fall in love with a Gypsie:
Blush not Dame Kate,                    355
For early or late

336 *omitted.*     337 After which the] The     348 hallow] hollow     [349 follow;] follow ᴧ     352 when.] when:]

B 336] so D²: om. D¹: Dance .2. 3. straine. H: Dance second, 3. strayne, N: 2 Dance. Staine 3. F     337 &c. *The Ladies' fortunes are present in* Con     337–8] *The Lady Marquesses by M*ʳ *Porter* Con     337 After which the] so H D² N F: The D¹     339 Hurle] Horle H     340 eve'r] e're D¹D²: ere H: euer NFCon     343 overtake] ouer take H: over-take N     345 pray thee] pry'thee H: prethee Con     depose] dispose HCon: despose N     346 shall be] shalbe H     347 signe] sighne N     348 hallow] so HF: hollow D¹D²: hallow (a *altered from* o) N     349 follow;] follow ᴧ D¹H Con: follow. D²F: follow, N     356 early] earelie H

w (*cont.*) *D²NFTan     beene] bin *D²NTan     386 Mars his] Mars-his N     387 Master] Maister N     388 honor] honour *D²F: hoʳ: N     389 beene] bin *D²NTan     389+] *see* 370.

## Windsor Version

(β)
    Since your name in peace or warres
    Nought shall bound vntill the starres    365
        Vp take you,

H
    And to all succeedinge veiwe
    Heauen a constellation newe
        Shall make you.

β
        *Dance 2. 3 straine.*    370

    *The Lord Chamberlaines by the*

    IACKMAN.

Though you, Sir, be Chamberlaine, I haue a key
To open your fortune a little by the way:
    You are a good man,    375
        Denie it that can,
    And faithfull you are,
        Denie it that dare:
You knowe how to vse your sword and your pen,
And you loue not alone the artes but the men:    380
The Graces and Muses eue'rie where followe
You, as you were theire second Apollo:
Onelie your hand here telles you to your face
    You haue wanted one grace
To performe what hath beene a right of your place; 385
For by this line, which is Mars his trenche,
You neuer yet help'd your Master to a wenche:
    Tis well for your honor hee's pious and chaste,
    Or you had most certainelie beene displac't.

---

*In* H *the Lord Chamberlaine's fortune (371–89) is misplaced as the last of the Lords' (before* 501*).*

---

385 has

w 367–9] *om.* \*D²NF      369+ *After the Ladies' fortunes* H *adds* At Windsor in place of the Ladies fortunes were spoken theise following of the Lordes.      370] *ed. conj.* : *before the Lord Keeper's fortune in* H\*D²NF      3. straine.] Straine 3. \*D²NF      371 &c. *Of the Lords' fortunes, those of the Lords Chamberlain, Keeper, Treasurer, and Steward are present in* Tan *and* Raw. 371–89] *in place of* 483–500 HTanRaw      371 Lo:] Lord \*D²FRaw Chamberlaines] Chamberlaine \*D²NF : Chamberleines fortune Tan : Chamberlens fortune Raw      371–2 by the Iackman] *om.* TanRaw 381 eue'rie] euerie HTanRaw : ev'ry \*D²NF      385 hath] has

(α)    I doe assure you it will be your fate:
Nor need you be once asham'd of it Madam,
He's as handsome a man as ever was Adam,
  A man out of wax
  As a lady would aks:
  Yet he is not to wed yee,
  H'has enjoyed you already,
  And I hope he has sped yee:
  A dainty young fellow:
  And though he look yellow,
  He neve'r will be jealous,
  But love you most zealous,
There is never a line in your hand but doth tell us.
And you are a soule so white and so chast,
A table so smooth, and so newly ras't,
  As nothing cald foule
   Dare approach with a blot,
   Or any least spot,
  But still you controule,
  Or make your owne lot,
Preserving love pure, as it first was begot.
  But Dame I must tell yee,
  The fruit of your belly
  Is that you must tender,
  And care so to render,
  That as yourselfe came
  In blood, and in name,
  From one house of fame,
   So that may remain
   The glory of twaine.

   369 There's never *or* There is not

361 aks] ak's   363 you *omitted*.   369 never] not   [359
Adam,] Adam.   368 zealous,] zealous.   369 us.] us,   372
foule₍] foule,   379 belly₍] belly,   385 remain₍] remain,]

B 357 will be] wilbe H   361 aks] *so* H : ak's D¹ : axe D²NF : aske Con
362 he is] *so* D¹HCon : he's D²NF   363 H'has] H'as H : hee has Con
you] *so* HD²NFCon : *om*. D¹   365 young] yonge NF   366 he]
you D²   367 neve'r] ne're D¹ : neu'r H : never D²NF : nere Con
will be] wilbe HN   369 There is never] *ed. conj.* : There is not D¹ :
there's neuer HD²NF : there is nere Con   371 ras't] rast H : ra'ste
D²NF : cast Con   373 Dare] dares H : doth Con   with] wᵗʰ H : wᵗᵉ N

w (*cont*.) Gypsie] *om*. Tan Raw   414 come] *so* *D²NFTanRaw: Come
Sʳ H   demaund] demand *D²FTan   415 sin'] Since *D²NF TanRaw
not for] for no *D²NFTanRaw

## Windsor Version

*The Lord Keepers by the* 390

### PATRICO.

As happie a palme Sir, as most i' the land;
It should be a pure and an innocent hand,
    And worthy the trust,
    For it sayes you'll be iust, 395
    And carrie that purse
    Without any curse
    Of the publique weale
    When you take out the seale;
    You doe not appeare 400
    A Iudge of a yeare.
    Ile venter my life
    You neuer had wife,
    But Ile venter my skill
    You may when you will. 405
You haue the Kings conscience too in your brest,
    And thats a good guest,
    Which you'll haue true touch of,
    And yet not make much of,
More then by truthe yourselfe forthe to bringe 410
The man that you are for God and the Kinge.

*The Lord Tresurers by the*

### 3 GYPSIE.

I come to borrowe, and you'll graunt my demaund Sir,
Sin' tis not for money; pray lend me your hand Sir: 415

---

*Lines 402–5 do not appear in* H *(copy-text* N*).*

---

    414 come Sir to    415 Since   for no

    409 much] mutch    414 come] Come S$^r$

w 390 The Lo: Keepers] The Lord Keepers Fortune *D²F Raw : The Lo: Keepers fortune N Tan    390–1 by the Patrico] *om.* Tan Raw    392 i'] in H Tan Raw    395 you'll] *so* *D² : you ll H : youle NF    396 that] the *D² : this Tan Raw    398 publique weale] Publicke-weale *D² : Publique-weale F    402–5] *in* *D²NF Tan Raw : *om.* H    402, 404 venter] *so* NF Raw : venture *D² Tan    406 too] to N    408 you'll] you will *D²NF : youle Tan Raw    409 much] *so* *D²NF Tan Raw : mutch H    412 The Lo: Tresurers] The Lord Treasurers fortune *D²F Raw : The Lo: Treasures fortune N : The lo: Treasorers fortune Tan (*in* Tan *and* Raw *this fortune is after the L. Steward's*).    412–13 by the 3

(α)

## Burley—Belvoir

### 2 *Dance.* Straine 4.

*After which the Countesse of Rutlands by the*

#### 3 GYPSIE.

You, sweet Lady, have a hand too,　　　　390
And a fortune you may stand too,
Both your brave'ry, and your bounty,
Stile you Mistris of the County.
You will find it from this night
Fortune shall forget her spight,　　　　395
And heape all the blessings on you,
That she can poure out upon you,
To be lov'd where most you love
Is the worst that you shall prove,
And by him to be imbrac'd,　　　　400
Who so long hath knowne you chast,
Wise, and faire, whilst you renew
Joyes to him, and he to you:
　　And when both your yeares are told,
　　Neither think the other old.　　　　405

β　　　　*And the Countesse of Exeters by the*

#### PATRICO.

Madam, we knew of your comming so late,
We could not well fit you a nobler fate
Then what you have ready made;　　　　410
　　An old mans wife
　　Is the light of his life,
A young ones is but his shade.

---

*The Countess of Exeter's fortune* (406–17) *does not appear in* D¹ *and may have been first spoken at Belvoir* (*copy-text* D²).

---

　　387 2 Dance.] Dance 4.　　Strain 4. *omitted.*　　388 After] In
392 and] O　　394 it *omitted.*　　400 imbrac'd] embrac'd
406–17 *omitted.*　　408 knew] know　　413 ones] one　　[390
You,] You‸　　Lady,] Lady‸　　394 night‸] night,　　398
love‸] love,　　408 Madam,] Madam‸　　409 fate‸] fate,
411 wife‸] wife,]

B 387] *so* D² : Dance 4. D¹ : Dance 2. 4. straine. H: 2 Dance 4 straine NF
388–9] the Countesse of Rutland Mʳ. Porter (*this fortune after the C. of
Buckingham's*) Con　　388 After] *so* HD²NF : In D¹　　392 brave'ry]
braverie D¹H Con : brav'ry D²NF　　and] *so* HD²NFCon : O D¹　　394 it]
*so* HD²NFCon : *om.* D¹　　395 shall] will H　　400 imbrac'd] embrac'd
D¹ : imbrac̃t H : imbrac't D² : imbra'st N : imbract F　　404 told]

## Windsor Version 147

(β) And yet this good hand, if you please to stretch it,
Had the errand beene money, could easilie fetch it:
You comaund the Kings treasure, and yet o' my soule
You handle not much, for your palme is not foule:
Your fortune is good and will be to sett            420
The office vpright and the Kinge out of debt,
To putt all that haue pensions soone out of theire paine
By bringing thExchequer in creditt againe.

*Dance 2. 4 straine.*

*The Lord Priuie Seales by the*            425

### 2 GYPSIE.

Honest and old:
In those the good parte of a fortune is told.
God send you healthe!
The rest is prouided, honor and wealthe,            430
All which you possesse
Without the makinge of any man less;
Nor need you my warrant, inioye it you shall,
For you haue a good Priuie Seale for it all.

*The Earle Marshalls by the*            435

### 3 GYPSIE.

Next the greate Master, who is the donor,
I read you here the preseruer of honor,
And spie it in all your singuler partes
What a father you are and a nurse of the artes;            440

429 you your healthe    440 and nurse
423 Exchequer] Excheque$^r$    424 *omitted*.    426 2 *omitted*.
428 parte] e *altered, perhaps from* r    440 $^2$a *omitted*.

w 417 the errand] the Errant *D²F Raw : therrand Tan    beene] bin NTan    418 o'] on *D²NF Raw : by Tan    420 will be] wilbe N Tan Raw    423 thExchequer] thExcheque$^r$ H : th'Exchequer *D²NF : the Exchequer Tan : thexchequer Raw    424] *ed. conj.*: *om*. H*D²NF    425 Lo:] Lord *D²F    by the] *om*. *D²FN    426 2] *so* *D²FN : *om*. H    427 old] Oulde N    428 parte] p't N    told] tould N    429 healthe] your healthe *D²NF    430 prouided] puided N    Honor] honour *D²F    433 inioye] enjoy *D²NF    435 by the] *om*. *D²NF    437 Master] Maister N    438 Honor] honour *D²F    440 $^2$a] *so* *D²NF : *om*. H

---

B (*cont*.) toulde N    405 old] ould H    406–17] *in* H D²NF Con : *om*. D¹    406–7] The Countesse of Exeter Con    408 knew] knewe HN : know *D²F    413 ones] *Simpson conj*. : one H*D²NF Con

148       *Burley—Belvoir*

(β)         You will not importune
          The change of your fortune;                           415
        For if you dare trust to my forecasting,
        'Tis presently good, and it will be lasting.

α                 *Dance 2.   Straine 5.*

        *After which the Countesse of Buckinghams by the*

                    4 GYPSIE.                                   420

        Your pardon Lady, here you stand
        (If some should judge you by your hand)
        The greatest fellon in the land
              Detected.
        I cannot tell you by what arts,                         425
        But you have stolne so many hearts,
        As they would make you at all parts
              Suspected.

        Your very face, first; such a one,
        As being view'd, it was alone                           430
        Too slippery to be look'd upon,
              And threw men:
        But then your graces they were such
        As none could e're behold too much,
        Both eve'ry taste, and eve'ry touch                     435
              So drew men.

        Still blest in all you thinke, or doe,
        Two of your sons are Gipsies too:
        You shall our Queene be, and see who
              Importunes                                        440
        The hurt of either yours or you,
        And doth not wish both George, and Sue,
        And every barne beside all new
              Good fortunes.

                    417 and will

    417 it *omitted.*      418 *omitted.*     419 After which the] The
    ²the] a       437 doe] o *blotted.*      439 see] he       444+]
    Dance 5.     [414 importune͜] importune,    433 such͜] such,]

      B 417 it] *so* H Con : *om.* *D²NF    will be] wilbe HN     418] *so* D² :
    *om.* D¹ : Dance .2. 5. straine. HNF    419–20 the Countesse of Bucking-
    ham (*this fortune before the C. of Rutland's*) Con    419 After which the]

(β)    By cherishing which a way you haue found
How they, free to all, to one may be bound;
And they againe loue theire bondes, for to be
Obliged to you is the way to be free.
But this is theire fortune; harke to your owne:    445
Yours shall be to make true gentrie knowne
From the fictitious; not to prise blood
So much by the greatenes as by the good;
To shewe and to open cleare vertue the way
Both whether she should and how far she may;    450
And whilste you doe iudge twixt valour and noise,
To'extinguishe the race of the Roringe Boyes.

        *The Lord Stewards by the*

        4 GIPSIE.

    I finde by this hand    455
    You haue the comand
Of the verie best mans house i' the land.
    Our Captaine and wee
    Ere long will see
    If you keepe a good table:    460
    Your Masters able,
And here be bountifull lines that say
You'll keepe no part of his bountie away.
    There's written francke
    On your Venus bancke    465
To proue a false Steward you'll find much adoe,
Being a true one by blood and by office too.

---

   446 shall be] shalbe    453 Stewards] Steward.    466 adoe] ado⟨

   w 442 they] the *D²NF    443 bondes] bond's N    446 shall be] so *D²F: shalbe HN    450 whether] whither *D²    452 To'extinguish] so NF: to extinguish H: T'extinguish *D²    453–4] the lo: Duks fortune Tan : The Lord Dukes fortune Raw (*in both this fortune is before the L. Treasurer's*).    453 Lord Stewards] so *D²NF: Lo: Steward H    by the] om. N    457 i'] so *D²NF: in HTanRaw    459 Ere] E're N    464–5] *in margin opposite* 462–3 N: *om*. TanRaw    464 There's written] Thus written to *D²NF    467 true] treve (v *altered from* w?) N

---

   B (*cont.*) so HD²NF: The D¹    ²the] so HD²NF: a D¹    422 *not in parentheses in* HD²NFCon    433 they] the N    434 behold] behould HN    435 eve'ry ... eve'ry] every ... every D¹HCon: ev'ry ... ev'ry D²NF    438 too] two N    439 see] he D¹D²    441 hurt] heart D²NF    443 beside] besides HD²NFCon    444+ D¹ *adds* Dance 5.

(α)

*The Lady Purbecks, by the*

2 GYPSIE.

Helpe me wonder! here's a booke
Where I would for ever looke:
Never yet did Gypsie trace
Smoother lines in hand or face:
Venus here doth Saturne move
That you should be Queene of Love,
And the other starres consent;
Onely Cupid's not content,
For though you the theft disguise,
You have robb'd him of his eyes;
And to shew his envy further,
Here he chargeth you with murther:
Sayes, although that at your sight
He must all his torches light;
Though your either cheeke discloses
Mingled bathe's of milk and roses;
Though your lips be bankes of blisses,
Where he plants, and gathers kisses,
And your selfe the reason why
Wisest men for love may dye;
  You will turne all hearts to tinder,
  And shall make the world one cinder.

*And the Lady Elizabeth Hattons, by the*

5 GYPSIE.

Mistresse of a fairer table,
Hath no history, nor fable;

470 4 GYPSIE.

445 The] In which the    469 And the] The    470 5] 4
[447 wonder!] wonder,   booke,] Booke!   451 move,] move,
452 Love,] Love;   453 consent;] consent,   454 content,]
content;   458 murther:] murther,   460 light;] light:
462 roses;] Roses:]

B 445–6] The La Purbecks by my Lord Feilding Con   445 The] so
HD²NF : In which the D¹   447 wonder,] wonder, D¹D²NF   booke,]
Booke! D¹ : booke, D²NF   450 hand] hands NF   454 Cupid's]
Cupid NF : Cupitts Con   456 robb'd] robd H : told *D²F : rob'd N
460 torches] troches F   461 cheeke] cheeks F   462 bathe's] so N : baths
D¹ : bathes HD²F   469–70] My Lady Hattons Con   469 And the] so
HD²NF : The D¹   Elizabeth] Eliz: HN   470 5] so HD²NF : 4. D¹   471
Mistresse] M<sup>rs</sup> N   472 no] noe N : not F : noe (e *altered from* r) Con

## Windsor Version

(β)

Dance 2. 5 straine.

*The Lord Marquess Hamiltons by the*

### 3 GIPSIE.

Onelie your hand Sir, and wellcome to Court! 470
Here is a man both for earnest and sport.
    You were latelie imployed,
    And your Master is ioyed
    To haue such in his traine 475
    So well can sustaine
    His person abroad
    And not shrincke for the loade.
    But had you beene here,
You should haue beene a Gipsie I sweare: 480
Our Captaine had somond you by a doxie
To whome you would not haue aunsweard by proxie,
One, had shee come in the way of your scepter,
'Tis ods you had laid it by to haue lept her.

γ

*The Earle of Buckclougs by the* 485

### PATRICO.

A hunter you haue beene heertofore,
    And had game good store,
    But euer you went
    Vpon a newe sent, 490
    And shifted your loues
As often as they did there smockes or theire gloues:
But since that your braue intendments are
    Now bent for the warre,

---

The Duke of Buccleuch's fortune (485–500) *appears only in* D²N F (*copy-text* N).

---

    471 hand and    and your wellcome

468 5] 4    469 Hamiltons] Hamilton    471 and] and yo$^r$
487 beene] bin    490 a newe] anewe    494 for] fo *or* fr

w 468] *om.* *D²NF    5] *ed. conj.* : 4 H    469 The] *om.* *D²NF
Lo:] Lord *D²F    Hamiltons] *so* *D²NF : Hamilton H    by the] *om.* N
471 S$^r$] *om.* *D²NF    and] *so* *D²NF : and yo$^r$ H    473 imployed]
imploy'd *D² : Employ'de NF    474 Master] M$^r$ N    ioyed] joy'd
*D²NF    479, 480 beene] bin N    482 aunsweard] answerd *D² :
answere'd N : answer'd F    484 'Tis] Ti's H : Tis *D²F : Tis' N
485–500] *in* *D²NF : *om.* H    487 beene] *so* F : bin *D²N    490 sent]
scent *D²    492 there] their *D²F    493 intendments] inten'dments N
494 for] *so* *D²F : fo *or* fr N

(α)
    Others fortunes may be showne,
    You are builder of your owne:
    And what ever Heave'n hath gi'n you,     475
    You preserve the state still in you:
    That which time would have depart,
    Youth, without the helpe of art
      You do keep still, and the glory
      Of your sexe is but your story.     480

        *Dance 2. Straine 6.*

*During which, enter the Clownes,
Cockrell, Clod, Townshead, and to them Puppy.*

---

    481 Dance 2.] Dance 6.     Straine 6. *omitted.*     [477 depart,]
    depart‸     478 art‸] Art,     480 sexe‸] Sexe,]

  B 475 Heave'n] Heaven D¹ Con : heau'n H D² N F     gi'n] given D² F :
giue'n (n *or* 'n *added*) N     481] (*see* w) Dance 6. D¹     (481 +] *see* w)
483 and to them] *om.* H N F     and] *om.* D²

---

  w (*cont.*) *is present in* Add.     506–7] *om.* *D² N F : The Gypsies. Patrico &
Iackman/ Add     513 Maior] Major *D²     514 'em] them *D² N F Add
520 He'is] H'is *D² N F : Hee's Add     523 o'] on *D² N F Add

## Windsor Version

(γ)
  The world shall see 495
  You can constant bee
  One mistres to proue
  And court her for your loue:
 Pallas shall be both your sword and your gage,
 Truth be your sheilde, and fortune your page. 500

α     *Dance 2. 6 straine,*
β    *which leades into Dance 3.*
H      *Dance 3.*
α   *During which enter the Clownes,*
  *Cockrell, Clod, Towneshead, Puppy,* 505
H  *whilst the Patrico and Iackman sing this song.*

     *Song.*

β  PATR.  Why this is a sport,
    See it northe see it southe,
    For the tast of the Court, 510
 IACK.   For the Courts owne mouthe.
    Come Windsor, the towne,
    With the Maior and oppose,
    Weel put 'em all downe,
 PATR.   Do-do-downe like my hose. 515
    A Gipsie in his shape
    More calles the behoulder
    Then the fellowe with the ape,
 IACK.   Or the ape on his shoulder;
    He'is a sight that will take 520
    An old Iudg from his wenche,
    I, and keepe him awake,
 PATR.   Yes, awake o' the benche;
    And has so much worthe,
    Though hee sitt i' the stockes, 525
    He will drawe the girles forthe,

    500 be] beare

w 497 Mistres] Mistris *D²F : M^es N   500 be] *ed. conj.*: beare *D²NF
*After* 500 *there is a row of ornaments in* *D²   501–6] *corresponding direction
after* 533 *in* D²NF   501] Dance 6. D¹   Dance 2] 2 Dance D²F
502] *om.* D¹   into] in't N   503] *om.* D¹D²NF   505 Puppy] and to them
Puppy D¹ : to them Puppy D²   506–33] *The duet of the Patrico and Jackman*

(α) COCK. O the Lord! what bee these Tom? dost thou know? come hether, come hether Dick, didst thou ever see such? the finest olive-coloured spirits: they have so danced and gingled here, as if they had beene a set of over-growne fayeries.

CLOD. They should bee morris dancers by their gingle, but they have no napkins.

COCK. No, nor a hobby-horse.

CLOD. O, he'is often forgotten, that's no rule, but there is no Maid-Marrian, nor Fryar amongst them, which is the surer marke.

COCK. Nor a foole, that I see:

CLOD. Unlesse they be all fooles.

TOWN. Well said Tom Foole! why thou simple parish asse thou, didst thou never see any Gypsies? these are a covy of Gypsies, and the bravest new covy that ever constable flew at: goodly game Gypsies! they are Gypsies o' this yeare, o' this moone, in my conscience.

CLOD. O they are called the Moon-men, I remember now.

COCK. One shall hardly see such gentleman-like Gypsies though, under a hedge in a whole summers day, if they be Gypsies.

TOWN. Male-Gypsies all! not a mort amongst them.

506 CLOD.

485 hether ... hether] hither ... hither    487 beene] bin
506 Town.] Clod.    [404 Tom?] Tom!    486 such?] such:
497 Foole!] Foole,    498 Gypsies?] Gypsies:    500 goodly,]
Goodly!    501 moone,] Moone,    504 Gypsies,] Gypsies,
though,] though,]

---

w (cont.) 549 newe Couie] newe come N : new-come F    550 goodlie,] Goodly! *D¹    game-Gipsies,] Game, Gypsies! *D¹ : game, Gipsies; N : game, Gipsies, F    551 ¹o'] of H : ô N    ²o'] ô HN    553–4 gentleman like Gipsies] Gentleman-/like Gypsies *D¹ : gentleman-like-Gipsies F    554 Gipsies, though,] Gypsies, though, *D¹F : Gipsies, though, N    556 Town] Clod. *D¹    amongst] amonge NF

(β) IACK.       I, forth i' theire smocks.
         Tut, a mans a man;
         Lett the clownes with theire sluttes
         Come mend vs if they can,                    530
   PATR.     If they can for theire guttes.
   Come mend vs, come lend vs theire showts and theire noise,
   BOTH. Like thunder, and wonder at Ptolomęes boyes.

α   COCK. O the Lord! what be theise Tom? dost thou
knowe? Come hether, come hether Dicke, didst thou  535
euer see such? the finest oliue colourd spirites! they haue
so dancd and gingled here as if they had beene a sett of
ouergrowne fayeries.
   CLOD. They should be morris dancers by theire gingle,
but they haue no napkins.                           540
   COCK. No, nor a hobby horse.
   CLOD. O, he'is often forgotten; thats no rule: but
there is no Maid-Marrian nor Frier amongst them,
which is the surer marke.
   COCK. Nor a foole, that I see.                   545
   CLOD. Vnles they be all fooles.
   TOWN. Well said, Tom Foole! why, thou simple
parishe-asse thou, didst thou neuer see any Gipsies? These
are a couie of Gipsies, and the brauest newe couie that
euer constable flewe at; goodlie game, Gipsies! they are  550
Gipsies o' this yeare, o' this moone, in my conscience.
   CLOD. O, they are calld the Moone men, I remember now.
   COCK. One shall hardlie see such gentleman like
Gipsies though, vnder a hedge, in a whole sommers day,
if they be Gipsies.                                 555
   TOWN. Male Gipsies all, not a mort amongst them.

                    556 CLOD.

      536 spirites] sprites        543 Maid-Marrian] Maidmarrian

   w  533  Ptolomęes] Ptolomies *D²F : Ptolomes N : Ptolomyes Add
533+] *Direction follows in* D²NF (*see* 501–5)    534 Lord_∧] Lord! D¹D²F :
Lord_∧ N       theise_∧ Tom_∧] these_∧ Tom! D¹D² : these, Tom_∧ N : these?
Tom_∧ F     535 hether . . . hether] hither . . . hither D¹D²F       hether_∧
Dicke_∧] hither_∧ Dick, D¹D²F : hether, Dick_∧ N      536 such_∧] such : D¹N :
such? D²F      spirites] *so* D¹D²NF : sprites H       537 beene] bin D¹D²N
538 Fayeries] Fayries D²NF       542 he'is] he's D¹D² : he is H : hees NF
543 Maid-Marrian] Maid-marrian D¹D² : Maidmarrian H : Maid Marian
N : Mayd-|marian F       545 see_∧] see: D¹N : see. D²F       547 said]
sed NF       548 parishe-] parish D¹D² : pish N : pish F       ¹thou_∧] thou,
D¹D²N : thou! F       Gipsies_∧] Gypsies: *D¹ : Gipsies; N : Gipsies? F

(α)  PUP. Where, where? I could never indure the sight of one of these rogue Gypsies: which be they? I would faine see 'hem.

CLOD. Yonder they are. 510

PUP. Can they cant, and mill? are they masters in their arts?

TOWN. No, batchellours these, they cannot have proceeded so farre, they have scarce had the time to be lowsie yet.

PUP. All the better, I would be acquainted with them 515 while they are in cleane life, they'll doe their tricks the cleanlier.

COCK. We must have some musick then.

PUP. Musick! we'll have a whole poverty of pipers: call Cheeks upon the bag-pipe, and Tom Ticklefoot 520 with his tabor; he could have mustred up the smocks
D¹ o'th two shires, and set the codpieces and they by the eares, I wusse: here's my two-pence towards it: Clod
α will you gather the pipe money?

CLOD. Ile gather'it an you will, but Ile give none. 525

PUP. Why well said; claw a churle by the arse, and he'll shite in your fist.

COCK. I, or whistle to a jade, and he'le pay you with a fart.

CLOD. That's all one, I have a wife, and a child in 530
D¹ reversion, you know it well enough, and I cannot fat pidgeons with cherry-stones: Ile venter my penny with you.

COCK. Well, theres my two-pence; Ile bee jovy: my name's Cockrell, and I am true bred.

TOWN. Come, there's my groat, never stand drawing 535

511 or mill     520 bag-pipes

507 indure] endure    511 Can they] They can    520 bag-pipe] Bag-pipes    532 venter] venture    [507 where?] where, 508 Gypsies:] Gypsies,    511 mill?] Mill,    513 No,] No&lt;sub&gt;∧&lt;/sub&gt; 519 pipers:] Pipers,    522 shires,] shires;    523 wusse:] wusse,]

B 532 venter] venture *D¹ (For other variants see w.)

---

w (cont.) bagpipe] Bag-pipes *D¹    575 gather'it] gather't *D¹ : gather it HNF    577 heel] he will *D¹    581 minstrell comes] ed. conj.: minstrellᵉ come H    582-3 Windsor∧ after him∧] Windsor∧ after him, N : Windsor; after him, F    583, 584 o'] ô HN    583 Yonder'is] yonders HN : yonder is F    Parkeᴧ] Parke. N : Parke, F    584 Francis] Frances NF    Castle∧] Castle; NF    585 Eaton∧] Eaton; NF

## Windsor Version

(α)   PVP. Where, where? I could neuer indure the sight of one of theise rogue Gipsies: which bee they? I would faine see 'hem.

CLOD. Yonder they are. 560

PVP. Can they cant and mill? are they masters in theire artes?

TOWN. No, batchelers theis; they cannot haue proceeded so farre, they haue scarce had the time to be lowsie yet.

PVP. All the better; I would be acquainted with them 565 while they are in cleane life, they'll doe theire trickes the cleanelier.

[β]   COCK. Wee must haue some musique then, *and take out the wenches.

PVP. Musique! wee'll haue a whole pouertie of pipers. 570 Call Cheekes vpon the bagpipe and Tom Ticklefoote with his tabour.

[Clod, will you gather the pipe monie?

CLOD. Ile gather'it an you will, but Ile giue none. 575

PVP. Why, well said: clawe a churle by the arse, and heel shite in your fist.

COCK. I, or whistle to a iade, and heel pay you with a fart.

H | CLOD. Fart? Its an ill winde blowes no man to proffitt! 580 see where the minstrell comes i' the mouth on't.]

β | COCK. I, and all the good wenches of Windsor after him. Yonder'is Prue o' the Parke,

TOWN. And Francis o' the Castle,

PVP. And longe Meg of Eaton, 585

---

*In place of* 572–81 NF *have only*:
  tabor, see where he comes. (Tabor; ... comes! F)

---

561 or mill    571 bag-pipes

561 and] or    564 the] theire    581 minstrell comes]
minstrellę come

w 557 where‸ where‸] Where, where, *D¹ F : Where? Where? F   indure]
endure *D¹ F    557–8 of one] *om.* F    558 Rogue Gipsies] rogue Gypsies
*D¹ : Rogue-Gipsies NF    559 'hem] *so* *D¹ : 'em HNF    561 Can they]
They can *D¹    and] *so* *D¹ : or HNF    Mill‸] Mill, *D¹; mill; N :
Mill? F    in] of NF    563 No,] *so* N : No‸ H*D¹F    564 the] *so*
*D¹ : theire HF : there N    566 they'll] they will *D¹H : thei'le N :
the'ile F    567 cleanlier] clenli'er N    571 Cheekes] cheekes NF

(D¹) indentures for the matter; we'le make a bolt, or a shaft on't now.

    CLOD. Let me see, here's nine-pence in the whole.

    PUP. Why there's a whole nine-pence for it: put it all in a piece for memory, and strike up for mirth sake. 540

    TOWN. Doe, and they'le presently come about us for lucke sake. But look to our pockets and purses for our own sake.

    CLOD. That's warning for me, I have the greatest charge I am sure. 545

α                      *Pipers.*

*A Country Dance.*
*During which the Gypsies come about them prying: and after the*

                PATRICO. 550

    Sweet doxies and dells,
    My Roses and Nells,
    Scarce out of the shells,
    Your hands, nothing ells,
    We ring you no knells 555
    With our Ptolomys bells,
    Though we come from the fells,
    But bring you good spells,
    And tell you some chances
    In midst of your dances, 560

556 Ptolomy

551 doxies] Doxes     553] *omitted.*     556 Ptolomys] Ptolemy
558 But] And     [556 bells,] Bells;]

---

w (*cont.*) 593 mirthe] mirthes H : Mirth NF (*cf.* *D¹ at B 540)     598 letts] lettę H: let's NF     'em] *so* NF : them H     599 Pipers] *so* *D¹N : Minstrell H : *om.* F     601 Francis] Frances F     Meg] Megge F     602 Contry] A Country *D¹ : Countrie N : Country F     605 doxies] Doxes *D¹     606 Nells] Knells F     607] *om.* *D¹     610 Ptolomęes] Ptolomy *D¹ : Ptolomes N : Ptolomies F     612 but] And *D¹

## Windsor Version

(β)    CLOD. And Christian o' Dorney.
     TOWN. See the miracle of a minstrell!
     COCK. Hee's able to muster vp the smockes o' the two shires.
     PVP. And sett the codpeices and they by the'eares at pleasure.
     TOWN. I cannot hold nowe; there's my groate: lets haue a fit for mirthe sake.
     COCK. Yes, and they'll come about vs for lucke sake.
     PVP. But looke to our pockettes and purses for our owne sake.
[*ƒ]    CLOD. I. I haue the greatest chardge, *gather the money.
     COCK. Come girles, here be Gipsies come to towne:
[*ƒ]    *letts dance 'em down!

α
*ƒ
α

           *Pipers.*
     *The Clownes take out their Wenches:*
     *Prudence, Francis, Meg, Christian.*
           *Contry Dance.*
*During which the Gypsies come about them prying, and after the*

           PATRICO.

Sweet doxies and dells,
My Roses and Nells,
Scarce out of the shelles,
Your hands, nothing elles:
Wee ringe you no knells
With our Ptolomęes bells,
Though wee come from the fells,
But bring you good spells,
And tell you some chances
In midst of your dances,

---

In 596 H *reads:* Chardge if I gather
In 597–8 H *reads:* towne if wee can lettę
The direction in 600–1 *appears only in* NF (*copy-text* N)

---

593 mirthes     610 Ptolomęe

592 groate] o *altered from* a    593 mirthe] mirthes    596 money.]
moneᑕ    597 letts] lettę    599 Pipers] Minstrell

w 588–91 cf. B 521–3.    588 o'] ô H : of NF    589 shires] sheeres
N : Shieres F    590 the'eares] the eares H : t'heares N : th'ea res F

(α)
> That fortune advances
> To Prudence or Francis,
> To Sisley or Harry,
> To Roger or Mary,
> Or Peg of the Dary,                                565
> To Maudlin or Thomas:
> Then doe not runne from us;
> Although we look tawny,
> We are healthy and brawny,
> What e're your demand is,                          570
> We'le give you no jaundis.

PUP. Say you so old Gypsie? 'slid these go to't in rime, this is better then canting by t'one halfe.

TOWN. Nay, you shall heare 'em, peace! they begin with Prudence, marke that. 575

PUP. The wiser Gypsies they, marry.

TOWN. Are you advised?

PUP. Yes, and Ile stand to't, that a wise Gypsie (take him at time o'th' yeare) is as politicke a piece of flesh, as most Justices in the county where he 580 maunds.

3 GYP. To love a keeper your fortune will be,
   But the dowcets better then him or his fee.

TOWN. Ha, Pru', has he hit you i'th teeth with the sweet bit? 585

PUP. Let it alone; she'll swallow'it well enough: a learned Gypsie.

TOWN. You'll heare more hereafter.

PUP. Marry and Ile listen: who's next, Jack Cockrell?

---

565 Meg    579 i'th time    o' yeare

565 Peg] Meg    579 at] i'th    583 then] than    [561 advances,] advances. (apparently).    564 Roger,] Roger, 565 Dary,] Dary.    566 Maudlin,] Maudlin,    Thomas:] Thomas,    567 us;] us,    576 they,] they,    577 advised?] advised.    582 be,] be.    589 listen:] listen,    Cockrell?] Cockrell.]

---

w (cont.) doucets F    then] than *D¹    638 Ha] so *D¹NF: Ho H
i'th] so N: in the *D¹H: it'h F    the] a NF    640 swallow'it]
ed. conj.: swallow it *D¹H: swallow'e N: swallow F    enough] inough (i
altered from e) N    643 next,] next, *D¹: next: N: next? F    Cockrell,
Cockrell: *D¹F

## Windsor Version

(α)
  That fortune aduances    615
  To Prudence or Francis,
  To Sisley or Harry,
  To Roger or Mary
  Or Peg of the Dairie,
  To Maudlin or Thomas:    620
  Then doe not run from vs;
  Although wee looke tawnie
  Wee are healthie and brawnie,
  What ere your demaund is
  Wee'll giue you no iaundis.    625

PVP. Say you so, old Gypsie? 'Slid, theise goe to't in rime; this is better then canting by t'one halfe.

TOWN. Nay, you shall heare 'em: peace, they begin with Prudence, marke that.

PVP. The wiser Gypsies they, marrie.  630

TOWN. Are you aduisd?

PVP. Yes, and Ile stand to't that a wise Gypsie (take him at time o'th' yeare) is as politique a peece of fleshe as most Iustices in the countie where he
[β] *stalkes.  635

3 GIP. To loue a keeper your fortune will be,
  But the dowcettes better then him or his fee.

TOWN. Ha Prue, has he hit you i'th teethe with the sweet bitt?

[*f] PVP. Let *her alone, shee'l swallowe'it well enough! A 640 learned Gypsie.

TOWN. Youll heare more hereafter.

[β] PVP. Mary, and Ile listen: *who standes next? Iack
            [Cockrell?

---

*In 640 H retains the reading of the Burley version.*

---

   619 Meg  633 i'th time  o' yeare

 627 this] that  633 o'th'] ô  politique] q *altered.*  638
 Ha] Ho

w 616 Francis] fraunes N : Frances F 619 Peg] Meg *D¹ Dairie] Dary *D¹NF 624 demaund] demand *D¹F 626 to't] too't NF 627 rime] rimes NF  this] *so* *D¹NF : that H t'one] to'ne H : tone NF 628 'em] them *D¹ 630 Gypsies] Gipsie's F they] the NF 632 to't] toot N : too't F 633 at] i'th *D¹ o'th'] *so* *D¹ : ô HN : o' F politique] pollique NF 637 dowcetts] doucet's N :

M

(α)  2 GYP. You'l steal your selfe drunk, I find it here true,  590
         As you rob the pot, the pot will rob you.
  PUP. A prophet, a prophet: no Gypsie, or if he be a Gypsie, a divine Gypsie.
  TOWN. Marke Frances now; she's going to't, the virginity o'th parish.  595
  PATR. Feare not, in hell you'll never lead apes,
         A mortifi'd maiden of five escapes.
  PUP. Bir-Lady, he toucht the virgin string there a little too hard; they are arrant learned men all I see. What say they upon Tom Clod? list.  600
  4 GYP. Clods feet in Christmas will goe neare to be bare,
         When he has lost all his hobnails at post and pare.
  PUP. H'has hit the hobnaile o'th head, his owne game.
  TOWN. And the very mettle he deales in at play, if you marke it.  605
  PUP. Peace, who's this? Long Meg?
  TOWN. Long and foule Meg, if she be a Meg, as ever I saw of her inches: pray God they fit her with a faire fortune, shee hangs an arse terribly.  610
  PATR. She'l have a tailer take measure of her britch,
         And ever after be troubled with a stitch.
  TOWN. That's as homely as she.
  PUP. The better: a turd's as good for a sow as a pancake.  615
  TOWN. Harke, now they treat upon Ticklefoot.
  4 GYP. On Sundayes you rob the poores boxe with
         [your tabor,
         The Collecters would doe it, you save 'em a
         [labour.

  590 find here       597 scapes

  592 he be] he must be    [598 Bir-Lady,] Bir-Lady_∧    599 hard;] hard,    600 Clod?] Clod:    607 this?] this_∧    611 britch,] britch.]

  B 590 it] *om.* H (*For other variants see* W.)

  W (*cont.*) Frances_∧ now; *D¹ : Frances, now_∧ F    to't]too't NF    649 o'th] *so* N : of the *D¹ : ô the H : o' the F    651 escapes] *so* *D¹ : scapes HNF    654 Tom_∧ Clod_∧ list_∧] Tom Clod: list. *D¹ : Tom Clod; list; N : Tom, Clod, List. F    655 4] 1 (N?) F    656 and] *so* *D¹NF : and at H    657 H'as] H'has *D¹ : Has NF    o'th] *so* NF : o' the *D¹ : ô the H    659 mettle] Mettall NF    661 this? Long Meg?] *so* HF : this_∧ Long Meg? D¹N    671 4] 1 (N?) F    672 'em] 'em (*altered from* them) H : them *D¹NF

## Windsor Version

*f|   2 GIP. You'le ha good lucke to horse flesh, o' my life,
        You plow'de soe late with the Vicars wife.    645
α   PVP. A prophet, a prophet! no Gipsie, or if he be a
Gypsie, a diuine Gypsie.
    TOWN. Marke Francis, now shee's going to't, the
virginity o'th parishe.
    PATR. Feare not, in hell you'll neuer lead apes,    650
        A mortified mayden of fiue escapes.
    PVP. By'r ladie, he touch'd the virgin stringe there a
little too hard. They are arrant learnd men all, I see.
What say they vpon Tom Clod? list!
[β]   4 GIP. Clods feete *will in Christmas goe neare to be bare, 655
        When he has lost all his hobnailes at post and paire.
[β]   PVP. H'as hit the *right naile o'th head: his owne
game.
    TOWN. And the very mettle he deales in at play, if
you marke it.    660
    PVP. Peace, who's this? Long Meg?
    TOWN. Long and foule Meg, if shee be a Meg, as euer
I sawe of her inches! praye God they fitt her with a faire
fortune, [shee hangs an arse terriblie.
    PATR. Shee'l haue a taylor take measure of her britch, 665
        And euer after be troubled with a stiche.
    TOWN. That's as homelie as shee.
    PVP. The better! a turd's as good for a sowe as a
pancake.
    TOWN. Harke, nowe they treate vpon Ticklefoote.] 670
    4 GIP. On Sundayes you rob the poores box with
                                  [your tabor;
        The Collectours would doe it, you saue 'em a
                                      [labor.

---

*At 644–5* H *retains the Burley version (copy-text* N).
*In place of 664–70* NF *have only:*
fortune.
    PVP. They slipp her, and treate vpon Tickle foote.
(Tickle-foot. F)

---

                        651 scapes

  644 2 Gip. *omitted.*       651 escapes] scapes       656 and] and at
  660 it.] i⟨     664 fortune,] fortu⟨     671 tabor;] tabo⟨     672
'em] them *with th crossed out and apostrophe added.*   labor.] l⟨

    w 644 2 Gip.] (*so* *D¹H) *om.* NF     o'] ô N     646 Prophet . . . prophet]
proffet . . . profett N         be] must be *D¹     648 Francis∧ now∧]

(α)   PUP. Faith but little, they doe it notwithstanding.
Here's my little Christian forgot: ha you any
fortune left for her, a strait lac'd Christian of sixteene?
   PATR. Christian shall get her a loose bodyed gown,
            In trying how a gentleman differs from a clowne.
   PUP. Is that a fortune for a Christian? a Turke Gypsie
could not have told her a worse.
   TOWN. Come, Ile stand my selfe, and once venter the
poore head o'th' towne. Doe your worst, my name'is
Townshead, and heres my hand Ile not be angry.
   3 GYP. A cuckold you must be, and that for three lives,
            Your owne, the Parsons, and your wives.
   TOWN. I sweare Ile never marry for that, an't be but
to give Fortune my foe the lye: come Paul Puppy you
must in too.
   PUP. No, I'am well enough: I would ha no good
fortune an I might.
   4 GYP. Yet looke to your selfe, you'l ha' some ill luck
            And shortly, for I have his purse with a pluck.

PATRICO.

Away birds, mum,
I heare by the hum,
If Beck-Harman come,
He'le strike us all dumbe,
With a noyse like a drum.
Lets give him our roome
Here, this way some,
And that way others,
We are not all brothers:
Leave me to the cheats,
Ile shew 'hem some feats.

629 2 GYP.

625 a *omitted.*   626 venter] venture   629 3] 2   638
*omitted.*   [620 forgot:] forgot,   637 pluck.] pluck,   639
birds,] Birds,]

w (*cont.*) or a N : Turke, or a F       679 a] *om.* *D¹*       680 venter]
venture *D¹*       681 o'th'] *so* *D¹* : ô the H : o' the NF       name'is] name
is *D¹* : names H : name's NF       683 3] 2 *D¹*       three] .3. N       685
an't] *so* *D¹*NF : and H       686 Come, Paul] Com Pan NF       688 I'am]
I am *D¹*H : I'me NF       enough] inough N       ha] have *D¹* : ha' NF
690 4 Gip.] 4 Gypsie. *D¹* : Patr H : Pat. NF       692 *ed. conj.*       695
Beckharman] Beck-Harman *D¹* : Beck-harman NF : Beckarman H       697
¹a] o N       698 roome,] roome, NF       699 Here,] here, H N       703
'hem] *so* *D¹* : 'em HNF

## Windsor Version

(α)[β]   PVP. Faith but little, they doe it *non vpstante.*
[β]   *TOWN. Here's my little Christian forgott! Ha you any
fortune lefte for her, a straite lac't Christian of sixteene? 675
   PATR. Christian shall get her a loose bodied gowne
         In tryeing how a gentleman differs from a clowne.
   PVP. Is that a fortune for a Christian? A Turke Gypsie
could not haue told her a worse.
   TOWN. Come, Ill stand my selfe, and once venter the 680
poore head o'th' towne. Doe your worst; my name'is
Towneshead, and here's my hand Ile not be angrie.
   3 GIP. A cuckould you must be, and that for three liues,
         Your owne, the Parsons, and your wiues.
   TOWN. I sweare Ile neuer marry for that, an't be but 685
to giue Fortune my foe the lie. Come, Paul Puppy, you
must in too.
   PVP. No, I'am well enough; I would ha no good
fortune an' I might.
   4 GIP. Yet looke to your selfe, youll ha some ill lucke— 690
[*ƒ]          And shortly, for I haue his purse *at a plucke.

### PATRICO.

         Away birdes, mum!
         I heare by the hum
         If Beckharman come                          695
         Heel strike vs all dumbe
         With a noise like a drum.
         Let's giue him our roome
         Here, this way some,
         And that way others;                        700
         Wee are not all brothers:
         Leaue me to the cheates,
         Ile shewe 'hem some feates.

---

*In* 691 H *retains the reading of the Burley version.*

---

683 2 GIP.

678 Turke] Turke w^th a    681 worst] s *altered from* t    683
liues,] )(    685 an't] and    690 4 Gip.] Patr    692 *omitted.*
695 Beckharman] Beckarman    703 'hem] 'em

w 673 little] a little NF    they] thei'le NF    vpstante] Vpstant N :
upstant F    674 Christian,] Christian. N : Christian, F    forgott]
forget NF    676 bodied gowne] bodide-gowne F    677 tryeing]
trying *D¹* : tri'mge NF    678 Turke] *so* *D¹* : Turke w^th a H : Turke

(α) PUP. What, are they gone? flowne all of a suddaine? 650
this is fine y' faith: a covy call yee 'hem? they are a
covy soone scattered me thinks, who sprung 'hem I
mar'le?

TOWN. Marry your selfe Puppy for ought I know,
you quested last. 655

CLOD. Would hee had quested first, and sprung 'hem
an houre agoe for me.

TOWN. Why, what's the matter?

CLOD. 'Slid, they ha' sprung my purse and all I had
about me. 660

TOWN. They ha' not, ha' they?

CLOD. As I am true Tom Clod ha' they, and ran-
sackled me of every peny: out cept I were with child of
an owle (as they say) I never saw such luck: it'is
enough to make a man a whore. 665

PUP. Hold thy peace, thou talkst as if thou hadst a
licence to lose thy purse alone in this company: 'slid
here be those can lose a purse in honour of the Gypsies,
as well as thou for thy heart, and never make word of it:
D¹ I ha' lost my purse too, and more in it then Ile speak 670
of, but e're I'de crye for't as thou dost———Much
good doe 'hem with all my heart, I doe reverence 'hem
for't.

α COCK. What was there i' thy purse?
was the lease of thy house in it? 675

PUP. Or thy granams silver ring?

CLOD. No, but a mill-sixpence of my mothers, I loved
as dearely, and two pence I had to spend over and
above, beside the harper that was gathered amongst us,
to pay the piper. 680

TOWN. Our whole stock, is that gone? how will Tom
Ticklefoot do to whet his whistle then?

659 ha'] *omitted.*    670 then] that    [650 What,] What_∧
gone?] gone,    suddaine?] suddaine;    672 heart,] *comma,*
*trace only.*    678 dearely,] dearely——]

B 670 then] *ed. conj.* : that *D¹

W (*cont.*) agoe] a goe H    for mee] *so* *D¹NF : *om.* H (*cf.*710).    713 ha]
*om.* *D¹    715 Tow.] So. F    716 Tom] *so* *D¹ : *om.* HNF    717
out cept] outcept NF    of] w^th N : with F    718 It'is] Its *D¹ : It is H :
It's NF    719 enough] inough N    721, 722 loose] lose *D¹ F    722 those]
*so* *D¹NF: them H    honor] honour *D¹NF    726 whimperinge] whininge
NF    728 of my mothers] *so* *D¹ : *om.* HNF    729 two] a 2 NF    730
beside,] besides_∧ N : besides; F    732 Tow] Tom. F    733 wet] whet *D¹

## Windsor Version

(α) PVP. What? are they gone? flowne all of a sudaine? This is fine i' faithe. A couie call ye 'hem? they are a couie soone scattered, me thincks: who sprung 'hem I marle.

TOWN. Mary, your selfe Puppie, for ought I knowe: you quested last.

CLOD. Would he had quested firste and sprung 'hem an hower agoe for mee.

[β] TOWN. Why, whats the matter *man?

CLOD. Slid, they ha sprung my purse and all I had about me.

TOWN. They ha' not, ha' they?

CLOD. As I am true Tom Clod, ha' they, and ransacled me of euerie penie; out cept I were with child of an owle (as they say) I neuer sawe such luck! It'is enough to make a man a whore.

PVP. Hold thy peace; thou talkst as if thou hadst a licence to loose thy purse alone in this companie. Slid, here be those can loose a purse in honor of the Gypsies as well as thou, for thy hart, and neuer make word of it: I ha lost my purse too.

[β] COCK. What was there i' thy purse *thou keepest such a whimperinge? was the lease of thy house in it?

PVP. Or thy grannams siluer ringe?

CLOD. No, but a mill sixpence of my mothers I lou'd as dearlie, and two pence I had to spend ouer and aboue, beside the harper that was gatherd amongst vs to pay the piper.

TOWN. Our whole stocke, is that gone? how will Tom Ticklefoote doe to wet his whistle then?

726 whininge

705, 706, 710 'hem] 'em    708 Town.] )ow    710 Clod.] )lod
firste] firste for me    711 agoe] a goe    for me *omitted*    716
Tom *omitted*    722 those] them    728 of my mothers *omitted*.

w 704 what?] What, *D¹ : What! F    gone?] gone, *D¹    sudaine?] suddaine; *D¹ : suddaine? N : sudden? F    705 i' faithe.] y' faith: *D¹ : i' faithe, H : ifaith? N : i' faith? F    ye 'hem] yee 'hem *D¹ : ye 'em H : yʷ'em N : y'em F    706 me thincks] mee thinke NF    'hem] so *D¹ : 'em HNF    707 marle,] mar'le? *D¹ : marle: N : marle? F    710 firste] so *D¹NF : firste for mee H (cf. 711).    'hem] so *D¹ : 'em H : yᵉᵐ (i.e. them) N : y'em F    711 hower] houre *D¹ : owre N : 'owre F

(α)    PUP. Marry a new collection, there's no musick else
Masters: he can ill pipe that wants his upper lip.
D¹    TOWN. Yes, a bag-piper may want both.                                    685
       COCK. Why they have rob'd Prudence of a    race of
ginger, and a jet ring she had to draw Jack Straw
hether a holy-dayes.
α     TOWN. Is't possible? fine fingered Gypsies y' faith.
D¹    COCK. And Meg has lost an inchanted nutmeg, all   690
guilded over,                      she had to put in
her sweet-hearts ale a mornings, with a row of pins,
which pricks the poore soule to the heart, the losse of
'hem.
       CLOD. And I have lost (beside my purse) my best bride-   695
lace,                              and a halpworth
of hobnails, and Francis

                        her thimble, with a skeane of Coven-
try blew she had to work Will: Litchfields hand-
kerchiffe.                                                                     700
       COCK. And Christian
her *Practice of Piety*, with a bow'd groat, and the
ballet of *Whoop Barnabee*, which grieves her worst
of all.
α     CLOD. And Ticklefoote has lost his clout, he says,    705
with a three-pence and foure tokens in'it, beside his
Tabouring stick, eve'n now.
       COCK. And I my knife and sheath, and a pair of
dogs leather gloves.
       TOWN. Ha' we lost neve'r a dog amongst us? where's  710
Puppy gone?

    688 hether] hither    690 Meg] Maudlin    703 ballet] ballad
    710 lost] left    [683 else‸] else:    684 Masters:] Masters‸
    689 possible?] possible,    692 mornings,] *possibly semi-colon.*
    705 clout,] Clout‸]

  B 688 hether] *so* HNF : hither *D¹    690 Meg] *ed conj.*: Maudlin *D¹
(*For other variants see* W.)

  W (*cont.*) 746–7 bride lace] (Bridelace *D¹) bridlace N : bride-lace F
747 Turnups] Turners NF    halp'orth] halpworth (*D¹) N : halpeworth F
749 beside] *ed. conj.* : besides NF    750 ha] haue NF    751–2
handkercheife] *so* NF : handkercheife H    755 ballett] (ballad *D¹)
Barnabe] (Barnabee *D¹) Barnabye N : Barnibie F    757 ha's] has
*D¹ : h'as F    758 three] three- *D¹ : 3. N    in'it] in it *D¹H in't NF
beside] *so* *D¹ : besides HNF    759 eue'n] even *D¹H : eu'n NF
762 Ha'] Have *D¹H : H'a NF    lost] left *D¹    neue'r] ne're *D¹ :
neu'r H : neuer NF    amongst] among'st N

## Windsor Version

(α)   PVP. Mary, a newe collection, theres no musique els Masters; he can ill pipe that wantes his vpper lip, *monie.* 735

] [β]
[*f*]   PRV. They haue robd me too of a *daintye race of ginger and a iett ringe I had to drawe Iacke Strawe hether a holidayes.

α   TOWN. Is't possible? fine fingerd Gypsies i' faith! 740

β
[*f*]   MEG. And I haue lost a nutmeg all guilded ouer, *was inchanted at Oxford *for mee, to putt i' my sweet hartes ale a mornings, with a rowe of white pinnes that pricke me to the very hart, the loss of 'hem. 745

CLOD. And I ha lost, beside my purse, my best bride lace I had at Ione Turnups wedding, and a halp'orth
[*f*]   of hobnailes. *Francis Adlebreech has lost somewhat
[*f*]   too, *beside her maidenhead.
[*f*]   FRA. *I ha lost my thimble and a skeine of Couen- 750 trie blewe I had to worke Gregorie Lichfeild a handkercheife.

CHR. And I, vnhappie Christian as I am, haue lost my *Practise of Pietie*, with a bowed groate, and the ballett of *Whoop Barnabe*, which greiues me ten times 755 worse.

α   CLOD. And Ticklefoot ha's lost his clowt, he sayes, with a three pence and fower tokens in'it, beside his tabouring sticke, eue'n now.

[β]   COCK. And I my knife and sheathe and *my fine 760 doggs leather gloues.

TOWN. Ha' we lost neue'r a dog amongst vs, wheres
[β]   Puppy*?

---

*At* 736 monie *appears only in* NF
*At* 737 daintye *appears only in* NF
*In* 742 H *reads:* ouer inchanted at Oxford I had to putt
*In* 748–50 H *reads:* of hobnailes and Francis Adlebreech has lost somewhat too | FRA. I. I. ha lost

---

747 Turners

735 Masters *omitted*.   741 a] an inchanted   745 'hem] 'em
749, 758 beside] besides   751–2 handkercheife] handkercheife

w 734–5 els͜, Masters;] els͜, H : else: Masters͜, *D¹ : else͜, Ma^rs; N : else͜, masters, F   740 Tow.] Tom. F   Is't] I'st H   741 a] *ed. conj.* : an inchanted HNF   743–4 white pinnes] white-pins F   745 'hem] (*so* *D¹*) 'em H : them NF   746 ha] haue (*D¹*) NF   beside] besides NF

(α) PUP. Here goodman Townshead: you ha nothing to lose it seemes but the townes braines you'are trusted with.

PATRICO.

O my deare marrowes,
No shooting of arrowes,
Or shafts of your wit,
Each other to hit,
In your skirmishing fit:
Your store is but small,
Then venter not all;
Remember each mock
Doth spend o' the stock:
And what was here done,
Being under the moone,
And at afternoone,
Will prove right soone
*Deceptio visus*,
Done *gratia risus*.
There's no such thing,
As the losse of a ring,
Or what yee count worse,
The misse of a purse:
But, hey for the maine,
And passe o' the straine,
Here's both come againe.
And there's an old twinger,
Can shew you the ginger:
The pins and the nutmeg,
Are safe here with slut Meg.
Then strike up your tabour,
And there's for your labour.
The sheath and the knife,
Ile venter my life,
Shall breed you no strife,
But like man and wife,

---

719 other] oth'r   722 venter] venture   741 slut Meg] Slutmeg   745 venter] venture   [724 stock:] stock;]

---

w (*cont.*) Disceptio NF   785 you] yee *D¹   788 o'] of HNF
791 yee] *so* F : you D¹ : *om.* H : yᵉᵉ (*altered from* you) N   793 slutt Megg] Slutmeg *D¹ : Slut-megge F   796–7] *as one line* NF   797 venter] venture *D¹

(α) PVP. Here, goodman Towneshead: you ha nothing to
loose it seemes but the townes braines you'are trusted 765
with.

### PATRICO.

O my deare marrowes,
No shooting of arrowes
Or shaftes of your witt 770
Eache other to hit
In your skirmishing fit!
Your store is but small,
Then venter not all;
Remember eache mock 775
Doth spend o' the stock.
And what was here done,
Being vnder the moone
And at afternoone,
Will proue right soone 780
*Deceptio visus*
Done *gratia risus*.
There's no such thing
As the loss of a ring,
Or what you count wurse 785
The misse of a purse,
But hey for the maine
And pass o' the straine
Heres both come againe.
And theres an ould twinger 790
Can shewe yee the ginger:
The pinnes and the nutt meg
Are safe here with slutt Megg:
Then strike vp your tabour
And there's for your labour: 795
The sheathe and the knife,
Ile venter my life,
Shall breed you no strife,
But like man and wife

767 Patrico.] ⟩atr.    777 here *omitted*.    791 yee *omitted*.

w 764 ha] haue NF    765 loose] lose *D¹F    townes braines]
Towne-braynes NF    you'are] you're *D¹ : you are HNF    767] om. NF
768 marrowes,] marrowes, *D¹N : marrowes! F    771 other] oth'r *D¹
772 fit,] fit: *D¹ : fit, N : fit? F    774 venter] venture *D¹    776 o']
ô HN    777 here] so *D¹F : heare N : om. H    781 deceptio]

(α)
>Or sister and brother,
>Keep one with another,
>And light as a feather, 750
>Make hast to come hether.
>The Coventry blew
>Hangs there upon Prue.
>And here's one opens
>The clout and the tokens; 755
>Deny the bow'd groat,
>And you lye i' your throat,
>Or the tabourers nine-pence,

β
>Or the sixe fine pence.
>As for the ballet, 760
>Or book what ye call it,
>Alas our society
>Mells not with piety:
>Himselfe hath forsooke it,
>That first undertooke it. 765
>For thimble or bridelace,
>Search yonder side-lasse.
>All's to be found,
>If you looke your selves round:
>We scorne to take from yee, 770
>We'had rather spend on yee:
>If any man wrong yee,
>The thiefe's among yee.

TOWN. Excellent y' faith, a most restorative Gypsie: all's here againe, and yet by his learning of leger- 775 demaine he would make us believe we had rob'd our selves, for the hobnailes are come to me.

COCK. May be he knew whose shooes lackt clouting.

PUP. I, hee knowes more then that, or Ile neve'r trust my judgement in a Gypsie againe. 780

COCK. A Gypsie of quality believe it, and one of the

754 here

754 here's] here  759–912] lost in D¹ : copy-text D²  781
and] omit.

w (cont.) mell's NF        818 bride lace] bridelace *D² : bride-lace F
819 side-lasse] side lasse NF    823 We'had] we had HNF : We'd *D²
827 Alls] Allę H : all's *D²NF    againe] agen NF    831 neue'r] neuer
HNF : ne're *D²    832 agen] againe *D²    833 and] om. *D²

## Windsor Version

(α)
    Or sister and brother 800
    Keepe one with another,
    And light as a feather
    Make haste to come hether:
    The Couentry blue
    Hangs there vpon Prue: 805
    And here's one opens
    The clowte and the tokens:
    Deny the bowd groate
    And you lie i' your throate;
    Or the tabourers nine pence 810

β
    Or the sixe fine pence:
    As for the ballett
    Or booke what you call it,
    Alas our societie
    Mell's not with pietie, 815
    Himselfe hath forsooke it
    That first vndertooke it:
    For thimble or bride lace
    Searche yonder side-lasse:
    Alls to be found 820
    If you looke your selues round;
    We scorne to take from ye,
    We'had rather spend on ye,
    If any man wrong ye
    The theifes among ye. 825

TOWN. Excellent i' faith, a most restoratiue Gypsie! Alls here againe, and yet by his learninge of legeirdemaine he would make vs beleiue we had robd our selues, [for the hob nailes are come to me.

COCK. May be he knewe whose shooes lackt clowting. 830

PVP. I, he knowes more then that, or Ile neue'r trust my iudgment in a Gipsie agen.]

COCK. A Gipsie of qualitie, beleiue it, and one of the

---

*The passage* 829 (for . . .)–32 *is not in* NF.

806 here
815 Mell's] mell'ꝭ    825 theifes] t *blotted, probably altered.*    827 Alls] Allę

w 800–1] *as one line* NF    803 hether] hither F    806 here's] here *D¹
809 i'] *so* NF: in *D¹ H    811 fine] yᵉ fine (yᵉ *perhaps erased*) N    813 booke] the booke F    you] ye *D¹    815 Mell's] mell'ꝭ H: Mells *D²:

(β) *Kings Gypsies this: a drinkalian, or a drinkebragatan,
aske him: the King has a noyse of Gypsies, as well as
of Bearewards.*

    PUP. *What sort or order of Gipsie I pray Sir?*     785

PATRICO.

> *A Flagonfeakian,*
> *A Divells Arse a Peakian:*
> *Borne first at Niglington,*
> *Bred up at Filchington,*     790
> *Boorded at Tappington,*
> *Bedded at Wappington.*

TOWN. *Fore me, a dainty deriv'd Gypsie.*

PUP. *But I pray sir, if a man might aske on you, how
came your Captaines place first to be cald the* 795
*Devills Arse?*

PATRICO.

> *For that, take my word,*
> *We have a record*
> *That doth it afford,*     800
> *And sayes our first lord,*
> *Cocklorrell he hight,*
> *On a time did invite*
> *The Devill to a feast;*
> *The taile of the jeast,*     805
> *Though since it be long,*
> *Lives yet in a song,*
> *Which if you would heare,*
> *Shall plainly appeare*
> H     *Like a chime in your eare.*     810

    787 Flagonfleakian     794 aske you

783 has] hath     785 Gipsie] Gipsies     789 Niglington] Ninglington     810] *omitted.*     [790 Filchington,] Filchington. 791 Tappington,] Tappington.     793 me,] me_∧     798 that,] that_∧     809 appeare_∧] appeare.]

---

w (*cont.*) H : Flagonfeakian *D² : Flagon-fekian NF      840 diuell*e*-ars-a-peakian] Divells Arse a Peakian *D² : Diuells-arse-a Pekian NF      841 Niglington] Ninglington *D²     843 boorded] boarded NF     846 on] so *D²NF : *om.* H     847-8 the Devills Arse] the Diuells-Arse N : the Devills-arse F (*both as separate line*).     852 it] so *D²F : *om.* H : if N     854 Cock-Lorell] Cocklorrell *D²NF     height] hight *D²NF     857 iest] jeast *D²F     858] *parentheses in H only.*     862] *om.* *D²NF

(β) Kings Gypsies this, a drinckalian or a drinckebragatan:
[*f*] aske him. The Kinge has *his noise of Gypsies aswell as  835
[*f*] of bearewards *and other minstrells.
    PVP. What sort or order of Gypsie, I pray Sir?

PATRICO.

    A flagonfeakean,
    A Diuelles-Ars-a-Peakian,  840
    Borne firste at Niglington,
    Bred vp at Filchington,
    Boorded at Tappington,
    Bedded at Wappington.

    TOWN. Fore me, a dainetie deriued Gypsie!  845
    PVP. But, I pray Sir, if a man might aske on you, how came your Captaines place firste to be called the Deuills Arse?

PATRICO.

    For that, take my word,  850
    Wee haue a record
    That doth it afford,
    And sayes our first lord,
    Cock-Lorell he height,
    On a time did inuite  855
    The Deuill to a feast:
    The taile of the iest
    (Though since it be longe)
    Liues yet in a songe,
    Which, if you would heare,  860
    Shall plainelie appeare
    Like a chime in your eare:

---

*In* 835 *the reading* has his noise *appears only in* NF.
*In* 836 *the words* and other minstrells *appear only in* NF.

---

836 as bearewards     839 flagonfleakean     846 aske you

  834 drinckebragatan] Drincke bragatan     836 of *omitted*.
  839] a flagonfleakean (*appended to previous speech*).     846 on *omitted*.     852 it *omitted*.

  w 834 Gypsies‸ this‸] Gypsies‸ this: *D² : Gipsies; this‸ F     Drinckalian] Drink-alian NF     Drincke bragatan‸] Drinkebragatan, *D² : Drink-braggatan, N : Drinke-braggatan? F     835 aske him] Aske him (*as a separate line*) NF     has] hath *D²     836 of] *so* *D²NF : *om.* H     837 Gypsie] Gipsies *D²NF     838] *om.* NF     839] *here in* *D²F : *appended to previous speech* H : *as heading* N     flagonfeakean] Flagonfleakian

β  *Ile call in my clarke*
*Shall sing't like a larke.*

*Come in my long sharke,*
*With thy face browne and darke;*
*With thy tricks and thy toyes,*      815
*Make a merry merry noise,*
*To these mad country boyes,*
*And chant out the farce*
*Of the Grand-Devills Arse.*

Song.      820

Cock-lorrel would needs have the Devill his guest,
And bad him once into the Peak to dinner,
Where never the Fiend had such a feast,
Provided him yet at the charge of a sinner.

His stomacke was queasie (he came thither coacht)      825
The jogging had made some crudities rise;
To help it he call'd for a Puritan poacht,
That used to turne up the egg's of his eyes.

And so recover'd unto his wish,
He sate him downe, and he fell to eate;      830
Promooter in plum-broth was the first dish,
His owne privy kitchin had no such meate.

Yet though with this he much were taken,
Upon a suddaine he shifted his trencher,
As soone as he spy'd the Bawd, and bacon,      835
By which you may note the Devil's a wencher.

         822 him into     829 to his     831 his first
812 sing't] sing     817 these] those     818–19] *as one line.*
818 farce] fart     825 (he came thither coacht)] (for comming
there Coacht)     826 made] caus'd     [812 larke.] larke,
817 boyes,] boyes.]

---

w (*cont.*) Cock-Lorell] Cock-lorel *D² : Cock-lorrell NF     877 once] *so*
*D²NF : *om.* H     880 there] *so* *D²F: their N     884 recouer'd vnto]
*so* *D²NF : recouered to H     886 Promooter] *so* *D²NF : Promoter H
the] *so* *D²NF : his H     888] *parentheses in* H *only.*     890 spied] spies H :
spy'd *D²NF

## Windsor Version

β       Ile call in my clarcke
        Shall sing't like a larke.

H   COCK. O, I, the song, the song in any case: if you 865
want musique wee'll lend him our minstrell.

### PATRICO.

β       Come in, my longe sharke,
        With thy face browne and darke,
        With thy trickes and thy toyes,      870
        Make a merrie merrie noyes
        To theise mad cuntrie boyes,
        And chaunt out the farce
        Of the Grand Deuilles Arse.

*Song.*     875

Cock-Lorell would needes haue the Diuell his guest,
    And bad him once into the Peake to dinner,
Where neuer the Feind had such a feast
    Prouided him yet at the charge of a sinner.

[γ] His stomacke was queasie (*for comminge there coacht) 880
[γ]     The iogging had *caus'd some crudities rise;
To helpe it he calld for a Puritan poach't,
    That vsed to turne vp the eggs of his eyes.

And so, recouer'd vnto his wishe,
    He sate him downe, and he fell to eate;    885
Promooter in plumbroth was the firste dishe,
    His owne priuie kitchen had no such meate.

Yet (though with this he much were taken)
    Vppon a suddaine he shifted his trencher
As soone as he spied the Baud and bacon,    890
    By which you may note the Deuills a wencher.

---

*In* 880 H *reads*: (he came thither coach't)
*In* 881 H *reads*: had made some
    *in both presumably retaining the reading of the Burley version.*

---

    877 him into     884 recouered to     886 his first
    877 once *omitted.*     880 there] their     884 recouer'd vnto]
    recouered to     886 Promooter] Promoter     the] his     890
    spied] spies

    w 864 sing't] sing *D²NF     865-7] *om.*D²NF     872 theise] those
*D²NF     873-4] *as one line* *D²NF     873 farce] fart *D²NF     876

(β)
    *Sixe pickl'd Taylers sliced and cut,*
    *Sempsters, Tyre-women, fit for his pallet,*
    *With Feathermen, and Perfumers put,*
    *Some 12 in a charger to make a grand sallet.*     840

    *A rich fat Usurer stew'd in his marrow,*
    *And by him a Lawyers head and green-sawce;*
    *Both which his belly took in like a barrow,*
    *As if till then he never had seene sauce.*

    *Then carbonado'd, and cook't with paines,*     845
    *Was brought up a cloven Serjeants face;*
    *The sauce was made of his Yeomans braines,*
    *That had beene beaten out with his owne mace.*

    *Two roasted Sheriffes came whole to the boord,*
    *(The feast had nothing beene without 'hem)*     850
    *Both living, and dead, they were foxt and fur'd,*
    *Their chaines like sawsages hung about 'hem.*

    *The very next dish was the Maior of a towne,*
    *With a pudding of maintenance thrust in his belly,*
    *Like a goose in the feathers drest in his gowne,*     855
    *And his couple of Hinch-boyes boyld to a jelly.*

    *A London-Cuckold came hot from the spit,*
    *And when the carver up had broke him,*
    *The Devill chopt up his head at a bit,*
    *But the hornes were very neere like to choake him.*     860

    *The chine of a Lecher too there was roasted,*
    *With a plumpe Harlots haunch and garlicke;*
    *A Panders pettitoes, that had boasted*
    *Himselfe for a captaine, yet never was warlick.*

    *A large fat pasty of Midwife hot,*     865
    *And for a cold bak't meate into the story,*
    *A reverend Painted Lady was brought,*
    *Was coffin'd in crust, till now she was hoary.*

         844 had never      853 The next

844 never had] had never     850 beene] bin     853 the Maior] a Major     857 Cuckold came] Cuckold,     860 choake] have choakt     865 Midwife] a Midwife     868 Was] And     [858 him,] him;]

---

w (*cont.*) ²the] a *D²     Maior] Major *D² : mayor NF     912 came] *ed. conj.*: *om.* H*D²NF     915 choake] have choakt *D²NF     916 too] to N     917 hanche] haunch *D²NF     920 midwife] a Midwife *D²NF     921 cold] *so* *D²NF : could H     923 ¹was] And *D²NF

## Windsor Version

(β) Sixe picled Taylors, slic'd and cutt,
    Sempsters, Tirewomen, fitt for his pallett,
With Fethermen and Perfumers putt
    Some twelue in a charger to make a grand sallet.   895

A riche fatt Vsurer stewed in his marrowe
    And by him a Lawyers head and greene sawce,
Both which his bellie tooke in like a barrowe
    As if till then he neuer had seene sauce.

Then, carbonado'd and cookt with paines,   900
    Was brought vp a clouen Serieantes face;
The sawce was made of his Yeomans braines
    That had beene beaten out with his owne mace.

Two rosted Sheriffes came whole to the bord,
    The feast had nothing beene without 'hem;   905
Both liuing and dead they were foxt and furd,
    Theire chaines like sausages hung about 'hem.

The very next dishe was the Maior of a towne,
    With a pudding of mainetainance thrust in his bellie,
Like a goose in the feathers drest in his gowne,   910
    And his couple of Hinche Boyes boyld to a iellie.

A London Cuckold came hot from the spitt,
    And when the caruer vp had broake him,
The Deuill chopt vp his head at a bit,
    But the hornes were very neare like to choake him.   915

The chine of a Letcher too there was rosted,
    With a plumpe Harlottes hanche and garlicke,
A Pandars pettitoes that had boasted
    Himselfe for a captaine yet neuer was warlicke.

A large fat pastie of Midwife hot,   920
    And for a cold bakt meate into the storie
A reuerend Painted Ladie was brought,
    Was coffind in crust till now she was hoary.

899 had neuer   908 The next

895 sallet.] sall⟨   905 'hem] em   907 'hem] 'em   908 very
omitted.   909 bellie,] bel⟨   912 came omitted.   921 cold] could

w 892 slic'd] sliced *D²NF   893 pallett] pallat NF   894 Per-
fumers] perfumes NF (corrected in some copies of F).   897 greene sawce]
Green-sawce *D²F : greensawce N   899 neuer had] had never *D²F
902 yeomans] Yeamans F   905] parentheses in D²NF   beene] bin *D² :
bene N   'hem] so *D² : em H : 'em NF   906 furd] fvr'd (v altered) N :
fu'rd F   907 'hem] so *D² : 'em HNF   908 very] so *D²NF : om. H

(β)     *To these an over-growne Justice of Peace,*
      *With a Clarke like a gizzard truss'd under each arme;*    870
      *And warrants for sippets, laid in his own grease,*
      *Set ove'r a chaffing-dish to be kept warme.*

      *The joule of a Jaylor serv'd for fish,*
      *A Constable sous'd with vinegar by;*
      *Two Aldermen lobsters a sleepe in a dish,*    875
      *A Deputy tart, a Churchwarden pye.*

      *All which devour'd, he then for a close,*
      *Did for a full draught of Darby call;*
      *He heav'd the huge vessell up to his nose,*
      *And left not till he had drunke up all.*    880

      *Then from the table he gave a start,*
      *Where banquet, and wine were nothing scarce;*
      *All which he flirted away with a fart,*
      *From whence it was called the Devills Arse.*

     PUP. An excellent song, and a sweet songster, and 885
would ha done rarely in a cage.

870 truss'd] thrust

---

w (cont.) 933 Darby] Derby NF    935 till] vntill N    938 flirted] *so*
*D² : blewe H : slirted NF    942 sent] scent *D²    before, & behinde]
*so* *D²F : hee left᳄behinde N    953 ha'] have *D²NF

## Windsor Version

(β) To theise an ouergrowne Iustice of Peace,
    With a Clarcke like a gizard truss'd vnder each arme, 925
And warrantes for sippettes laid in his owne greace,
    Sett oue'r a chafingdishe to be kept warme;

The ioule of a Iaylor, seru'd for fishe,
    A Constable sousd with vineger by,
Two Aldermen lobsters a sleepe in a dishe,     930
    A Deputie tart, a Churchwarden pye.

All which deuourd, he then for a close
    Did for a full draught of Darby call;
He heau'd the huge vessell vp to his nose
    And lefte not till he had druncke vp all.     935

Then from the table he gaue a start,
    Where banquett and wine were nothing scarce,
All which he flirted away with a fart,
    From whence it was calld the Deuills Arse.

γ And there hee made such a breach with the winde,     940
    The hole too standinge open the while,
That the sent of the vapour before and behinde,
    Hath foulye perfumed most parte of the ile.

And this was tobacco, the learned suppose,
    Which since in countrye, court, and towne,     945
In the Diuells glister pipe smokes at the nose
    Of pollcat and maddam, of gallant and clowne.

From which wicked weede, with swines flesh and linge,
    Or anye thinge else thats feast for the Feinde,
Our Captaine and wee crie God saue the Kinge,     950
    And send him good meate and mirth without ende.

β    pvp. An excellent song and a sweet songster, and would ha' done rarelie in a cage with a dish of water

---

*The three additional stanzas (940–51) do not appear in* H, *which presumably retains the Burley version (copy-text* N*).*

---

  925 truss'd] *originally* trust *then* ²t *altered to* s *and* 'd *added.*     938 flirted] blewe     939 was] *apparently begun as* wal *or* wol     942 before and behinde] hee lefte⸌behinde     953 ha' *interlined.*

w 925 truss'd] thrust *D²NF     927 oue'r] ouer H : o're *D²NF

*The passage* 978–82 (*copy-text* N *opposite*) *originally ran as follows* (*copy-text* H):

PVP. Tutt they haue other manner of guiftes then telling of fortunes or picking of pocketṭe

COC I an if they please to shewe them or thought vs poore Contrie folkes worthy of them

PVP. what might a man doe to be a gentleman of yo<sup>r</sup> Companie S<sup>r</sup>

*and was first revised thus* (*copy-text* *D²):

PUP. Tut, they have other manner of gifts, than telling Fortunes, or picking pockets.

COCK. I, and they would bee pleased to shew 'hem, or thought us poor mortall country folkes worthy of them.

PUP. What might a man doe to be a gentleman of your company sir?

---

    W 963 vpon me  976 pocket pickt  993 Or brother

  W 955 vnderstand] vnderstood  963 vs] me  965 beene] bin
  972 (for] ₐfor

W 955 vnderstand] *so* *D²NF : vnderstood H  956 now] *om.* *D²
957 prentice₍ Sir₎] Prentise Sir? *D²F 962 i'] *so* *D²NF : in H 963
vs] *so* *D²NF : me H  965 ha] have *D²NF beene] *so* *D²F :
bin HN shall be] *so* *D²NF : shalbe H 966 venter] venture *D² at]
*om.* *D² 967 appoint₍] appoynt, D²NF prefer] pferre N Captaine₎]
Captain; *D²F : Captaine, N 971 then] than *D² made] made
for *D² 971–2 Deuill (for] Devill₍ for H : Devill, for *D²F : Diuell, for N
972 neue'r] neuer H : ne're *D²N : nere F diett)] dyet, *D²F : dyet,) N
975 it₍ A] it: A *D² : it; A NF 976 purse] pocket *D²NF  978
guiftes] gifts (*D²) F then] (than *D²)  980 shewe 'hem] shewe
'em N : shew'em F (shewe them H : shew 'hem *D²)  983 Coc.] *om.* NF
(*but a fresh speech*) ordi'narie] ordinarie H*D² : Ord'narye NF  989
yee] You *D² : y<sup>es</sup> (*i.e.* thes) N : Ye F misterie] Mistorye N  990
worthy] Worthis N 992 ere] E're *D²NF you] yee *D²  993 a]
*om.* *D²NF o'] ô H : of NF

## Windsor Version

(β) and hempseed; a fine brest of his owne! Sir, you are a Prelate of the order, I vnderstand, and I haue a terrible grudging now vpon mee to be one of your companie: will your Captaine take a prentice Sir? I would binde my selfe to him, bodie and soule, either for one and twentie yeares, or as many liues as he would.

CLOD. I, and put in my life for one, for I am come about too. I am sorrie I had no more money i' my purse when you came first vpon vs Sir: if I had knowne you would haue pickt my pockett so like a gentleman, I would ha beene better prouided. I shall be glad to venter a purse with your worship at any time you'll appoint, so you would prefer me to your Captaine: Ile put in securitie for my truthe and serue out my time though I die to morrowe.

COCK. I, vppon those tearmes Sir, and in hope your Captaine keepes better chere then he made the Deuill (for my stomack will neue'r agree with that diett) wee'll be all his followers. Ile goe home and fetch a little monye Sir, all I haue, and you shall picke my pockett to my face, and Ile avouch it a man would not desire to haue his purse pickt in better companie.

*f* PVP. Tut, they haue other manner of guiftes then pickinge of pockets or tellinge fortunes, if they would but please to shewe 'hem, or thought vs poore cuntrye mortalls worthye of them. What might a man doe to be a gentleman of your companie Sir?

β COCK. I, a Gipsie in ordi'narie, or nothing.

### PATRICO.

Freindes, not to refell ye
Or any way quell ye,
To buy or to sell ye,
I onelie must tell ye
Yee aime at a misterie
Worthy a historie.
There's much to be done
Ere you can be a sonne
Or a brother o' the moone;
Tis not so soone

w 996 bene-] ben-

w 996 bene-] ben- H : beane- *D² : ben⸗ N : Ben- F     999 ye . . . ye]
yᵉ . . . yᵉ N     1000 auowes] arowse F     ye] yᵉ N     1001 ye] you NF
1005 be] be left *D²     1006 o'] of *D²NF     1007 and] or NF
1015 one or] One, *D²     1017 beamesˏ] beames; F     1021 a] om. NF
1025 ye] you *D²NF     1026 Ptolomęes] Ptolomies *D²F : Ptolomes N
1030 hoggs greace] Hogges-grease *D²F     1031 dogs greace] Dogs-
grease F     1032 to] om. *D²     1034 haue] hath NF

(β) Acquird as desird; 995
You must be bene-bowsy
And sleepie and drowsie
And lazie and lowzie
Before ye can rowse ye
In shape that auowes ye; 1000
And then ye may stalke
The Gypsies walke
To the coopes and the pens,
And bring in the hens;
Though the cock be sullen 1005
For loss o' the pullen,
Take turky and capon
And gammons of bacon;
Let nought be forsaken.
Wee'll let you go loose 1010
Like a foxe to a goose,
And shewe you the stie
Where the little piggs lie,
Whence if you can take
One or two, and not wake 1015
The sowe in her dreames,
But by the moone beames
Soe warilie hie
As neither doe crie,
You shall the next day 1020
Haue a licence to play
At the hedg a flirt
For a sheet or a shirt.
If your hand be light
Ile shewe ye the slight 1025
Of our Ptolomęes knott,
It is, and 'tis not;
To change your complexion
With the noble confection
Of wall nuttes and hoggs greace, 1030
Better then dogs greace;
And to milcke the kine
Ere the milcke mayd fine
Haue opend her eyne.
Or if you desire 1035
To spitt or fart fire,
Ile teache you the knackes

(β) COCK. *O hee would chirpe in a paire of stocks sumptuously.*

PUP. *O' my conscience he feares not that:*
*I protest I admire* 890
*him.*

PATRICO.

*Is this worth your wonder?*
*Nay then you shall under-*

w (*cont.*) 1055 Be'it]–be it H : Be it *D²F : bee'it N    1059 twere] it were *D²NF    1060 'hem] yᵉᵐ (*i.e.* them) N : 'em F    1062 fleshlie] fleshy *D²    1063 Pup.] Clod. *D²    1064 Clod] Pup. *D²    1067 are] were NF    1068 and] an *D²    1069 protest] ptest N    1072 yᵒʳ] y (*with a superior letter apparently altered and indecipherable, but not* r) N

## Windsor Version

(β)
    Of eating of flaxe,
    And out of your noses
    Drawe ribons for poses,         1040
    As for example
    Mine owne is as ample
    And fruitfull a nose
    As a witt can suppose;
    Yet it shall goe hard         1045
    But there will be spard
    Eache of you a yard,
    And worthe your regard,
    When the culler and sise
    Ariue at your eies.         1050
    And if you incline
    To a cup of good wine
    When you sup or dine,
    If you chance it to lacke,
    Be'it claret or sacke,         1055
    Ile make this snoute
    To deale it about,
    Or this to run out
    As twere from a spout.

TOWN. Admirable trickes, and he do's 'hem all *se* 1060 *defendendo*, as if he would not be taken in the trap of authoritie by a fraile fleshlie constable.

PVP. Without the ayd of a cheese.

CLOD. Or help of a flitch of bacon.

COCK. Oh, he would chirpe in a paire of stockes 1065 sumptuouslie: I'ld giue any thing to see him play loose with his handes when his feet are fast.

PVP. O' my conscience, he feares not that and the Marshall himselfe were here: I protest I admire him.     1070

### PATRICO.

    Is this worthe your wonder?
    Nay then you shall vnder-

---

1042 as] *interlined.*     1053 sup] s *altered and illegible.*     1062 by] b *altered from* f.

w 1038 flaxe] flacks N    1039 yo<sup>r</sup>] theire NF    1040 ribons] Ribbons *D² : Ribbands NF    for] and NF    poses] Posies *D²NF    1044 a] *om.* *D²    1046 will be] *so* *D²NF : wilbe H    1049 the] they NF    culler] colour *D² : Coulor N : collour F    1051 incline] encline F

(β)
  *Stand more of my skill,*   895
  *For I can (and I will)*
  *Here at Burlye o'th' Hill,*
  *Give you all your fill,*
  *Each Jacke with his Gill,*
  *And shew you the King,*   900
  *The Prince too, and bring*
  *The Gypsies were here,*
  *Like Lords to appeare,*
  *With such their attenders,*
  *As you thought offenders,*   905
  *Who now become new men*
  *Youle know 'hem for true men;*
  For he we call Chiefe,
  (Ile tell't you in briefe)
  Is so farre from a thiefe,   910
  As he gives you reliefe,
  With his bread, beere, and biefe,

α
  And tis not long syne
  Yee dranke of his wine,
  And it made you fine,   915
  Both clarret and sherry;
  Then let us be merry,
  And helpe with your call
  For a hall, a hall!
  Stand up to the wall,   920
  Both good-men and tall,
  We are one mans all;
  Make it a jolly night,
  If not a holly night,
  Spight o' the constable,   925
  Or Mas Deane of Dunstable.

---

*At Belvoir* 897 *was presumably omitted:* 908 *ff. opposite.*

 896 and] for   905 With] And   909 tell't] tell   911 As
 he] He   912 bread, beere, and] Beere and his   926 Mas]
 May-   [901 bring,] bring,   922 all;] all,]

B 909] *no parentheses in* NF.   tell't] *so* HNF : tell *D²   you] yᵉᵉ N :
ye F   911 As] *so* HNF : *om.* *D²   you] ye HF : yᵉᵉ N   912 bread,
beere, and] *so* HNF : Beere and his *D²   biefe] beife HF : be'efe N
913 sine] since NF   914 Yee] yᵉᵉ N   915 you] ye H   921
good-men] goodmen H : good men NF   924 Holly] holie HN : holy F
925 o'] *so* H : of D¹D²NF   926 Mas] *so* D²NF : May- D¹ : *om.* H

(β)
    Stand more of my skill.
    For I can (and I will)           1075

    Giue you all your fill,
    Eache Iack with his Gill,
    And shewe ye the King,
    The Prince too, and bring
    The Gipsies were here           1080
    Like Lordes to appeare,
    With such theire attenders
    As you thought offenders,
    Who nowe become newe men
    You'll knowe 'hem for true men.     1085

---

    At Belvoir lines 908 (*presumably*) to 924 *were replaced by the following* (*copy-text* D²):

β
        The fift of August           908¹
        Will not let saw-dust
        Lie in your throats,
        Or cob-webs, or oates;
        But helpe to scoure yee.     908⁵
        This is no Gowrie
        Hath drawne James hether,
        But the good man of Bever,
        Our Buckinghams father;
        Then so much the rather     908¹⁰
        Make it a jolly night,
        For tis a holy night,

                908⁷ Has

[908¹ August‸] August,     908⁵ yee.] yee,]
908⁷ Hath] *so* H : Has *D²NF     hether] *so* HN : hither *D²F
908¹² tis] ti's H

---

              1075] I can for I will

    w 1075 For] *so* *D² : *om.* HNF     and] *ed. conj.*: for H*D²NF (*parentheses in* *D²NF)     1078 ye] you *D²NF     1079 too] to N     bring‸] bring, *D² : bring; F     1082 wᵗʰ] And *D²     theire] there NF     1085 'hem] *so* *D² : 'em H : yᵉᵐ (*i.e.* them) N : them F     true] Trve (ve *altered from* os ?) N

(α) OMNES. A hall, a hall, a hall!

*The Gypsies chang'd.*

*Dance.*

[927 hall!] Hall.

w (*cont.*) *D²F  1099 by] With *D²NF  1102 Master] Mr N
1103 faster] fas'ter N  1104 then] Than *D²  1110 art] heart *D²
1114 knight] knigt N  1119 Clo.] Clow. *D²NF

## Windsor Version

α ALL. A hall! a hall! a hall!

*The Gypsyes chang'd.*

*Dance.*

β         PATRICO.

    Why, now ye behould         1090
    Twas truth that I tould
    And no deuice;
    They'are changd in a trice,
    And so will I
    Be my selfe by and by;         1095
    I onelie nowe
    Must studie howe
    To come of with a grace
    By my Patricos place:
    Some short kinde of blessing,         1100
    It selfe adressing
    Vnto my good Master,
    Which light on him faster
    Then wishes can flie;
    And you that stand by         1105
    Be as iocound as I,
    Eache man with his voice
    Giue his heart to reioyce,
    Which Ile requite
    If my art hit right.         1110
    Though late now at night
    Eache clowne here in sight
    Before day light
    Shall proue a good knight,
    And your lasses pages         1115
    Worthy theire wages,
    Where fancie engages
    Girles to theire ages.

CLOD. O, any thing for the Patrico: what ist? what ist?
PATR. Nothing but beare the bob of the close;     1120
    It will be no burthen you well may suppose,

        1099 With

w 1090 ye] y$^{ee}$ N     behould] behold *D²NF     1091 tould] told *D²F     1093 They'are] they'r H : They are *D²NF     1098 of] off w 1154 Or a paire

w 1122 Soue'raigne] Soveraingne    1128 *omitted.*    1143 file] *written after* stile *deleted.*    1149–50 *omitted (copy-text* N).    1150 Meant] meane    1156 then] them

w 1122 the] y N    Soue'raigne] Soveraingne H : Sov'raigne *D² : Sou'raine NF    1123 and] an NF : And so *Simpson conj.*    1124 Clo.] Clow. *D²    Soue'raigne] soueraigne H : Sov'raigne *D² : Sou'raine NF    1126–7 *as prose* *D²    1126 'em] them *D²NF    1128] *om.* H : Pat. *D²F : Pa: N    1129–81] *stanzas numbered* 1 *to* 5 *D²NF    1130 torninge] turning *D²NF    1134 and] which *D²F : wᶜʰ (*interlined above* and) N    vglie] Ouglie NF    beside] besides *D²NF    1135 that] the *D²NF    1137 wheresoere] where soere N : Wher so'ere F    ha'] *so* *D²NF : haue H    1138 Soue'raigne] soueraigne H : Sov'raigne *D²N : Sov'raine F    1144 stile₍] Stile. *D²F : stile, N    1146 Iune₍] Iune. *D²F : Iune, N    1148–50] *in* *D²NF : *om.* H    1150 Meant] *so* *D² : meane NF    1152 Soue'raigne] soueraigne H : Sov'raigne *D² : Souraigne N : Sov'raine F    1154 and] Or *D²NF    1156 then] *so* F : them H : than *D² : yᵉⁿ N

## Windsor Version

(β)  But bless the Soue'raigne and his sences,
And to wishe away offences.
CLOD. Let vs alone: Bless the Soue'raigne and his senses.
PATR. Weel take 'em in order, as they haue being;
And first of seeinge.

### PATRICO.

From a Gypsie in the morninge,
   Or a paire of squint eies torninge,
From the goblin and the spectre,
   Or a drunckard, though with nectar,
From a woman true to no man
   And is vglie beside common,
A smock rampant and that itches
   To be putting on the britches,
Wheresoere they ha' theire beeing,
Blesse the Soue'raigne and his seeinge.

From a foole and serious toyes,
   From a lawier three partes noise,
From impertinence, like a drum
   Beat at dinner in his roome,
From a toung without a file,
   Heapes of phrases and no stile,
From a fidle out of tune
   As the cuckow is in Iune,
From the candle stickes of Lothbury
   And the loud pure wiues of Banbury,
γ   Or a longe pretended fitt
   Meant for mirth but is not itt,
β   Onelie time and eares out wearinge,
Blesse the Soue'raigne and his hearing.

From a strowling tinckers sheete
   And a paire of carriers feete,
From a ladie that doth breathe
   Worse aboue then vnderneathe,
From the diet and the knowledg
   Of the studentes in Beares-Colledg,
From tobacco with the type
   Of the Diuells glister pipe,

(β)  Or a stincke all stinckes excelling,
    A fishemongers dwelling,
Blesse the Soue'raigne and his smelling.

From an oyster and fryd fishe,
    A sowes babie in a dishe,             1165
From anie porcion of a swine,
    From bad venison and worse wine,
Ling, what cooke so ere it boyle,
    Though with musterd sauc'd and oyle,
Or what else would keepe man fasting,     1170
Bless the Soue'raigne and his tasting.

Both from birdlime and from pitche,
    From a doxie and her itche,
From the bristles of a hog,
    Or the ring worme of a dog,         1175
From the courtship of a brier,
    Or Saint Anthonies old fire,
From a needle or a thorne
    I' the bed at eue'n or morne,
Or from any gouts least grutching,       1180
Bless the Soue'raigne and his touching.

Bless him too from all offences
    In his sportes as in his sences,
From a boy to crosse his way,
    From a fall or a foule day.          1185

Bless him, ô blesse him heaue'n, and lend him long
    To be the sacred burthen of all song,
The actes and yeares of all our Kings to'outgoe,
    And while hee'is mortall, wee not thinck him so.

      1166 Anie    1175 in a    1177 From

1166 From] *omit.*    1169 and] an    1177 Or] from    1179
I' the] i'th the    1189 hee'is] i *imperfectly formed.*

w 1163 Soue'raigne] soveraigne H : Sov'raigne *D²F : Souraigne N
1166 From] om. H    1168 so ere] soe're *D² : soere N : so'ere F    1169
and] *so* *D²NF : an H    1171 Soue'raigne] soueraigne H : Sov'raigne
*D²F : Souraigne N    1174 bristles] Brisles *D²F : brissles N    1175
of] in *D²NF    1177 Or] *so* *D²NF: from H    Saint] Sᵗ HN: St. *D²F
1179 I' the] *so* NF: i'th the H: Ithe *D²    eue'n] euen H: Ev'n *D²F: eu'en N
1180 grutching,] grutching, *D²N : grutching. F    1181 Soue'raigne]
soueraigne H : Sov'raigne *D²F : Souraigne N    1181+] 6 *D²    1186
heaue'n] heau'n H *D²F : heau'en N    1188 to'outgoe] to outgoe H :
t'out-go *D² : t'out goe NF    1189 hee'is] he's *D² : hee's NF

(α)    *After which, ascending up, the Jackman sings.*    930

### Song 1.

The sports are done, yet doe not let
Your joyes in suddaine silence set;
Delight and dumbnesse never met
    In one selfe subject yet.    935
If things oppos'd must mixt appeare,
Then adde a boldnesse to your feare,
    And speake a hymne
    To him
Where all your duties doe of right belong,    940
Which I will sweeten with an under song.

### CAPTAINE.

Glory of ours, of grace of all the earth,
How well your figure doth become your birth?
As in you forme, and fortune equall stood,    945
And onely vertue got above your blood.

### Song 2.

Vertue! his kingly vertue which did merit
This isle intire! and you are to inherit.

### 4 GYPSIE.    950

How right he doth confesse him in his face,
  His brow, his eye, and eve'ry mark of state,
As if he were the issue of each Grace,
  And bore about him both his fame and fate?

### Song 3.    955

Looke, look, is he not faire!
And fresh, and fragrant too!
As summer skye, or purged ayre,
  And lookes as lyllies doe,
That were this morning blowne.    960
4 GYP. O more, that more of him were knowne.

---

945 you] your    954 fate?] ? *doubtful.*    959 lookes] looke

---

w (*cont.*) face? D²    1212 eue'rie] every D¹H : ev'ry D²F : eur'ye N
1214 fate!] fate? D¹ : fate. HD²F : fate, N    1216 faire₍] faire! D¹ :
faire, D²NF    1217 ²and] *om.* NF    too?] too! D¹ : too₍ HF : too, D²N
1218 summer] *so* D¹D²NF : sum̃ers H    1219 lookes] looke D¹    1221
¹more₍] more, D¹N : more! D²F

## Windsor Version

α    *After which, ascending vp, the Iackman sings.*    1190

### Song 1.

The sportes are done, yet do not let
Your ioyes in sodaine silence set:
Delight and dumbnes neuer met
    In one selfe subiect yet.    1195
If things opposd must mixt appeare,
Then ad a boldness to your feare,
    And speake a hymne
      To him
Where all your duties doe of right belong,    1200
Which I will sweeten with an vndersong.

### CAPTAINE.

Glorie of ours, and grace of all the earthe,
  How well your figure dothe become your birthe,
As in you forme and fortune equall stood,    1205
  And onelie vertue gott aboue your blood!

### Song 2.

Vertue! his kinglie vertue, which did merrit
This ile intier, and you are to inherit.

### 4 GYPSIE.    1210

How right he doth confesse him in his face,
  His browe, his eie, and eue'rie marke of state,
As if he were the yssue of eache Grace,
  And bore about him both his fame and fate!

### Song 3.    1215

    Looke, looke, is he not faire,
      And freshe and fragrant too?
    As summer skie or purged aire,
      And lookes as lillies doe
    That were this morning blowne.    1220
4 GYP. O more, that more of him were knowne!

    1194 Delight] g *altered.*    1204 birthe,] bir⟨    1218 summer] sum̃ers

  w 1191 1] *om.* N      1193 sodaine] suddaine D¹D²N : sudden F
1198–9] *as one line in* D²NF    1203 earthe] Eath F    1204 birthe˰(?)] birth?
D¹ : birth. D² : birth, NF      1205 in you] in your D¹ : if your D²NF
1206 blood˰] blood. D¹D²F : blood, N      1208 vertue!] Vertue; D²NF
1209 intier˰] intire! D¹ : entire, D²F : intyre, N    1211 face˰] face, D¹F :

(α)
### 3 GYPSIE.

Look how the winds upon the waves grown tame,
   Take up land-sounds upon their purple wings,
And catching each from other, beare the same     965
   To eve'ry angle of their sacred springs:
So will we take his praise, and hurle his name
   About the globe in thousand aëry rings,
If his great vertue be in love with fame,
   For that contemn'd, both are neglected things.    970

### Song 4.

Good princes soare above their fame,
   And in their worth
   Come greater forth,
      Then in their name:    975
Such, such the father is,
Whom eve'ry title strives to kisse;
Who on his royall grounds, unto himselfe doth raise
The worke to trouble fame, and to astonish praise.

### 4 GYPSIE.    980

Indeed he is not lord alone of the estate,
But of the love of men, and of the empires fate:
The muses, arts, the schooles, commerce, our honours, lawes,
And vertues hang on him, as on their working cause.
2 GYP.    His hand-maid, Justice is,    985
3 GYP.    Wisdome his wife,
4 GYP.    His mistris Mercy,
5 GYP.    Temperance his life.
2 GYP. His pages Bounty and Grace, which many prove,
3 GYP. His guards are Magnanimity and Love,    990
4 GYP. His ushers, Councell, Truth, and Piety,
5 GYP. And all that followes him Felicity.

971 4 *omitted.*    972 Fame] m *impression defective.*    975 Then] Than    [965 same₍ₐ₎] same,    968 rings,] rings:    969 fame,] fame:    977 kisse;] kisse:]

---

w (*cont.*) 1237 eue'rie] every D¹H : ev'ry D²F : eu'rye N    1241 he is] he's D² : heeis (*altered from* hees) : hee's F    1243 (*for punctuation see note*) 1245 handmaid] hand-maid D¹D²F : hand mayd N    is₍ₐ₎] is, D¹NF : is. D² 1246 wife₍ₐ₎] wife, D¹N : Wife: D² : Wife; F    1247 Mercie₍ₐ₎] mercy, D¹N : Mercy: D² : Mercie; F    1248 life₍ₐ₎] life. D¹D²F : life, N    1249 proue₍ₐ₎] prove, D¹D²NF    1250 Loue₍ₐ₎] love, D¹ : love. D²F    1251 pietie₍ₐ₎] Piety, D¹NF : Piety. D²

## Windsor Version

(α)
### 3 GYPSIE.

Looke how the windes, vpon the waues growne tame,
   Take vp land soundes vpon theire purple wings,
And catching eache from other, beare the same      1225
   To eue'rie angle of theire sacred springs!
So will we take his praise, and hurle his name
   About the globe in thousand ayrie rings,
If his greate vertue be in loue with fame,
   For, that contemn'd, both are neglected things.     1230

### Song 4.

Good princes sore aboue theire fame,
   And in theire worthe
   Come greater forthe
     Then in theire name;      1235
Such, such the father is,
Whome eue'rie title striues to kiss,
Who on his royall groundes vnto himselfe doth raise
The worke to trouble fame and to astonishe praise.

### 4 GYPSIE.      1240

[γ] Indeed, he is not lord alone of \*all the state,
But of the loue of men and of the empire's fate,
The muses, arts, the schooles, commerce, our honors, lawes,
And vertues, hang on him as on theire working cause.
2 GIP.    His handmaid Iustice is,      1245
3 GIP.      Wisdome his wife,
4 GIP.    His mistresse Mercie,
5 GIP.      Temperance his life,
2 GIP. His pages Bountie and Grace, which many proue,
3 GIP. His guardes are Magnanimitie and Loue,      1250
4 GIP. His vshers Counsell, Truthe, and Pietie,
5 GIP. And all that followes him Felicitie.

---

*In* 1241 H *retains the reading of the Burley version.*

---

    1228 ayrie] ayerie    1230 things.] thi⟨    1239 praise.] pr⟨

w 1224 land sounds‸] Land-sounds‸ D¹ : Land sounds‸ D²F : land sounds; N    1226 eue'rie] every D¹H : ev'ry D²F : eur'ye N    springs‸] springs: D¹D² : springs. F    1228 ayrie] ayerie H : aëry D¹ : ay'ry D²NF    1229 Loue] lore F    1230 contemn'd] Contem'nd H : contem'd F    1231 4] *om.* D¹    1232 sore] soare D¹D²NF    1235 then] Than D¹

(α)                    *Song* 5.

  O that we understood
   Our good:         995
 There's happinesse indeed in blood,
   And store,
   But how much more,
  When vertues flood
 In the same streame doth hit!      1000
As that grows high with yeares, so happinesse with it.

### CAPTAINE.

  Love, love his fortune then,
   And vertues knowne,
  Who is the top of men,        1005
 But make the happinesse our owne;
Since where the Prince for goodnesse is renoun'd,
The subject with felicity is crown'd.

### *FINIS.*

993 5] *omitted.*  1003–4] *as one line.*  [1006 owne;] owne.]

## Windsor Version

(α)        *Song* 5.

      O that we vnderstood
          Our good!              1255
There's happiness indeed in blood
          And store,
      But how much more
      When vertues flood
   In the same streame dothe hitt!    1260
As that growes highe with yeares, so happines with it.

         CAPTAINE.

Loue, loue his fortune then
     And vertues knowne,
  Who is the top of men,            1265
    But make the happiness our owne;
Since, where the Prince for goodnes is renownd,
The subiect with felicitie is crownd.

        *The End.*

    1263–4] *as one line.*

w 1253 5] *om.* D¹    1260 hitt,] hit! D¹ : hit? D²F : hit, N    1263–4] *ed. conj.: as one line in* D¹HD²NF.    1266 make] makes D²F    1269 The End.] Finis. D¹ : *om.* D² (*in its place a row of ornaments*).

## The Epilogue.

β

At Burley, Beuer, and now last at Windsor
(Which shewes wee are Gipsies of no common kind Sir)
You haue beheld, and with delight, theire change,
And how they came transformd may thinck it strange,
It being a thing not touchd at by our poet;
Good Ben slept there, or else forgot to shewe it.
But least it proue like wonder to the sight
To see a Gipsie, as an Æthiop, white,
Knowe that what dide our faces was an oyntment
Made and laid on by Master Woolfs appointment,
The Courtes *Lycanthropos*, yet without spelles,
By a meere barbor, and no magicke elles:
It was fetcht of with water and a ball;
And to our transformation this was all,
Saue what the master fashioner calls his,
For to a Gypsies metamorphosis
(Who doth disguise his habit and his face,
And takes on a false person by his place)
The power of poesie can neuer faile her
Assisted by a barbor and a taylor.

### FINIS.

1281 Court     1284 this is all     1289 poetry

1275 by] b *altered from* oʳ     1279 oyntment] oyntmen⟨ (ᴵt *blotted*).

w 1270 Epilogue] Epiloge N     1272 ed. parentheses.     Sʳ˄] sir. *D² : Sʳ, N : Sir: F     1274 strange˄] strange. *D²F : strange, N     1278 as an Æthiop *in parentheses in* H     white,] white. HF : white: *D² : white, N     1279 dide] dy'd *D²NF     1280 Master] Mʳ HN : Mr. *D²F     1281 Courtꜱ] Court *D²NF     1282 Barbor] Barber *D²NF     1283 of] off *D²F     1284 was] is *D²F : is (*interlined above* was) N     1286 a] *om.* *D²NF     1289 poesie] Poetry *D²NF     1290 Barbor] Barber *D²NF     Taylor] Tayler *D²     1291] *so* *D²F : om.* HN

# NOTES

THE following notes are devoted almost exclusively to textual matters and discuss questions of interpretation only in so far as they affect the readings. They are mainly concerned with the choice between variants, either defending the copy-texts or explaining main departures from them. For many minor departures see Introduction, pp. 109 ff. There are a few additional notes on pp. 231–2.

B 1. The original heading was evidently *At the Kings Entrance* as in D¹, and that this remained in all the hypothetical manuscripts is shown by its retention in N. H adds *at Burley* to distinguish the speech from the prologue *at Windsor*; and F adopts the more elaborate form *The Speech . . . at Burleigh*, with the spelling it also has on the title-page. Clearly these are expansions in the individual authorities, and illustrate the freedom with which these treat headings and directions throughout. I have availed myself of this latitude to adopt whatever form appeared most helpful, rather than endeavour to arrive at that of the original (Introd. p. 109). On the order of the two prologues in NF see Introduction, p. 39. Strictly speaking, this speech of welcome by the porter on the King's arrival at Burley forms no part of the masque (Introd. p. 26).

B 3. The forms *uttred* (D¹) and *vttered* (β) are indifferent, and may pass as variant spellings, but it seems more likely that there was normalization in β than that the less usual was substituted for the more usual form.

B 8. The line contains a difficult reading, in which the variants are anomalous, D¹N reading *affects* and HF *effectes*. There is no doubt that *effectes* is the easier reading, and possibly on that account suspect. 'Affect' is a word of somewhat wide connotation, and though it is difficult to define its exact meaning here, its association with *love* gives it plausibility, in spite of its less likely association with *life*. If *affects* was original, there are two possibilities. Either *effectes* was substituted independently in H and F, which is quite possible; or else it was substituted in β, and N reverted to *affects* through the influence of *love*, which though possible is less probable. If, on the other hand, *effectes* was original, then we must suppose that D¹ and N independently substituted the less obvious *affects*, which is frankly incredible. I assume, therefore, that *affects* is correct, and that there is coincident error in H and F.

B 10. *sperrittes* is an eccentric spelling in H, which, as Simpson says (p. 549), it is difficult to believe due to Jonson.

B 11. All the extant texts read *sillables*. It was Cunningham who proposed to read *sillabes*, and Simpson notes that *syllabe* is Jonson's invariable form, e.g. throughout *The English Grammar*. Since its restoration here reduces the line to normality, there can be little doubt that it was intended.

The omission of *w*, as in D¹, is inadmissible, and was probably a mere slip, though it may have been prompted by the metrical redundancy due to the form *sillables*. On the other hand, *as* could have been omitted with less damage.

B 13. The presence or absence of *hath* is really indifferent, but its presence is perhaps slightly preferable, and omission seems more likely than insertion, especially as it makes the metre more regular and D¹ has been guilty of omission just before. It is probable that Jonson wrote *bounty'hath* as in N.

B 15. *Which shews* (D¹) has the support of *f* and (coincident error apart) must be correct: H alone reads *As showes*. The singular *shews* following on the plurals of the previous line is in any case awkward, but *Which* may be intended to have a more general reference—'all which shows'. H's reading has the air of being more idiomatic. But to have relative force 'as' requires an antecedent 'such' or demonstrative pronoun (*O.E.D.*, sense 24). The latter may be found in *those* of the line before, but that would tie the singular *shews* yet more closely to *favours* and *increases*. This the scribe of H seems to have overlooked when he made his stylistically attractive alteration.

B 20. The rather unusual contraction *neu'r* is frequent in H: still more unusual is N's *ne'uer* (cf. *eu'erye* in B 17). They may point to a Jonsonian *neue'r* of which *never* in F and *ne're* in D¹ are normalizations. See Introduction, pp. 113 ff.

B 21. The substitution, in γ or *f*, of *heape* for *poure* was clearly made to avoid the unpleasant jingle of *poure on more*. Though not perhaps beyond the capacity of a scribe, it is the sort of alteration one would naturally ascribe to the author. It cannot, of course, have been made for the Windsor performance (since the speech was only spoken at Burley) but Jonson may have made it casually at the same time as the other revisions. Since it was in any case made after the Burley–Belvoir performances it cannot, of course, be admitted into the present text.

B 25. If Jonson tinkered with B 21 he may have done so here too. For ²*him* in D¹ H, γ or *f* substituted *them*, which appears to be a grammatical correction in view of the plural antecedent *Him, and his house*. There seems at first sight no reason why the *search* should exclude the *house*, and one might suspect that in α *him* was nothing but a slip for the Jonsonian *'hem*. On the other hand, *thanks* and *vowes* (B 26) are more likely to be found in a person than a building, so that *him* may be correct.

W 3. *Ptolomęes* (H). For the spelling see note on W 30.

W 16. The *proue* that N substitutes for *growe* cannot, of course, be original, but the change was probably deliberate. The scribe must have failed to see, or thought readers might fail to see, that *growe* can mean 'become' as well as 'cultivate', and therefore preferred what he thought a less ambiguous word.

W 26, B 33. Concerning the term *Iackman* see W 53.

W 28, B 35. *Ammon* in D¹ can be nothing but an error. But to a scribe or compositor who knew nothing of Aymon the connexion between Ammon and Egypt might seem obvious.

W 30, B 37. In D¹ the *e* in *Ptolemy* must be a misprint, for the spelling with two *o*'s is elsewhere consistent and though incorrect clearly original. In H the name is regularly spelled *Ptolomęe*, as already at W 3. This 'ę' is a graphic form of 'æ', and the spelling *Ptolomæus* duly appears at W 132 both in D¹ and H (where NF have *Ptolomeus*). But such an ending as '-aee' does not seem to be a possible Jonsonian spelling, and must be put down as a scribal peculiarity in H: I have, however, retained it, though it is found in no other text (but see note on W 200).

W 32, B 39. The agreement of D¹ and *f* appears to warrant the originality of *strooke*, and I have ventured to reject H's *strucke* as a formal modernization rather than a mere variant spelling.

W 35, B 42. ²*her*, omitted in D¹, is not necessary to the sense and may not be original, but its presence seems natural.

W 36, B 43. The repetition of *greate* after *she*, in β but not in D¹, is not necessary and may not be original, but it serves to emphasize the antithesis, and omission seems in general more likely than insertion.

W 37, B 44. In D¹ *for the same time* must be an error due to confusion with the similar phrase 'at the same time'.

W 38, B 45. Either *at the last* (D¹) or *at last* (β) might be original, and there is little to choose between them. Again, omission is perhaps more likely than insertion, and there may be an intentional parallelism between *for the time* (B 36–7) and *at the last*. I therefore follow D¹, although its authority is rather invalidated by w 37.

w 42, B 49. Here *of* (β) and *in* (D¹) seem completely indifferent, though the former is possibly slightly more idiomatic. But *the most stone iuges of the kingdome* of course means *in the kingdome*, and a scribe or compositor might be unconsciously influenced in favour of the more literal *in*, as he might be by *in picture* just before. I follow β partly as in general the more accurate text.

*wretchock*, the smallest or weakest of a brood, is a term recorded from Skelton onward, proving that *f*'s *wretchcock* (anyhow unoriginal) is nothing but a scribal error, though (as appears from *O.E.D.*) it gave rise to a ghost-word.

w 43, B 50. Either *were* (β) or *was* (D¹) might be original; but after *though* Jonson may have preferred the subjunctive even when stating a fact, and the change from subjunctive to indicative is perhaps more likely than the reverse.

The insertion of *verye* in *f* is rather unexpected, but is hardly likely to be due to revision.

w 47, B 54. In D¹ *Quinguinever* is clearly the result of a succession of graphic errors, but suggests that the 'n' may not have been doubled in α: *f*'s *Guinquennium* is a simpler and more obvious corruption, which implies that the capital was not in the source.

w 52, B 59. To 'beat the hoof' is a common expression for to go afoot, and there is no reason why in D¹ *beate it on the hoofe* should not be original. But the alliterative expansion *beate it on the hard hoofe* in β looks genuine. Therefore, although omission in D¹ is perfectly possible, we are bound to assume revision in β.

Here H has *ben* and D¹*f bene*: at w 996 H*f* have *ben-* and D² *beane-*. There is no doubt of the length (see *O.E.D.*, s.v. Bein, *adj*.) and I have therefore departed from the peculiar spelling of H. *bene bowse* is a regular canting term for good drink, but here, coupled with *stauling ken*, it seems rather to mean an alehouse.

w 52–3, B 59–60. A *stauling ken* or 'stalling-ken' is a canting term for a house where stolen goods are disposed of, a receiver's. *Starlinge* is, of course, an error of *f*, and the punctuation shows that it was not understood.

w 53, B 60. To *nip a ian* is to cut a purse. According to *O.E.D.* to *cly* is thieves' slang for to procure or steal, and a *iarke* is a counterfeit licence, particularly the seal to it. Either *or* (D¹) or *and* (β) might be original, but the disjunctive here balances that in the previous line; they would go to the tavern to steal and to the 'fence's' to get a faked licence.

In *f Iacke* is an obvious corruption, but perhaps influenced by *Iackman*, the form Jonson uses throughout. It should be 'Jarkman', an educated beggar or forger of 'jarks', so defined in Awdelay's *Fraternity of Vagabonds*, 1561. As explained in *O.E.D.*, the form *Iackman* originated in a misprint in the 1575 edition of that work.

w 55–8, B 62–5. These four lines are italicized in the two printed texts (D¹, F) and unless this is a case of contamination, which is unlikely (Introd. pp. 15–16), they were probably distinguished in script in the original. This may mean that they were sung. The Jackman was, it seems, the chief vocalist of the cast.

w 55, B 62. *cheates* (stolen) goods, cf. w 702.

w 56, B 63. *Harman-beckage* apparently a fanciful deformation of 'beckharman', a constable (cf. w 695).

w 57, B 64. To 'lib' is to sleep, and 'libken' is therefore a sleeping place: *libkins* in D¹*f*, though apparently original, is a false formation ('ken' = house), but there is independent support for it. A *crackmans* is cant for a hedge. Either *theire* (β) or *the* (D¹) may be original, but the former seems more natural, and *the* may have been substituted under the impression that *he* (w 53) was the subject, whereas this is more likely to be the collective *equipage*.

w 58, b 65. A *skipper* is a barn or shed used by vagabonds to sleep in. A 'blackman' was a seller of blacking or perhaps of black metalware (at least in the droll so called), but *blackmans* is not recorded in any sense relevant here. It is, no doubt, a variant of 'darkmans', a recognized canting term for 'night'.

w 59, b 66. The *2 Gypsie* is, of course, simply the other Gipsy, the leader of the second horse. Whether he is the same as the one so called later (w 321, &c.) is doubtful. If he was, he was Lord Feilding (Introd. pp. 71–2), and it seems unlikely that any of the noble masquers came on before the Captain (Buckingham) at w 86. If he was not, he was presumably the Patrico, even though he here plays second fiddle to the Jackman. A 'Patrico' is defined in *O.E.D.* as 'A priest or parson; *esp.* a hedge-priest': according to Harman's *Caveat for Cursitors*, 1567, 'a Iarkeman and a Patrico, bee in the old briefe of vacabonds'. In Brome's *Jovial Crew*, 1652, one of the 'especial Beggars' is called Patrico.

w 69, b 76. *'hem* Concerning the adoption of this Jonsonian form see Introduction, pp. 113–14.

w 70–1 : b 77–8. There is a slight difficulty here. By its punctuation $D^1$ associates the couplet with what precedes rather than with what follows: NF do the reverse: H, as usual, affords no help. Moreover, the couplet itself is ambiguous. *So* would most naturally mean 'thus', but in that case we should expect *will* rather than *may* to follow. With *may* the meaning of *So* would rather be 'provided that', but this hardly fits the passage as a whole. Connected with what precedes the former interpretation would be necessary; connected with what follows, the latter, and this seems to be excluded. I conclude that, in spite of the difficulty of *may*, the punctuation of $D^1$ is correct: it is also in general a somewhat better authority than *f*. Perhaps *So* has the force of 'in order that'.

w 71, b 78 and w 73, b 80. See Additional Notes on p. 231.

w 74, b 81. We can hardly doubt that when Jonson wrote this line he expected the part of the Captain to be taken by the Prince and not by George Villiers.

w 75, b 82. On the whole I do not think that H's *to* for *too* can be anything but a slip (Introd. p. 113).

w 78, b 85. *then* appears to have been the original form throughout, and commonly survives, as here, in the two manuscripts, whereas the prints often substitute the modern *than* (Introd. p. 112).

w 80, b 87. Either *doubt* (β) or *doe doubt* ($D^1$) might be original. In general omission seems more likely than insertion, but here *doe* may very easily have arisen through accidental dittography, *do doubt*, in $d^1$.

w 85–7, b 92–3. I take 'to dance to a stand' to mean to dance till one comes to a stand at the end of the measure. If so, the direction in $D^1$ would seem to be more original than β's, in which the meaning of the phrase is obscured. This was evidently felt when in *f* (or γ) *to a stand* was changed to *attendant*. This is not likely to have been due to revision since there is no evidence that Jonson concerned himself with the form of the directions. Indeed, from the muddle over the fortune-dances at Windsor (Introd. p. 50) it is clear that he did not.

The text recognizes five speaking parts for 'Gipsies', the Captain being the First. The direction here calls for seven in all. The other two are, of course, the Patrico and the Jackman. But in that case the direction is faulty, for the Jackman at least is already on the stage ready to join in and make music for the dance (w 83). The *2 Gypsye* of w 59 (whether the Patrico or not) has doubtless gone off with the horses and now re-enters.

The difficulty can be resolved by supposing that the direction originally read simply *Dance 1 The Captain with sixe more to a stand*. Then in an attempt to be more explicit D¹ inserted *danceth forth*, (which is consistent with *to a stand*), and β *The Entrance of* (which is not); further H inserted *being*, and *f* (or γ) *Which is* (N retains the capital of the following *The*) at the same time removing the absurdity of *to a stand* by substituting *attendant*.

w 98, B 105. Without knowing what they wanted the *Shelles* for, I cannot guess whether *or* (D¹) or *and* (β) is the more likely to be correct, but there seems no reason why they should not have both, and I therefore follow the generally more authoritative text, especially as Robert Johnson's setting in *The Musical Companion*, 1672 (Cole, p. 15), has *and*.

w 104, B 111. For the Windsor revision in this line see Introduction, p. 30.

w 105, B 112. *yee* (D¹) is, of course, required by the rime, and H's *you* is in any case a bad oversight. But the slip may have been in β and survived in *f*, for the scribe of N first wrote *you* and corrected it to *yee*. In that case F made the correction independently.

w 106, B 113. The agreement of D¹ and *f* convicts H of error in *your*: revision cannot appear in a single text.

B 116–19. All texts include this stanza, but it is clear that the last two lines at any rate can only have been sung at Burley (Introd. pp. 29, 30). It is possible of course, though unlikely, that a revised version has been lost.

w 111, B 120. Respecting the Patrico see w 59.

w 121–6, B 130–40. For the revision here see Introduction, pp. 26–7, 30. The substitute is written in the right margin of a recto page in H opposite B 130–4, and stands thus:

> At Beauer
> There be Gentry Co⟨
> Coues here
> Are the Cheife of⟨
> the shire.

The leaf must have been trimmed while the manuscript was still in the hands of the scribe, for when the end of the word *Coues* in the second line was cut away he repeated it at the beginning of the third. (Cole read the remaining letters of the mutilated word correctly: Simpson read them as *lo* and supposed the scribe to have begun to write *lords*; but the *C*, though different from that in the repeated word, is exactly the same as in the *Coue* of B 130.)

The passage raises two problems: first, How came it to be written for Burley? and second, Why was it altered at Belvoir? The Burley version is devoted to flattery of Buckingham, the King's host there, but these lines refer to the Earl of Rutland, as is clear from mention of *the Beaver-ken*, Belvoir Castle. Of course, as the King's prospective host two days later, Rutland was a suitable object for incidental compliment; but why is he called *top of the shire*? Here I must call attention to the misleading punctuation of all texts except H, which as usual has none at all. D¹NF all put a comma after shire, so that it is at least possible to read the passage to mean that the *Gentry-Cove* was *the top of the shire* and *Of the Beaver-ken*. But remove the comma (as I have done in the text) and the meaning is that he was top of the shire of Belvoir, that is of Leicestershire, of which county Rutland had in fact been Lord-Lieutenant since 1612. (At the same time Jonson may not have had the distinction between the counties of Leicester and Rutland always in mind: he certainly speaks of the *two shires* at B 522, but at B 393 he describes the Countess of Rutland as *Mistris of the County* in a passage that we are bound to suppose was spoken at Burley.)

Why then was the passage altered at Belvoir, where it would appear that it was really more appropriate than at Burley? One answer would be that it was not, and that in H's heading *Beauer* is a slip for *Windsor*. (This I understand to be the explanation favoured by Dr. Simpson.) But I think we can trust H. At Belvoir Rutland had replaced Buckingham as host and become the principal character. Later on *the good man of Bever* was duly celebrated in a revisional passage (B 908¹⁻¹²), and there was no need to extol him personally here. But Buckingham was also present, and it was politic that the powerful favourite (who, moreover, had presumably commissioned the masque) should not be forgotten. So, just as later *the good man of Beuer* is celebrated as *Our Buckinghams father*, so the present passage is altered to include Rutland's son-in-law as well as himself, the *Gentry Coues* that are *cheife of the shire* being the neighbouring county magnates.

It almost looks as though Jonson thought he might have been a little indiscreet in extolling Rutland as *top of the shire* at Burley, since he was careful to add (in lines later omitted: B 138–40) that great as he might be the King and Prince and perhaps Buckingham were greater still.

B 133. Either *among* (β) or *amongst* (D¹) might be original and there is no intrinsic probability in favour of either (Introd. pp. 112–13). In such cases I follow β as generally the correcter text.

W 123, B 134. On the use of 'you' and 'ye' see Introduction, p. 111. I merely follow the copy-text, unless obviously wrong as at W 105.

W 127, B 141. *Roome Mortes* or 'rum morts' are great ladies: 'rum' a canting term for 'Good, fine, excellent; great' (*O.E.D.*), and 'mort' the ordinary word for a woman. Harman's *Caveat* (1567) gives '*Rome mort*, the Quene'. It is thus parallel to *Gentry Coues*. In Brome's *Jovial Crew*, 1652, 'an Old Beggar-Woman' is called Autumn-Mort.

W 129, B 143. Either with (β) or without (D¹) *theire* the line might be original, but the presence of the word seems natural and D¹ is somewhat given to omission.

For *iolly* H has the eccentric and incorrect, though recognized, spelling *ioylly*, which there is no reason to suppose original. It is mainly a fifteenth-century form, due to mistaken association with 'joy'.

W 149, B 163. The passage, discussed in the Introduction, pp. 61–2, is obscure and possibly corrupt. The near agreement of D¹ and *f* of course convicts the reading of H as a scribe's sophistication. Whether either D¹ or *f* can be original is another matter. There may have been corruption in α. The question turns, I suspect, on the correctness and meaning of *paginæ* in the line before. It will be noticed that Jonson more than once uses the word *table* in connexion with the reading of fortunes (W 256, B 471), and since he also speaks of a *booke* (B 447) in the same connexion, there can be little doubt that he thought of the *hand*, or the *hand and face* (B 450), as a writing tablet on which were inscribed the character and fate of the owner. And Jonson was doubtless aware that in classical Latin 'pagina' and 'tabula' might equally mean an inscribed slab or tablet. It seems possible, then, that Jonson uses 'pagina' here in the same sense as he uses *table* later on, in spite of the rather misleading *all*. In that case *f* offers the preferable reading. Still, in so obscure a matter, I have thought best to follow the authority of D¹.

W 150, B 164. *all miste'ry*. The shortened form is of course necessary for the rime; still, the reading of D¹ may point to a Jonsonian apostrophus (Introd. p. 114).

W 156, B 170. A 'simper-the-cocket' or more usually 'simper-de-cocket' means a woman of affected coquettish airs (*O.E.D.*). It appears to be formed from the verb 'simper' and the adjective 'cocket', which is perhaps a confusion of 'coquette' and 'cocky'. Since the first element at least is certain, I have altered the spelling *semper*- in D¹.

w 162, b 176. *minte* i.e. money. This was the original meaning of the word, but from the sixteenth century on is only found in slang and may represent a borrowing from Low German (cf. G. *münze*: O.E.D.). It was perhaps not understood when *f* (or γ) altered it to *mine* (but cf. the error *meane* for *meant* at w 1150).

w 164, b 178. In view of the singular *pot* and *braine* that follow, the plural *Tuns* in D¹ must be held an error. In *f towne* is of course a misreading of *tonne* as in H.

The curious form *brew'ell* in D¹ may be an eccentricity of the compositor's. It is doubtful whether *brew'well* would be possible as a Jonsonian apostrophus.

w 173–80. For the Windsor revision see Introduction, p. 31.

b 189. *knackets* The variants here are discussed in the Introduction, p. 36.

b 191–2. Here *Nancies* is evidently used generically for girls, and *trickets* and *tripsies* seem to be fanciful formations of like meaning. The first may be fashioned (with the same suffix as *knackets*, b 189) from the obsolete adjective 'trick' (perhaps an adaptation of the north-country 'trig') meaning adroit or trim: the second more obviously from the verb 'trip', to step daintily. In *f trinkits* (N) or *trinkets* (F) is due to confusion with a more familiar word.

w 180. The agreement of H and N, here and at w 1098, appears to warrant the originality of *of* in place of *off*, and we know that Jonson sometimes affected this spelling (Introd. p. 113).

w 186–7, b 199–200. The support of *f* proves that D¹ is correct in giving these lines in what is obviously their natural order. The inversion in H was presumably accidental, and the fact that the scribe enclosed what he made the second line in parentheses (which was the only way to make it intelligible) suggests that he was prepared to vamp his text rather than correct it (Introd. pp. 60–1).

w 190–9. For the Windsor revision see Introduction, p. 31.

w 200, b 206. The spelling *Ptolomee* is unusual in any text but H, and its appearance here in D¹ and F and in both versions in N, goes some way towards guaranteeing the habitual form in H (see note on w 30).

w 204, b 210. The reading of D¹, *drops*, is impossible, and inexplicable except as a mere slip for *draughts*, as in H (corrupted to *draught* in γ or *f*). Jonson could never have written *drops*, even in a first draft, so that the question of revision does not arise.

w 205, b 211. In D¹ *thee* can only be an error for *there* through accidental loss of the 'r'. It cannot be admitted as a possible variant, for throughout the speech the Captain is addressed as 'you'.

w 208, b 214. D¹ has *strict watches* and β *longe watches*, and it is not altogether easy to see the variant as merely scribal. It is true that *longe* appears the weaker reading; at the same time it is the length rather than the strictness of a watch that may be expected to induce sleep, so that if the more colourful *strict* was original there might be motive for the change. It is wiser, therefore, to admit the possibility of an author's revision.

For *winke* (D¹H) *f* (or γ) substituted *shrinke*, a change that can, of course, have nothing to do with that earlier in the line. It is not easy to account for, unless the scribe was unfamiliar with the use of 'wink' in the sense of 'sleep'. Two lines below *royall* (NF) is doubtless a mere slip for *loyall*.

w 209, b 215. The punctuation of this line is troublesome. None of the composite texts has any internal stop (except N, which puts an absurd comma after *by*). But the following *As* makes it necessary to connect *so* with *kept*, and I have therefore made *commaunded by you* parenthetical. D¹ places a comma after *But* and another after *you*. This is plausible enough, though it virtually means understanding a second *so* before *kept*; I have allowed it to stand, since the sense is not really affected.

## Notes

W 211, B 217. Either *yett did* (β) or *did yet* (D¹) is possible and might be original. It is true that *yett did* is so much the more expected order that one is naturally disposed to assume it to be correct: at the same time if Jonson wrote *did yet*, inversion would be almost inevitable sooner or later. Revision seems improbable.

W 213, B 219. F puts a comma before *that*, perhaps in a rather clumsy attempt at emphasis to indicate that it is the demonstrative adjective and not the conjunction.

W 215, B 221. The support of *f* makes an original *Charta* as in D¹ probable; but H's *Carta* may pass as a mere difference of spelling.

W 224, B 230. Presumably, therefore, it is the Patrico who sings the following song.

W 227–8, B 233–4. This one-line speech (and prefix) appears only in D¹, and is there misassigned (Introd. p. 55). Obviously there must have been a rime to W 226, and an accidental omission in β is therefore indicated.

W 229, B 235. D¹ has *Dance 2* only. Concerning the dances and the directions for them in the several texts see Introduction, pp. 46–51.

W 241, B 247. The absence of the article before *Captaine* suggests that the words *goes up to the King*, which appear in no other text, were simply added to the speaker's name in D¹. As Gifford observed, the Captain does not in fact approach, or at any rate address, the King till two lines later. To the speaker's name Gifford therefore added the note 'surveying the company'. But it is not certain whether *my sweete Masters, the ould and the younge* refers to the company in general or particularly to the King and Prince, who would presumably be seated somewhat apart from the rest. The latter seems the more likely, since *my sweete Masters* could hardly include the Ladies.

W 242–3, B 248–9. The agreement of D¹ and N in the spelling *yong* points possibly, but not necessarily, to the original form of the word. The spelling is a common one. It is perhaps to some extent confirmed by N's spelling *tonge* in the next line, where D¹ and F have the modernized *tongue*. The spelling in H is uncertain, for all but the first three letters are cut away. The third letter looks like a 'u', but the distinction between 'u' and 'n' is not always clear. Still the scribe seems more inclined to write 'n' for 'u' than the other way about (Introd. p. 19, note 2). Both Cole and Simpson complete the word as *tounge*, and in view of the rime-word *younge* I have allowed this to stand.

W 246–7, B 252–3. See Additional Notes on p. 231.

W 248, B 254. In D¹ *time* for *line* is of course a graphic error, helped probably by misunderstanding.

W 250–1, B 256–7. The complicated variation in these lines has been fully discussed in the Introduction, pp. 63–4. But in the second line either reading might be original.

W 251, B 257. The contracted form of the second *of* found in *f* is here rejected in order to preserve parallelism with the first (Introd. p. 116).

W 252, B 258. Either *territorie* (D¹) or *territories* (β) might be original, and I have allowed the alternative. At the same time Con's *teritoryes* probably convicts D¹ of error (Introd. pp. 74–5).

W 253, B 259. See Additional Notes on p. 231.

W 254, B 260. The variant in and the meaning of this line are discussed in the Introduction, p. 61.

W 261, B 267. The omission of *haue* in *f* (or γ) must have been accidental: had revision been intended *of* must have been changed to *for*.

W 262, B 268. With this line D² becomes available, replacing D¹ in Dᵇ.

w 264–7, B 270–3. D¹ peppers these lines with points of exclamation. H has no punctuation and N none of significance. D² and F, however, show a marked similarity (*here?* . . . *Monarch;* . . . *appeare!* . . . *Just:*), which may point either to originality or to imitation (Introd. pp. 15–16).

w 271, B 277. To follow H in printing the line without internal punctuation is to risk a misunderstanding from which D¹ is saved by a comma. Yet to carry through such punctuation is hardly possible; D¹ confines it to the first two lines, and even Simpson, who inserts five internal commas, is not consistent.

w 281–2, B 287. Again (cf. w 241) there appears to have been originally merely the speaker's name; but in this instance D¹ and β have both embroidered after their own fashion. Con alone (omitting the song) indicates a dance, but this is not of any authority. The form of its direction is clearly, however, somehow related to that of β (cf. B 369, note).

w 288, B 293. The whole stanza is obviously a question, but F is the only text that puts a question-mark at the end.

w 294, B 299. The stanza is without grammatical construction, and we ought perhaps to put a mark of exclamation at the end, though no text has any but a full stop. Simpson puts a question-mark, but I do not see how the stanza can be grammatically connected with the preceding.

w 299, B 304. *amongst* must be an individual variant in H: the majority's *among* is somewhat equivocally supported by *amonke* in Con (Introd. pp. 112–13).

B 306–8. On these lines, and their relation to the Windsor version, see Introduction, p. 32 and note.

w 305. Either *fortunes* (H) or *fortune* (γ) might be original, though I think the sense favours the former.

w 306. Here, on the contrary, the sense is decisive for *fortune* (H) as against *fortunes* (γ).

w 309. Either *would* (H) or *could* (γ) might, of course, be original. On the whole I think *would* is the more likely, but *could* has a superficial plausibility that would make it an easy substitute. This, however, is a purely subjective feeling.

w 319, B 309. Both D¹ and D² have *Dance 3*. For the former, and for its omission of *Straine 2.*, see Introduction, pp. 46–51. The latter seems due to contamination (Introd. pp. 58–9).

w 320, B 310. If the *In* of D¹ is anything more than a slip it is still obviously less appropriate than the *After* of β. Even if the fortune was spoken during the measure, which there is no reason to suppose, it could not be said to be offered in it. The same phrasing is found at B 388 and B 445, but since it does not appear at B 337 or B 419 it may very well be due to the scribe of *d¹*. In that case the original headings contained only the names of the persons whose fortunes were told, but even if the phrase *After which* first appeared in β, it probably represents the action correctly.

w 328, B 318. D² alone has *Starres* for *states*. Since at w 334 a king is called a *starre*, we cannot perhaps pronounce *starres* intrinsically impossible here. But it is, of course, an error, and suggests that the scribe or compositor glanced ahead.

w 329, B 319. Either *shall* (β) or *should* (D¹) might be original. I have a personal preference for *should*, but if Con is independent its agreement with β is conclusive, and it is best to allow it to decide.

w 332–3, B 322–3. The division of a word between two lines is of course unusual in serious verse, and it may be thought more appropriate at w 1073–4. But Jonson uses the device elsewhere (*Sejanus*, II. 360–2):

> Pray AVGVSTA then,
> That for her owne, great CAESARS, and the pub-
> lique safetie, she be pleas'd to vrge these dangers.

w 335, B 325. The construction here is obscure. It looks as though there had been confusion between *One, the noblest nowe that is*, and *One of the noblest nowe that are*, but what Jonson really had in mind may have been *One, the noblest of all that nowe are*. However, it is wiser not to attempt any punctuation.

w 339, B 329. D¹ and H concur in the spelling *Height*, where all other texts, including Con, have the normal *Hight*. Whether this is coincidence or originality it is hard to say. At w 854 H again has *height* where D²NF have *hight*. While the spelling of 'height' (from 'high') has varied widely, the spelling 'hight' for the present and past tenses of the verb appears to have been almost constant from the sixteenth century at least. But I do not feel justified in departing from the copytext.

w 342, B 332. It is, no doubt, possible to read the passage in such ways that either *For* (β) or *Of* (D¹) would be correct, and they must be allowed as alternatives. *For*, however, gives the better and more natural sense, and β has the support of Con for what it is worth.

w 345, B 335. D¹ naturally ends the stanza with a question-mark, and so do D² and F although the sentence runs on. (D² may, of course, have merely followed D¹: it is less likely that F should have followed D².) This points to an original manuscript that did indeed end at this point and to which the following four stanzas were actually an addition: it is significant that no text has the question-mark needed after *laughter* in w 351. This should be borne in mind when considering the relation of the texts at this point (Introd. p. 32 and note).

w 367–9. These lines were accidentally omitted in γ, so that H is here our only authority.

B 336. Concerning the dance-directions for the Ladies' fortunes see Introduction, pp. 46–50.

B 337. For the form of this and later directions see note on w 320.

B 339. It is uncertain whether H's spelling *Horle* is significant. The scribe possibly inclined to *o*-spellings: he has *Ho* for *Ha* at w 638, and *torninge* for *turninge* at w 1130 (but this may be merely due to its riming with *morninge*). However, all texts have *hurle* at w 1227. On the other hand, in his autograph *Masque of Queens* (l. 391) Jonson has *hoorl'd* riming with *world*, which seems to have retained the *o*-sound.

B 345. However written, *pray thee* would probably be shortened in speech, and the contracted form may easily have been introduced in H (and Con). It is less likely that expansion took place independently in D¹ and γ.

The variant *depose* : *dispose* is discussed in the Introduction, pp. 62–3.

B 348. For the error *hollow*, common to D¹ and D², see Introduction, p. 58.

B 349. See Additional Notes on p. 231.

B 361. There is no sense in the apostrophe in *ak's* in D¹, and I therefore follow H.

B 362. It appears that γ had a contraction for *he is*, but this throws an emphasis on *he* that contradicts the sense. I therefore retain the full form of D¹ and H, supported by Con (Introd. p. 116).

B 363. The omission of *you* is a mere slip in D¹.

B 369. We are bound to admit the possibility that either *There's never* or *There is not* may be original, but the reading *There is nere* in Con seems to make the full form *There is never* more likely. See Introduction, p. 75. But even if we accept the argument there advanced, the relation might still be D¹ (β Con) though a direct derivation of Con from β would be ruled out. That would imply an additional hypothetical manuscript, but it would reconcile the evidence of w 281–2 with a measure of independence on the part of Con.

B 389. There is a difficulty here, of which I know no solution. All texts agree in giving the fortunes of the Marquess of Buckingham and her mother, the Countess of Rutland, to the Third Gipsy, that is, according to Con, to Endymion Porter. But it is surely unlikely that he originally spoke twice in succession. Con avoids this by giving the Countess of Buckingham precedence over the Countess of Rutland. This has the effect of bringing Buckingham's wife and mother together: it would have been possible at Burley but hardly at Belvoir, where Rutland was the host. But in that case D¹ (like β) has the Belvoir order and Con alone the Burley order, and this is unlikely, since Con, which includes Lady Exeter's fortune, apparently represents a later state of the text than D¹, which lacks it.

B 392. In D¹ *O* is of course a slip for *and*: in some hands '&' might possibly be mistaken for an 'O'.

B 393. When Jonson styled the Countess of Rutland *Mistris of the County* he must have been thinking of the Belvoir performance, and we may see in it evidence that the two earlier versions were prepared at the same time (Introd. p. 28). It is strange that the couplet should have been spoken at Burley at all, and it could, of course, easily be omitted. We might find in it support for Simpson's belief that the Countess of Rutland was not present at Burley, but this was based on a textual misapprehension (Introd. p. 27, note 3).

B 394. The omission of *it* in D¹ makes no difference to the sense, but metrically it makes the line too irregular for us to admit it as possibly original.

B 404–5.    And when your yeares rise more, then would be told,
       Yet neyther of you seeme to th'other old

Jonson had written in 1613 on the occasion of the marriage of the Earl of Somerset and the Countess of Essex (*Jonson*, viii. 384).

B 406–17. The Countess of Exeter's fortune is not in D¹, though Con, which purports to give the Burley version, contains it (Introd. p. 27). It is admittedly a late addition, and the necessity of introducing it at short notice accounts for its being entrusted to the Patrico, who was doubtless played by a professional.

B 408. H's *knewe*, supported by Con, is obviously right: *know* is an error of γ, conjecturally corrected in N.

B 413. The error *one* is in all texts and was first corrected to *ones* by Simpson. β is here our ultimate authority, but the appearance of the error in Con suggests that it may go back farther: it may well be a slip of the author's.

B 417. Either with (H) or without (γ) *it* the line might be original. But omission is probably more likely than insertion, and H, which is anyhow a better authority than γ, is supported by Con.

B 419. D¹ has *a* for ²*the* by an obvious slip.

B 438. See Introduction, p. 72.

B 439–41. For the interpretation of this obscure passage, assuming coincident error in D¹ and D², see Introduction, p. 58.

## Notes

B 445. For the position of the fifth dance in D¹, after instead of before the Countess of Buckingham's fortune, see Introduction, p. 50.

B 447. D¹ alone recognizes the exclamatory nature of the apostrophe here, but its mark after *booke* is of course impossible.

B 456. The curious blunder *told* in γ, presumably a graphic error for *robd*, was conjecturally corrected in N.

B 469. The facts that there is no *And* here in D¹ and none at B 445 in β suggests that it may have been added by the scribe of β here and at B 406.

B 470. D¹ is alone in giving this speech to the Fourth instead of the Fifth Gipsy. Either might be original. Con does not help since it identifies neither. The Second (Feilding) and Third (Porter) speak two fortunes each, and it seems more likely that the Fourth and Fifth spoke one apiece than that the Fourth spoke two and the Fifth none. There can hardly have been any reason for altering the speakers at Belvoir.

B 480. After this H has the note recording that at Windsor the Lords' fortunes replaced those of the Ladies (Introd. p. 29).

W 370. For the dances in the Lords' fortunes consult the Introduction, pp. 50–1.

W 371–89. On the misplacing of the Lord Chamberlain's fortune in H see Introduction, pp. 40–1.

W 385. Either *hath* (H) or *has* (γ) may be original: I merely follow the generally more reliable text.

W 396–401. The *purse* (396) is of course the bag in which the Great Seal is carried and from which on occasions it may be taken out (399). Since I am not aware that the seal plays any part in the judicial functions that the Lord Keeper exercises *vice* the Lord Chancellor, I follow Simpson (who, however, puts a full stop after *seale*) in taking 399 in connexion with what precedes rather than what follows; but the sense of the passage is not very clear to me, and none of the texts help—they either have no punctuation or else a series of commas.

W 402–5. For these lines, probably an addition in γ, see Introduction, p. 41. For the forms *venter* (*f*) and *venture* (D²) see Introduction, p. 112.

W 408. Although γ has the full form *you will*, H's contraction is here necessary.

W 409. Though *mutch* (H) is a recognized sixteenth-century spelling, it is here eccentric and there is no point in preserving it (Introd. p. 110).

W 411 *for* may of course mean 'in respect of', but *'fore* would perhaps be rather more natural.

W 414. H has another *Sir* after *come*, and this may, of course, be original. It even makes the line slightly more regular, but the repetition is clumsy, and it is better away.

W 415. There are two alternative readings in this line. Either *Sin'* (H) or *Since* (γ) and either *not for* (H) or *for no* (γ) might be original. But obviously in the first H's reading is likely to be correct (cf. B 913), and there is no reason to displace it in the second.

W 417. H's spelling *errand* has the support of N and Tan; the other texts have *errant*. The *t*-spelling had crept in during the sixteenth century, and custom had not yet become fixed.

W 422. It may be remarked that Jonson was himself a pensioner, and had his pension increased on this occasion (Introd. p. 36).

w 423. H's *Excheque<sup>r</sup>* might stand, on the analogy of 'o<sup>r</sup>' 'yo<sup>r</sup>', for *Exchequeur*, and a spelling in *-our* is recorded from the sixteenth century; but it is at best eccentric, and probably a mistake.

w 429. Either *health* (H) or *your health* (γ) might, of course, be original. But the insertion is quite uncalled-for, and why Simpson should have accepted it I do not know. In H the line is exactly equivalent metrically to 427, and if neither *honor* or *wealth* (430) requires *your*, why should *health*?

w 440. Either *nurse* (H) or *a nurse* (γ) might be original, and in such a case as this omission and insertion seem equally likely. To my mind the line reads rather better with *a*, and I therefore add it: Simpson seems to have felt this much more strongly, for he too introduced it into H.

w 442. No doubt it is possible to make sense of *the free to all* (γ), i.e. 'what is free to all', but it would be a very awkward mode of expression here, since *they* (H) clearly refers to *artes* (440) and we get a parallel *they* in the next line. I think it may safely be rejected.

w 450. D² alone has the modern spelling *whither*, but that with *-e-* was common down to the eighteenth century.

w 464. For the absurdity in γ see Introduction, p. 66. The scribe may have had some excuse for his misunderstanding, for even H capitalizes and italicizes *Francke* as though it were a proper name.

w 471. I suspect that the line is corrupt both in H and γ. The former reads *your hand Sir, and your wellcome*, which is plethoric; the latter *your hand, and wellcome*, which is deficient. Presumably *Sir* and ²*your* were meant as alternatives, only one of which was intended to stand. I choose *Sir*, since the polite address is usual.

w 485–500. For the absence of the Earl of Buccleuch's fortune in H see Introduction, p. 41. It may not have been known that he was to be present till after Jonson had composed the rest of the fortunes and H been transcribed. It should be noticed, as possibly significant, that it gives the Patrico a second fortune among the Lords, and that among the Ladies it was to him that was assigned the additional fortune for Lady Exeter.

w 490. D² alone has the modern spelling *scent*, but the unetymological *c* first appeared in the seventeenth century.

w 500. Here our only authority is γ, and it is not a very reliable one. It may have preserved the line as Jonson wrote it, but if so Jonson wrote nonsense (Introd. p. 67). I have substituted *be* for *beare*.

w 501–6. It is clear that the form and the position of this direction in the Windsor version are alike due to the scribe of H (Introd. p. 41), and it is one of his merits that he cleared up the confusion in which the insertion of the duet, along with the Lords' fortunes, had left the manuscript. The awkward collocation of the duet and the last fortune did not disturb the scribe of *f*, but it evidently did the printer of D², since he introduced a row of ornaments at this point. The arrangement in H is clearly right, for we are bound to believe that the fortunes ended with a dance, namely the final strain of the Second Dance, and if this led into the Third and the Clowns entered during the Third (both being vouched for by γ), then the duet must also have been sung whilst the dance went on, unless it followed the entrance, which would be contrary to the whole evidence.

B 483. D¹ has *to them Puppy*, and the fact that D² alone of the other texts agrees with it clearly proves imitation (Introd. p. 59). Both, moreover, centre Puppy's name in capitals as though it were that of the first speaker, though they give *Cock.* as a prefix in the next line. The phrase *to them* was probably added by the scribe of *d*¹ to indicate that Puppy comes on after the others: he arrives just in time to hear Townshead's remark at w 556.

w 534, B 484. We are hampered here by the lack of punctuation in H. $D^1$ and $D^2$ put a mark of exclamation after *Tom*; F puts a question-mark after *theise*, and finds some support in N. The agreement of $D^1$ and $D^2$ ought to be decisive, but the possibility of contamination makes it uncertain. I feel bound to follow $D^1 D^2$, but a good deal could be said in favour of *f*. Tom is Clod, and Dick, Townshead.

w 536, B 486. In view of the agreement of $D^1$ and γ, we are bound to treat H's *sprites* as a scribal vagary, though coincident normalization is of course possible. But the forms had probably not yet been differentiated in sense and are hardly more than variant spellings.

w 538, B 488. It is worth noticing that $D^1$ and H agree in the spelling *Fayeries* where γ has *Fayries*. At w 231 $D^1$ has *faiery*, β *faery*.

w 545, B 495. $D^1$ and N have a colon because the sense is carried on by the next speaker; but the speech is not itself incomplete. Actually the sense runs on from 544 to 545 in much the same way.

w 548, B 498. From *Gipsies* in this line to w 810 inclusive $D^2$ is absent, $D^1$ being retained in $D^b$.

w 550, B 500. The line can be read in several ways. The simplest interpretation would be, 'they are fine sprightly Gipsies', but this is inadmissible, for the adjective 'game' is not older than the eighteenth century. The sense ultimately depends on the punctuation. H has no points at all apart from a hyphen between *game* and *Gipsies*, which would allow us to punctuate after *they are*: to do so, however, would be to neglect the whole of the other evidence. $D^1$ has points of exclamation both after *Goodly* and *Gypsies*, but the former makes no sense and may be disregarded (there is no hyphen). F has only a comma after *Gipsies* (and no hyphen). N has a comma after *game* and a semicolon after *Gipsies*. Clearly, then, we must punctuate after *Gipsies*, and the exclamation-mark of $D^1$ is the most satisfactory point. But the absence of any mark after *game* (as in $D^1$ and F) still leaves the meaning ambiguous. We may choose between the hyphen in H and the comma in N. With a hyphen the sense is, 'they are fine Gipsies for hunting', and that, I suppose, is how Simpson took it since he followed H. The objection (not perhaps conclusive) is that *O.E.D.* records no instance of the attributive use of 'game' (except in the compound 'Game-Act') before the nineteenth century. But H's hyphen might be a mistake for a comma as in N. So pointed, the sense is, 'they are goodly game, are Gipsies', and this seems particularly appropriate after *flew at*. I have therefore followed N in the Windsor text, while leaving the Burley text ambiguous as in $D^1$.

w 554, B 504. As usual H has no stops. N reads *Gipsies though,* (comma), which, like Simpson, I take to give the only reasonable sense. But $D^1$ and F agree in placing the comma after *Gipsies*, and this also gives a possible, but surely not an acceptable, meaning. Either we must suppose a curious coincidence (or improbable contamination) or else an original error that the scribe of N, who was alert and given to conjecture, corrected.

w 556, B 506. β gives the speech to Townshead, $D^1$ to Clod. Either might be original, and there seems no reason to suspect revision. But the speech fits Townshead as the best-informed of the Clowns.

w 561, B 511. *They can* must be a slip in $D^1$. Later either *and* ($D^1$) or *or* (β) might be original. But there seems no reason for the disjunction. To 'cant' is to beg (primarily to whine like a beggar) and to 'mill' is to steal, and any master-Gipsy would be able to do both.

w 563, b 513. N is the only text with the intelligence to put the necessary comma after *No*. Simpson supplies a colon.

w 564, b 514. β's *theire* can hardly be correct, though Simpson keeps it, and *the* in D¹ is unexceptionable, if unnecessary.

w 568, b 518. We find here the first instance of revision in the antimasque, the addition of *and take out the wenches*, sc. to the dance. It is significant that it gives prominence to the country girls, who play an altogether more important part in the Windsor version.

w 570, b 519. *pouertie* is an 'Alleged name for a company of pipers' says *O.E.D.*, quoting the Book of St. Albans, 1486. The book went on being printed in various forms to the end of the sixteenth century and may well have been known to Jonson.

w 571, b 520. Either *bagpipe* (β) or *bag-pipes* (D¹) may be original. The latter is conformable to modern usage, and may therefore be due to the printer: the former was well recognized at the time.

Ticklefoot is the more important throughout, and it is to him that refers the *he* of what follows in b (cf. w 581). Cheeks maintains a rather shadowy existence; but the *pouertie* implies that there was more than one piper. Ticklefoot, observe, is not called a tabourer (except at w 810), we are merely told that he had a tabour. I think he had a pipe as well—not a bag-pipe of course. A well-known drawing represents Tarleton playing on the pipe and tabour at once (*Shakespeare's England*, ii. 258). This justifies the *Pipers* at w 599.

b 521–3. Most of the passage in b here suppressed in w was used later in w 588–91.

w 580–98, b 530–46. For the important revision here, which introduces the Wenches formally and by name, see Introduction, p. 33. It will be observed that the collection of the pipe-money, including Puppy's changing the odd nine pence for a single coin (b 539–40) is suppressed, though the incident is later on assumed at w 730 (b 679).

b 532. For *venter* D¹ has *venture*: see Introduction, p. 112.

w 581. The uncertainty about the number of musicians, already seen at b 520–1, crops up in aggravated form here, where the *minstrelles come* (in a speech only preserved in H) is followed by a reference to *him*, and we have the singular again at 587. There is no course but to recognize an error in H and correct it.

w 583–5. Again there is distinct recognition, in the punctuation of N and F, of the continuity of the speeches (cf. note on w 545).

w 584. H spells the name *Francis* throughout; all other texts vary between -*is* and -*es* (see w 601, 616, 648, 748). Only in the last instance do all texts agree. I follow the copy-text.

w 593. Either *mirthes* (H) or *mirth* (*f*) might, of course, be original. I prefer the latter because it is the form found at b 540 in D¹, albeit this is not parallel, and because all texts have *lucke sake* in the next line. But how much such spellings are a matter of chance is shown by the fact that at w 248 all texts except N and Con have *luckes sake*.

w 596. Clod's remark in b 545–6 is clear enough, since he has just appeared as gatherer of the pipe-money. But in w it was some time before that he assumed this office, and in revision β sought to make the meaning plain by adding *if I gather the money*. But the phrase was not happy, for he must be supposed to have already gathered it (cf. 592). There can, I think, be little doubt that an attempt was made to remedy this in further revision in *f* (or γ) by placing a stop after *chardge* (comma in N, semicolon in F) and omitting *if I*. It is true that this makes it a little obscure and it is just possible that the *I* was deleted by mistake. However, I leave it as it stands in N.

w 598. This is one of the additions made in w to give greater prominence to the Wenches. Originally the phrase *letts dance 'em down* was qualified by prefacing *if wee can* (H), but these words disappeared in *f* (or γ), and the improvement is so marked that we are bound to suppose it due to further revision.

w 599, B 547. D¹ has *Pipers* and since this is also found in N (in the headline: F omits it) it must be original. H's *Minstrell* is therefore due to interference by the scribe. He presumably preferred it to *Pipers* owing to doubt whether Ticklefoot had more than a tabour (see note on 571), but his choice of the singular is in any case wrong, and perhaps merely due to repetition from 587. The direction no doubt means that they here strike up for the dance.

w 600–1. This direction was first supplied in *f* (or γ), whether by the author in revision or by the scribe there is nothing to show (but see note on w 85–7).

w 602, B 548. H's etymological spelling *Contry*, though recorded as late as the sixteenth century, might be regarded as eccentric did it not recur at w 980 (H).

w 605, B 551. In D¹ *Doxes* is evidently a slip, like F's *Knells* in the next line.

w 607, B 553. Since we cannot suppose this otiose line to have been added in revision, we must conclude that it was accidentally omitted in D¹.

w 610, B 556. The bells are presumably those that *gingled* in the dance (w 537). We might think *Ptolomy* (D¹) preferable to *Ptolomęes* (β), but cf. w 1026 where all the texts have the possessive.

w 612, B 558. *But* (β) is so clearly preferable that we may suppose *And* (D¹) to have been caught up from the next line.

w 616–20, B 562–6. The significance of this list of names is discussed in the Introduction, pp. 21–5.

w 616, B 562. *Francis* is here apparently a man's name, whereas among the rustics it is a girl's. D¹ H spell it *-is*, NF *-es*, but no distinction can be intended (see note on w 584).

w 619, B 565. Either *Peg* (β) or *Meg* (D¹) might be original: both are, of course, familiar forms of Margaret. There can hardly have been any reason to substitute one for another in revision. But there is a *Meg* among the Wenches, and D¹ may perhaps have substituted her name here by mistake, as it appears to have mistakenly borrowed *Maudlin* from the list at B 690.

*Dary* is an unetymological spelling, recognized in the sixteenth century, and here used for the sake of the rime—an eye-rime at least. It appears to have been original since it is in NF as well as D¹. H's *Dairy* is therefore a normalization, which may possibly be supported by the ear-rime (Shakespeare rimes 'mane' with 'again' in *Venus and Adonis*, 271, 273).

w 627, B 573. The agreement of D¹ and *f* in *this* shows H's *that* to be an error.

w 633, B 579. Either *at time o' yeare* (β) or *i'th time o'th' yeare* (D¹) might be original. But the meaning seems to be 'at (or in) the right (or a certain) time of the year' (cf. 'in the season of the year' of the Lincolnshire song) and if so, *at* (β) rather than *i'th* (D¹) and *o'th'* (D¹) rather than *o'* (β) seem preferable. Of course *at time* may stand for *at'time*, i.e. *at the time*; and failure to perceive this may have led to the substitution of *i'th*.

w 635, B 581. There can, of course, be no doubt that *maunds* (D¹) is Jonson's own word, but there are also reasons to suspect that he may have altered it to *stalkes* in revision. The matter is discussed in the Introduction, p. 57.

w 638, B 584. For *Ho*, peculiar to H, see note on B 339; but if not a slip, it must be held an eccentric spelling.

w 640, B 586. The substitution of *her* for *it* in *f* (or γ) is so obvious an emendation that it may have been made even unconsciously. But being undoubtedly an improvement on an earlier reading, itself quite possible (Introd. p. 60), it is safer to treat it as probably due to revision.

*swallowe'it* D¹ and H have *swallow(e) it*: N and F omit the *it*. But N has the extraordinary form *swallow'e*. I conjecture that this stood in *f*, and was normalized to *swallow* in F, but really represented a form *swallow't* in γ. I therefore adopt a contracted form.

w 643, B 589. D¹ has *who's* where β reads *who standes*: the latter has the support of w 680. The former may, of course, be an error, but it is a perfectly sound reading in itself, and it will therefore be better to assume revision in β.

No text has a question-mark after *Cockerell*, but I think the intention must be the same as at w 661, where even H is emphatic in its punctuation. Here Simpson follows F.

w 644–5, B 590–1. β evidently retained the B-version, but a different couplet was substituted in γ or *f*. It was presumably in making the substitution that the speaker's name got lost, but there is no reason to suppose that any alteration was intended.

B 590. Either with (D¹) or without (H) *it* the line might be original, but the metre seems more likely with it.

w 646, B 592. D¹ alone reads *if he must be a Gypsie*. I am completely at a loss to explain Simpson's introduction of *must* into the text of H, for so far as I can see it makes no sense whatever. We find *if they be Gipsies* used similarly at w 555, and *if shee be a Meg* (whatever that may mean) at w 662. At the same time the insertion of *must* can hardly have been accidental: it may have originated in some misunderstood alteration in α.

w 647, B 593. See Additional Notes on p. 231.

w 648, B 594. There are no stops in either H or N in the earlier part of the line, and the exact meaning may have been left ambiguous in the original. Thus the semicolon after *now* in D¹ and the comma after *Frances* in F probably represent no more than the interpretations of the two compositors. Neither was remarkable for intelligence, and the difference between their interpretations is slight. I have allowed F to decide the punctuation of w, while following the copy-text in B.

w 651, B 597. There is no difference of sense between *escapes* (D¹) and *scapes* (β)— both mean amorous adventures—and either might be original. But metrically *scapes* is awkward enough to warrant its rejection.

w 655, B 601. Here, and again at w 671, *f* (or at any rate F) substitutes the First for the Fourth Gipsy. This must, of course, be wrong, for the First Gipsy is the Captain and is always called so. But a study of N shows how easily, in some hands, a '4' could be mistaken for a '1'.

D¹ has *in Christmas will*, β *will in Christmas*, and either might be original. Accidental inversion in either text is possible; but while the order in D¹ is quite possible, that in β is metrically so much easier that we are bound to admit the possibility of revision (cf. w 211).

w 656, B 602. 'Post and pair' is the name of a card game, and H's 'at post and at paire', in any case condemned by the agreement of D¹ and *f*, is therefore an error.

w 657, B 603. The phrase 'to hit the nail on the head' was current a century before Jonson, and the reading of D¹ appears to be a humorous adaptation of it, since it is of hobnails that the talk is. The reading of β drops the allusion but emphasizes the idea of hitting aright. The change might be a scribe's, but it might also have occurred to Jonson that the expression in D¹ was a little far-fetched. The possibility of revision should therefore be recognized.

w 673, b 619. Either *f* or *γ* made two alterations in this line, reading *a little* for *little* and *thei'le* for *they*. Nothing can be said in favour of the first, and this makes it unlikely that any authority attaches to the second, in spite of its superficial plausibility—*they doe it* rightly indicates habitual behaviour. It is unnecessary to see revision.

Since it would be far-fetched to suppose that the D¹ translated *non vpstante* as *not withstanding*, we must suppose that Jonson introduced the Latin phrase (β) in revision. The perversion is, of course, deliberate.

w 674, b 620. It is, of course, possible that in D¹ the accidental loss of a speaker's name led to the erroneous fusion of two speeches. Supposing, however, D¹ to be original, the division would be an obvious improvement to make, and on the evidence we are bound to assume revision in β.

w 677, b 623. D¹ has the normal spelling *trying*, H has *tryeing*. Probably β had *trieing*; for N and F both have the extraordinary error *tri'mge*, clearly a graphic error in *f* for *tri'inge* in *γ*.

w 678, b 624. Concerning the presumed error in β here see Introduction, p. 56.

w 679, b 625. (*told her*) *worse* in D¹ is not necessarily wrong, but in the context *a worse* (β) is so much more natural that I think we may assume an accidental omission. It seems quite unnecessary to suppose revision.

w 682, b 628. No text has a stop after *hand* and there is no need to supply one. But the remark is capable of two meanings, and perhaps both are implied. The obvious sense (without stop) is, 'I give you my word not to be angry'. But it may also be read to mean, 'here is my hand (for you to read), and I will not be angry (whatever you find in it)'. This would properly require a comma at least after *hand*. There is also, of course, an antithesis between (Towns)head and hand.

w 683, b 629. D¹ gives the couplet to the Second Gipsy, β to the Third. Either may be original, and since there seems no telling which, I follow β as the generally more reliable text.

w 685, b 631. Concerning the error *and* for *an't* in H see Introduction, p. 61.

w 690, b 636. Concerning the muddle over the speakers here and two lines below see Introduction, p. 55.

w 691, b 637. No doubt *with* (D¹) is a possible reading, and is probably original, the primary sense of *pluck* being 'snatch'. But *at* (NF) seems so much more idiomatic that one would gladly accept it as an author's revision in either *γ* or *f*, and as such I have treated it.

w 698–9, b 644–5. See Additional Notes on p. 231.

b 705, b 651. Here, and again at w 710, F has the curious contraction *y'em*. But the cases are not parallel. In the first *y'em* is a further contraction of *ye 'em*, as in H, and probably occurred in *γ* or *f*, for N, seeking to restore a more intelligible form, hit on the aberrant *y$^w$ 'em*. In the second *y'em* is an error, for the original reading was not *ye 'hem* (as in 705) but *'hem*: and *y'em* is a misunderstanding of *y$^{em}$* (i.e. *them*) as in N.

w 710–11, b 656–7. *for me*, i.e. for all I care. H places the words after *firste* instead of at the end of the speech. This may be thought a stylistic improvement, and was presumably so intended by the scribe. It cannot be a revision of the author's since it occurs in only one text.

w 711, b 657. The *h* of *hower* was silent, as shown by the *an* in all texts—it always was in English—and there is no point in the spelling *owre* (N), *'owre* (F). Probably the *h* was accidentally dropped in *f* (or γ) and the compositor added the apostrophe for distinction's sake.

w 712, b 658. Unless there was accidental omission in D¹, *man* must obviously have been added in revision in β, and it has been so treated. But that omission is not impossible is shown from the absence of *ha* in the next line.

w 716, b 662. *Tom* is in D¹ only, but since we cannot suppose that it was added in that text and still less that it was removed in revision, its absence from β must be accidental (cf. w 728).

w 717, b 663. The apparently meaningless *with child with* in *f* is presumably due to accidental repetition.

w 721–2, b 667–8. The spelling *lose . . . lose* in the two printed texts (D¹, F) is a good example of their tendency to modernize (as again at w 765). Presumably the original spelling was *loose*, a form that persisted till the eighteenth century. Since the vowel-sounds in 'lose' and 'loose' had been assimilated, the spelling naturally tended to follow suit.

w 722, b 668. In place of *those* H has *them*, which might be thought fitting in rustic speech, and as such may have been introduced by the scribe. Alternatively, if *them* was original, D¹ and *f* (or γ) may have normalized it independently. As at w 536 I feel bound to follow the evidence, though with some hesitation.

w 724, b 670–3. The reason for the cutting in β is not very clear, but accidental omission seems unlikely. That the reviser was on the alert is shown by the addition in the next line.

b 672. The uncertain punctuation in D¹ leaves the construction ambiguous.

w 726. We cannot, of course, be certain whether *whimpering* (H) or *whining* (*f*) was original in the revision, but the former seems the more individual word, and the latter may be due to the accidental loss of medial letters. Further revision may be ruled out.

w 728, b 677. Since there can have been no possible reason for the omission of the words *of my Mothers* (D¹) we are bound to believe that the loss in β was accidental. Simpson restored them (though he did not restore *Tom* at w 717).

w 735, b 684. Here *Masters* is absent from H only; clearly an accidental omission, though Simpson did not restore it. The punctuation of D¹ is of course possible but improbable.

w 736, b 685. For *money*, added in revision in γ or *f*, see Introduction, p. 43. The omission of Townshead's reply (D¹), presumably intentional, had already occurred in β.

w 737. The addition of *daintye* (not in either D¹ or H) is a revisional touch in γ or *f*.

w 741–3, b 690–2. The passage was of course recast in β and again slightly altered in γ or *f* (Introd. p. 43). But when the phrase *inchanted at Oxford* was inserted, the earlier *inchanted* was left standing by what I assume to have been an oversight: I therefore read *a nutmeg*. For the final version N and F are our only authorities, and they both put a comma after *for mee*; I have felt bound to follow them, though I suspect that it should come after *Oxford*.

b 690. In the Windsor version the Wench in question is called *Meg*, and it is quite clear from b 740–1 and b 607–8 that she was *Meg* at Burley too. Here, however, D¹ calls her *Maudlin*, a name borrowed from b 566, apparently through some confusion. See Introduction, p. 24.

w 747. I feel bound to admit *f*'s *Turners* as possibly original, though I have no doubt myself that it is a 'normalization' of H's more distinctive *Turnups*. Revision is, I imagine, out of the question.

w 748–50. Here is more revision in γ or f. When the words *beside her maidenhead* were added, the *and* was omitted in the line before, and naturally Frances's assenting *I* in the line after. The insertion, of course, alludes to her fortune at w 650–1.

w 751–2, B 699–700. *handkercheife* The scribe of H accidentally wrote his *-es* contraction (often, as here, indistinctly formed) in place of *-e*.

w 755, B 703. The *ballad* of D¹ has been altered to *ballet*, as almost certainly a compositor's spelling (Introd. p. 111).

w 757, B 705. It would, of course, be possible to explain the *ha's* in β (F *h'as*) as a contraction (i.e. 'Ticklefoot, he has'), but the reading of D¹ is simpler and more natural, and an apostrophe in *has*, where no contraction is intended, is quite common both in manuscript and print.

w 760, B 708. *my fine (gloues*: β) is, I think, a nice revisional touch for *a pair of* (D¹).

w 762, B 710. In D¹ the gross error *left* is of course a graphic perversion of *lost*.

w 763, B 711. *gone* (D¹) may, of course, have been accidentally lost in β, but it is superfluous, and its absence sufficient of an improvement to make revision possible.

w 771, B 719. *oth'r* (D¹) seems a strange form for a compositor to introduce even by a slip, but if original and intended as a contraction, it is erroneous, and in either case must be corrected.

w 772, B 720. F has a question-mark after *fit*, an error presumably for one of exclamation.

w 777, B 725. H's omission of *here* is obviously accidental; Simpson restores it.

w 787–8, B 735–6. The demands of Skeltonical riming have rather disguised the conjurer's formula *hey pass*.

w 791. Since the scribe omitted the word there is no means of telling whether H would have agreed with D¹ in *you* or with *f* in *yee*, but since it is my practice to supplement H by N, I here print *yee* (Introd. p. 111). That the scribe of N first wrote *you*, erased the *ou*, and interlined *ee*, can only be a coincidence.

w 806, B 754. Either *here* (D¹) or *here's* (β) might be original, but the latter is obviously the more likely (cf. w 790).

B 759–912. These lines are not in D¹ owing to the loss of four leaves from our only copy of Dᵃ. Exactly what these leaves included is of course conjectural—though certainly less than the corresponding text of β—and the details unknown. The matter is discussed in the Introduction, pp. 36–8. I have printed a conjectural reconstruction, using as copy-text D², which becomes available again at this point (w 811).

w 815, B 763. See Additional Notes on p. 231.

w 829–32, B 777–80. Although the reason for the omission of this passage in *f* is less clear than, and certainly different from, that which prompted the omission of two earlier passages (w 573–81 and 664–70), it warrants the conclusion that it was probably also in *f* rather than in γ that those passages were suppressed.

w 833, B 781. The omission of *and* in D² is, of course, a proved error.

w 834, B 782. The punctuation of D² is the more plausible, and like Simpson I have accepted it: but that of F, with the stop after *Gypsies*, is also possible, if we take *this* as equivalent to 'this is', as we perfectly well may. But F's authority here is weakened by its treating the clause as interrogative (with a question-mark after *Drinckebragatan*), being misled apparently by the following *aske him*.

w 835, B 783. In *f* the words *Aske him* stand as a line by themselves, and so do *the Diuells-Arse* at w 847–8. In the latter case the words might be supposed to have been mistaken for some sort of heading, but no such explanation will fit here. We may suppose that in γ the words happened to be on a line by themselves, and that though correctly rendered in D², the arrangement was for some reason mistaken in *f*. In H *the Deuills Arse* does happen to be a separate line.

The agreement of H and *f* shows the *hath* of D² to be an individual error.

The substitution of *his* for *a* in *f* may, of course, be an error or conjecture, but since it does seem to be preferable the possibility of revision must be recognized, especially in view of a clear case of revision in the next line.

w 835–6, B 783–4. Either *as* (H) or *as of* (γ) might be original, and intrinsically there is nothing to choose between them, but the latter is perhaps preferable if *f*'s addition is to be accommodated, and omission may be more likely than insertion.

w 837, B 785. The Patrico's reply and Townshead's remark at w 845 prove that here γ is in error in reading *Gipsies*.

w 838, B 786. There was evidently some confusion here that went back at least as far as β. We may assume that the arrangement in D² is correct. But the speaker's name was probably misplaced in the original: it is omitted in *f*, and H tacks w 839 onto the end of Puppy's speech, whereas in N it is written as a sort of heading.

w 839, B 787. Either *flagonfleakean* (H) or *flagonfeakian* (γ) might be original (since the meaning of the second element of the compound is unknown) but the former looks as though it might be due to an accidental repetition of the *l* (just as we get an erroneous duplication of *n* in D² in the next line but one).

w 841, B 789. In D² *Ninglington* is an obvious corruption, for the name is formed from the verb 'niggle', i.e. 'to have to do with a woman carnally' (*O.E.D.*), just as *Filchington* is formed from 'filch'.

w 846, B 794. Either *aske you* (H) or *aske on you* (γ) might be original, but here omission seems much more likely than insertion.

w 848, B 796. See note on *aske him* at w 835.

w 852, B 800. The omission of *it* is an obvious error in H.

w 854, B 802. For the spelling *height* see note on w 339.

w 857, B 805. The spelling *jeast*, found in the two printed texts, is peculiar to the sixteenth and seventeenth centuries. Here it is probably due to the compositor's desire for an eye-rime.

w 858, B 806. The parentheses, found only in H, serve to make it immediately clear that *since* is temporal, not causal.

w 862, B 810. There can have been no reason to suppress this line; its omission in γ must have been accidental.

w 864, B 812. For *sing't* (H) γ has *sing*: an evident error.

w 865–6. The absence of these lines in γ might, of course, be accidental. But there is some reason to suppose that they were inserted in revision (Introd. p. 45). Revision in β itself (as distinct from β') would of course be anomalous; but if the lines were added in α' they may have been overlooked in the first instance by the scribe of β and only later added in the margin, and this may have led to their being again overlooked by the scribe of γ. The probability is that they were not in α, and therefore not in the lost D¹.

w 872, B 817. For *theise* (H) γ has *those*; probably a mere slip.

w 873–4, B 818–19. By a grotesque error γ substituted *fart* for *farce*, and since this destroyed the rime, it proceeded to write the two lines as one (Introd. p. 66).

## Notes

w 875, B 820. Who the singer is remains uncertain. We should expect him to be the Jackman, and since this name is never used in the text, it is possible that it is he whom the Patrico calls his *clarcke* (w 863). Indeed, a jackman or jarkman would need to be something of a clerk (see note on w 53).

w 877, B 822. Either *him into* (H) or *him once into* (γ) might be original, but omission is perhaps more likely than insertion, and revision is improbable.

w 880–1, B 825–6. We must assume that in these lines H preserved the reading of the Burley version (i.e. of the lost D¹). For the purely parenthetic *he came thither coach't* revision in γ substituted the syntactical *for comminge there coacht*, and in the second line altered the colourless *made* to the more forceful *caus'd*.

w 884, B 829. No text has any relevant punctuation, but it seems more natural to connect *so* with *sate him downe* than with *recouer'd*, and I have therefore inserted a comma in w (cf. note on w 209).

*vnto* (γ) seems metrically more probable than *to* (H), but either might be original.

w 886, B 831. *Promooter* i.e. an informer. *O.E.D.* notes that the form with -*oo*- was confined to this sense, and on the strength of it I have thought justified for substituting γ's spelling in w.

I have also preferred γ's *the* to H's *his*, if only to avoid the frequent repetition of the pronoun: either might be original.

w 890, B 835. H's *spies* is obviously a slip for *spied* (γ *spy'd*), though Simpson allows it to stand.

w 899, B 844. The metre makes H's *neuer had* probable: γ had the inversion *had neuer*, but N reverted to H's order, perhaps unconsciously. On the other hand, *had never* (D²F) might be original, altered independently in H and N to the metrically smoother reading. The possibility must, I think, be allowed.

w 908, B 853. *The next* (H) may, no doubt, be original, but on metrical grounds *The very next* (γ) seems much more likely.

D² has *a Major*. The *a* is necessarily an error, and the spelling *Major* eccentric, though not in fact uncommon. *O.E.D.* seems to imply that it was a distinct (etymological) form, but if so, it is here an error.

w 912, B 857. I think the co-ordinate clause in the next line implies a verb in this; I therefore supply *came* as in w 904.

w 915, B 860. For *to choake him* (H) γ substituted *to haue choak't him* (N), thereby improving the sequence of tenses at the cost of destroying the rime (Introd. p. 67).

w 920, B 865. The unnecessary insertion in γ of *a* before *Midwife* makes a metrically awkward line, which there is no need to suppose original. The dishes usually of course have the article; but 'a pasty of midwife' is parallel, not with 'the chine of a letcher' (w 916) but rather with 'a deputy tart' (w 931).

w 921, B 866. H's spelling *could* for *cold* (γ) is ambiguous and, though current in the sixteenth and seventeenth centuries, eccentric, and there seems no need to keep it.

w 923, B 868. The substitution in γ of *And* for *Was* at the beginning of this line may have been due either to failure to recognize that the clause was relative, or to a desire to avoid the close repetition of *was*, or both. But the alteration perverts the sense.
For *coffind* see Additional Notes on p. 232.

w 925, B 870. From the alteration made by the scribe in H we may infer an original spelling *trust* for *truss'd*, and for this *thrust* as in γ, would be a very likely substitute, especially if the scribe recalled w 909.

w 938, B 883. The substitution in H of *blewe* for *flirted* is discussed in the Introduction, pp. 67–8.

w 940–51. These three stanzas, found only in γ, must be supposed to have been lacking in the lost D¹ as well as in H.

w 942. *sent*. The unetymological *c* of the modern spelling appears only in D², cf. w 490.

N's reading *hee lefte⸗behinde* is necessarily unoriginal, though a distinct improvement. Being found in only one text, it cannot be due to revision.

w 955. I accept *vnderstand*, the reading of γ, in preference to H's *vnderstood*: the present is obviously more natural than the past. It has, indeed, been suggested (Simpson, p. 546) that when Puppy speaks of *a Prelate of the order* he is harking back to his earlier phrase *What sort or order of Gypsie* (w 837)—this idea was originally Cole's (p. 23)—and that he uses the past tense as referring to a particular occasion. But nothing was then said about the Patrico being a *Prelate*. That comes from a much earlier passage (w 118–20) where he calls himself the *mouth of your order, As Priest of the game And Prelate of the same*. This was long before the Clowns were present, and Puppy must therefore be referring to what he knows, not to what he then learned. It follows that *vnderstood* can only be a slip in H.

w 957. *prentice Sir?* This is the punctuation of D² and F, and seems reasonable. There is none in H or N, and it would obviously be possible to put the question-mark after *prentice*. On the other hand, at w 963, where D² has a colon and F a semicolon after *Sir*, N has a full point, and only H is without punctuation.

w 963. Either *me* (H) or *vs* (γ) might be original, but I think the latter is more likely. The Gipsies came upon the yokels as a body, and *me* might easily be substituted in a context in which Clod is speaking particularly about himself.

w 967. Again the punctuation is ambiguous. D² and F connect *so you . . . Captaine* with what precedes, reasonably enough: H has no stops, N only commas.

w 972. A closing parenthesis after *diett* in H and N (which has a comma as well) shows that the whole phrase *for my . . . diett* was meant to be parenthetic. The printed texts have commas.

w 975. A question of interpretation arises here. The texts are in substantial agreement, with a capital *A*, except that H has no point before it, whereas the others have a colon or semicolon. Simpson, without citing variants, prints a full stop, apparently taking *auouch* in the sense of 'allow'. This is not the usual meaning, though some senses come near it. I cannot doubt that the real meaning is 'I will maintain that a man' &c. It is common enough to find an indirect statement beginning with a capital and preceded by a heavy stop.

w 976. In place of *purse* (H) γ has *pocket* and either might be original. If *purse* is correct, *pocket* may be due to assimilation with w 975 and 979, and I therefore follow H. There is nothing to suggest that it was altered as part of the revision that follows.

w 978–82. The passage presumably originated in β, and revision was carried out in two stages, in γ and *f*. The final amalgamation of the first two speeches was a clear improvement: the inclusion of the third followed, if the speaker were not to be changed.

w 983. In the course of the final revision this speech (which was not altered) lost its prefix, but the intention that it should remain a separate speech is quite clear both in N and F. There seems no reason to suppose that the speaker was meant to be changed.

w 993. Either *brother* (γ) or *a brother* (H) might be original, but the latter seems preferable, and H is in general the better authority.

w 996. For *bene-bowsy* see note on w 52.

w 1005. The reading of D², *left sullen*, is rather attractive, but it would be rash to assume omission independently in H and *f*. We find D² tinkering at B 912.

w 1028–34. There is no principal verb in these lines: perhaps they depend loosely on *Ile shewe ye* in 1025. I have therefore placed a semicolon only at 1027, where D² has a full stop (*f* a comma).

w 1039. The error *theire* (*f*) for *your* presumably originated in the ambiguous use of the contraction *y*ʳ; but *and* in place of *for* in the next line was mere carelessness.

w 1040. See Additional Notes on p. 232.

w 1044. On the omission of *a* in D² see Introduction, p. 68.

w 1062–4. The continuity of grammatical construction in these speeches was perhaps recognized. F puts a comma after 1063: N to all three lines—but then it often ends a speech so. It is also noticeable that H has no capitals to 1063 and 1064, though it regularly begins speeches with them hereabouts. D² accidentally reverses the prefixes on 1063 and 1064.

w 1065, B 887. See Additional Notes on p. 232.

w 1067. In *f* we have *were* in place of *are*, and the subjunctive is perhaps more natural after *I'ld*. The change may have been made unconsciously: it is hardly likely to be due to deliberate revision.

w 1075, B 896. β presumably read *I can for I will* as in H: γ inserted the parentheses: D² prefixed *For*, by way of emendation apparently. I accept the conjecture, though insufficient by itself, and to make sense change ²*for* to *and*. This makes at least a possible reading; but *an'* would do as well as *and*. Simpson was content to leave H alone, but I do not know how he interpreted the line.

B 897. The line is in all the extant texts, but must obviously have been omitted at Belvoir and Windsor.

w 1082, B 904. D² has *And* in place of *With*, an indifferent variant, but of course unoriginal.

B 908 ff. This passage, with its specific praise of Buckingham (*he we call chiefe*), can only have been spoken at Burley. Its extent is not very clearly defined, but there is no convenient break down to 926. The Belvoir alternative (B 908¹⁻¹²) is preserved in some form in all texts, except of course D¹, which becomes available again at 913. It is, as we know, at 925 that this Belvoir revision joins up again with the Burley original, and we must conclude that the twelve lines of the revision replaced seventeen (908–24) of the original. At Windsor neither the Burley nor the Belvoir version can have been spoken; and we are left to assume that the whole nineteen lines of the original (908–26) were simply omitted. This means that neither at Belvoir nor at Windsor was the call for *A hall* at w 1086 led up to by the admonition of B 919, but this was of no consequence (Introd. pp. 28, 34–5).

B 909. D² has *tell* in place of *tell't*, an equally possible reading, though of course unoriginal.

B 911. D² omits *As*, another possible but unoriginal reading.

B 912. D² has *his Beere and his Biefe* in place of *his bread, beare, and beife* (H): an evidently deliberate alteration, which gives a slightly smoother line, but effects no material improvement: it cannot, of course, be due to the author.

B 913. The normalization *since* in *f* destroys the rime.

B 908⁷. Either *Hath* (H) or *Has* (γ) may be original: in an indifferent case H takes precedence.

The very imperfect rime requires *hether* rather than *hither*: the latter is a normalization of the printed texts.

B 923–4, 908¹¹⁻¹². It seems so obvious that here the Belvoir version is original and the Burley an adaptation, that we are bound to conclude that the Belvoir alternatives were written concurrently with the original text, as is indeed inherently probable (Introd. p. 28).

B 926. *Mas* 'A vulgar or jocular shortening of *master*, usually followed by a proper name or official title.' Of such use *O.E.D.* quotes examples from 1575 to 1625; but it appears not to have been familiar to the scribes, for D¹ corrupted it to *May-* and H left it out altogether.

w 1087, B 928. This is evidently a direction for the entrance of the gentlemen masquers in their own shape, having shed their Gipsy disguise. The Patrico, no doubt a professional actor, does not change, though he speaks of doing so at w 1094–9. Nothing is said of the Jackman, but he reappears as such at w 1190.

w 1098. The two manuscripts guarantee *of*; the printed texts normalize (Introd. p. 113).

w 1099. The proper construction after 'come off', in the sense to get rid of, is doubtful, and either *By* (H) or *With* (γ) may be original; but the former is to be preferred, if only because of the *with* in the previous line.

w 1110. D² has *heart* for *art*, presumably by repetition from 1108.

w 1119. Through a misunderstanding γ has *Clow.* (i.e. Clown) in place of *Clo.* (i.e. Clod) as in H: D² repeats the error at 1124.

w 1122. *Soue'raigne* The exact form of the word varies a good deal, and the contraction, in any case purely graphic, is not found in H. I have made the spelling consistent throughout. Jonson has *sou'raignes* in *Sejanus*, II. 278, but *soueraigntie* at II. 359.

w 1123. Simpson inserts *so* after *And*. He apparently assumed that 1122–3 both referred to the blessing of the King's senses, and that the meaning of the lines (if meaning it can be called) was 'wish away offences by blessing his senses'. But I think he is here mistaken: only 1122 refers to the blessing of the senses; 1123 refers to the blessing *from all offences* that follows. The clowns are invited to join in the *bob* (the last line) of the five stanzas that follow, and also in the four lines w 1182–5. The text is perfectly correct as it stands.

w 1128. γ has the speaker's prefix, though not as a separate line. H takes it as implied in 1126.

w 1129 ff. It was apparently in γ that the five stanzas of the blessing were first numbered. D² carries on the numbering to the supplementary lines 1182–9, which it prints as a single stanza.

w 1130. H's *torninge*, where γ has the normal *turning*, is no doubt for the sake of the rime; but in view of the Latin 'tornare' it may possibly be original.

w 1133–6. In H we get two parallel constructions: in the first the relative clause *And* [who] *is . . . common* is coordinate with the adjectival phrase *true to no man*; in the second the relative clause *and that . . . britches* is coordinate with the adjective *rampant*. In both cases γ appears to have misunderstood or disapproved of the construction: in the first it altered *And* to *Which*, in the second *that* to *the*. It is difficult to account for the apparent alteration in N: we can hardly suppose that *Which* was introduced into three texts independently (there is a similar instance at 1284). *A smock rampant* is, of course, a masterful woman.

w 1146. The phrase occurs in 1 *Henry IV*, III. ii. 75, 'He was but as the cuckoo is in June, Heard, not regarded', but there is no need to suppose that Jonson recalled it.

w 1149–50. On these 'typical Jonsonian lines', as Simpson calls them, accidentally omitted in H, see Introduction, pp. 45–6. The only authority is γ, and only D² has the correct reading *Meant*.

w 1154. Either *Or* (γ) or *And* (H) might be original: it makes no difference. I follow H.

w 1156. By a slip H has *them* for *then*.

w 1162. Simpson records that the very unreliable Dobell manuscript (Introd. p. 10) reads *A fishmonger and his dwelling*. He also notes that Gifford, evidently seeking to make the line normal, printed *From a fishmonger's stale dwelling*. But the line is structurally anomalous, intruding itself in the final couplet of the stanza, and there is no reason to suppose that metrically it was meant to conform.

w 1166. No doubt *From* is not strictly necessary to the line and may have been originally absent, as in H. Still the passage reads more naturally with it.

w 1169. By a slip H has *an* for *and*.

w 1175. Either *of* (H) or *in* (γ) might be original: there is really nothing to choose, and I follow H. I do not understand how Simpson came to substitute *in*, unless for the sake of variety. It might perhaps be argued that H is more likely to have assimilated the phrase to that in the previous line than γ is to have varied it. But it might also be argued, if we care to press the strict logic of the phrase, that the disease *of* the dog would trouble no man so long as it remained *in* the dog.

w 1177. Either *Or* (γ) or *From* (H) might be original, but the balance seems better with *Or*.

w 1192, B 932. *yet* is evidently what Jonson wrote: *but* would have avoided an unpleasant jingle (cf. B 21).

w 1193, B 933. O.E.D. notes that *sodaine* (H) is by far the commonest spelling in the First Folio of Shakespeare: it may be original here in spite of the other texts.

w 1205, B 945. The variants are discussed in the Introduction, p. 62. If H's reading *As in you* is original, the resemblance between D¹, *As in your*, and γ, *As if your*, must be accidental. The reading of D¹, though senseless, could arise very easily through writing *your forme* under the influence of *your figure* just above. That of γ might easily come about through a scribe who misunderstood *As* [if] *in you* substituting *As if your*. (This seems the most likely explanation.) Or else (not to multiply hypothetical manuscripts) γ may have made the same error as D¹, and D² and *f* may have independently emended it in the same way. (This is more far-fetched.) Or, thirdly, we might suppose that D¹ reproduces an original error in α, which also survived in β, and that H on the one hand and γ on the other emended it in the only two possible ways, the one presumably correct, the other mistaken. (But it is doubtful whether the scribe of H had the ability to do this: emendation was not his strong point.)

w 1213, B 953. D¹ and D² (alone) do not capitalize *Grace*, but I suppose that an allusion to the Gratiae or Charites must be intended.

w 1218, B 958. H's *summers* is, I think, too awkward to be original.

w 1219, B 959. D¹ has *looke* for *lookes*, an evident slip, perhaps through assimilation with w 1216.

w 1223, B 963. See Additional Notes on p. 232.

w 1228, B 968. In D¹ *aëry* looks like an original spelling, though three syllables are not metrically admissible: perhaps it was only intended to indicate length. H's *ayerie* (a form also implied by *ay'ry* in γ) is a hybrid and has been altered to *ayrie* (Introd. p. 10, note 2). (Cf. *Troilus and Cressida*, l. iii. 144, Q *ayrie*, F *ayery*.)

W 1231, B 971. D¹ accidentally omits the number of the song both here and at W 1253.

W 1241, B 981. The verse requires the full form *he is* as in D¹ and H. This was recognized by the scribe of N, when having written *hees* (in obedience to his copy) he altered the *s* to *i* and added another *s*. The contracted form in γ shows, of course, that scribal tendency was not always towards expansion.

The original reading *the estate* (D¹ H) was altered in γ to *all the state*, apparently to avoid the rare use of *estate* in the sense of state or kingdom. Whether it was Jonson himself who made the alteration is of course uncertain, but the possibility of revision must be admitted.

W 1243, B 983. This is the most difficult line in the masque, at least so far as punctuation is concerned. The exact form it takes (including italics) in the several texts is as follows:

D¹ The Muses, Arts, the Schooles, Commerce, our Honours, Lawes,
H The *muses arts* yᵉ *schooles commerce* oʳ *honors Lawes*
D² The *Muses* Arts, the *Schooles* commerce, our *Honours* lawes,
N yᵉ *Muses* Arts, yᵉ *Schooles*, comerce, oʳ honoʳˢ, lawes,
F The *Muses* Arts, the *Schooles* commerce, our honoures lawes,

There are obviously two ways in which the line can be read, indicated most clearly in D¹ and D² respectively. The first presents a series of single items; in the second they are grouped into pairs, *Muses*, *Schooles*, and *Honours* being possessives, and *the Schooles commerce* meaning the business or intellectual intercourse of the schools. (In either case *commerce* would probably be accented on the second syllable, a pronunciation current down to the eighteenth century.) H seems at first sight to support D², but this is only because of its always heavy and often eccentric use of italic script; in fact its testimony is neutral. N clearly inclines to D¹, whereas F supports D² in a suspiciously exact manner (Introd. pp. 15–16). The interpretation put upon the line in D² is certainly ingenious, but the only internal argument in its favour, beyond the disposition of articles and pronoun, is the tautology of *Muses* and *Arts* if taken separately. Against it is the isolated position in which *vertues* is left in the next line, the rather strained meaning assigned to *commerce*, and the fact that in English an alexandrine usually has a pause after the third accent. I conclude that the interpretation offered by D¹ (supported in the main by N) is probably correct. It would, of course, be possible to take *Muses* and *Arts* together and the rest separately, as in N, and this is, in fact, the solution adopted by Simpson.

W 1245–52, B 985–92. All texts except H (which has no punctuation at all) to some extent recognize the continuity of these lines. All but N put a full stop after W 1248, but there seems to be no ground for the distinction. For some reason that I do not fathom, Simpson puts full stops after W 1249 and W 1251, commas elsewhere.

W 1263–4, B 1003–4. All texts agree in making one line of these, and so it must have stood in α, but the need of a rime to *men* (W 1265) shows that *then* must have been intended to end a line.

W 1266, B 1006. The variant here is discussed in the Introduction, p. 59. The agreement of D¹ and H guarantees the originality of *make*, and proves γ's *makes* to be an error. N restores *make* (Introd. p. 65), which is curious, seeing that either reading is possible, and *makes* perhaps the more obvious—at least Simpson presumably thought so when he chose it in preference to that of H.

W 1281. Either *Courtes* (H) or *Court* (γ) might be original, but *Courtes* seems to me preferable, and the change to *Court* is certainly the more likely.

# Notes

w 1282. In place of H's *barbor* (both here and at 1290) γ has *Barber*, a spelling said in *O.E.D.* to be rare before 1700: the usual spelling was 'barbour'.

w 1284. Either *was* (H) or *is* (γ) might be original, but *was* seems the more logical and *is* may have been attracted to the present in the next line. Again (cf. w 1134) I am unable to account for the alteration in N. The scribe originally wrote *was* with two letters following, then erased these two letters and interlined *is* with a caret under the *was*.

w 1286. The omission of *a* must be a mere slip in γ, since the next line shows that *Gypsies* cannot be plural.

w 1289. Either *poesie* (H) or *poetry* (γ) might be original. It might be thought that the former was rather too poetic for the style of the Epilogue, but I am not sure how far this would have been felt at the time, and if it was, it may have been intended humorously: *poesie* is perhaps more suitable for a quasi-personification.

w 1291. The *Finis* is found only in the two printed texts: doubtless the compositors were responsible.

## ADDITIONAL NOTES

w 71, B 78. *Barnabee*  I suppose the King's game-keeper.

w 73, B 80. Taken in conjunction with the next line it is evident that *Geruice* was the name of one of the Lords who took, or was expected to take, the part of a Gipsy. Since the identity of the Fifth Gipsy is unknown (Introd., p. 72), we cannot tell whether he actually appeared or not.

w 246–7, B 252–3. There is no punctuation in H. Simpson puts a comma after *alreadie* and a full stop after *art*, evidently because the manuscript has a capital to the following *Heres*. This gives, of course, a possible interpretation, though to my mind a less likely one. But capitalization in H is erratic, and I see no reason to doubt the punctuation of D¹, though it is true that F has a semicolon after *art*. N has only commas.

w 253, B 259. There is little to choose between *and were* (β) and *but were* (D¹). One might suppose that the change from the more emphatic *but* to the less emphatic *and* was more likely than the reverse: on the other hand *but* may have been introduced to avoid the succession of *and*'s in this line and the next. I follow β as on the whole the more reliable text: moreover it is here supported by Con.

B 349. The punctuation of D¹, linking this line with what follows, gives of course a possible sense; but this seems so much the less likely that we are justified in supposing the lack of a stop to be an error.

w 647, B 593. *divine* i.e. divining, prescient, prophetic. The only quotation for this Latinism in *O.E.D.* is from Milton (*Paradise Lost*, ix. 845), 'Yet oft his heart, divine of something ill, Misgave him'.

w 698–9, B 644–5. Simpson puts a colon after *roome* and no stop after *Here*. H as usual has no stops; N a comma after *roome* only; F commas in both places. But in this doubtful case D¹ seems our only clear guide.

w 815, B 763. *mell's*  The apostrophe, which is in all texts but D², is evidently original. It presumably indicates, however clumsily, that the word was taken to be a contraction of 'meddles'. In fact 'mell' and 'meddle' are distinct words in English, derived from variant forms in Old French.

w 923, B 868. *coffind* So Webster, *The White Devil* (1612), IV. ii. 19–21: 'you speake as if a man Should know what foule is coffind in a bak't meate Afore you cut it up.'

w 1040. In H *poses* (γ *Posies*) is an unetymological spelling adopted for the sake of the rime.

w 1065, B 887. It will be noticed that there is nothing in what precedes in the Windsor version to suggest the idea of *chirpe*, which goes to confirm the suggestion that the line originally followed on w 953.

w 1223, B 963. Would it be hypercritical to suggest that one can hardly see *the winds . . . Take vp land soundes*? The awkwardness would have been avoided had Jonson written *List* or *Hark*. But the figurative use of *Looke* was formerly of wide extension.

## *Distribution of errors* (pp. 81–98).

I regret to find that two mistakes (at least) have crept into the lists here given. On p. 90 the intrinsic error credited to γ at w 899 has no business there: it is properly a residual variant and duly appears as such on p. 100. On p. 92 the inferential error credited to *f* at w 88 occurs in a heading and should not have been included. I have not attempted to correct these errors, since to do so would upset the details of the calculations and figures on pp. 93 and 96 without appreciably affecting the final results.

# VERBAL INDEX

*The spelling is usually, but not always, that of the text: some of the forms listed are to be sought in the apparatus. References are to the Windsor version unless preceded by* B.

aery, B 204, nestlings, brood.
aëry, 1228, airy.
affects, B 8.
aks, B 361, ask.
Alchindus, 145.
among, amongst, *see* p. 112.
angle, 1226, corner, nook.
apes, lead, 650, to die a maid.
apostrophus, *see* p. 114.
avouch, 975, declare.
Aymon, the four sons of, 28.

ball, 1283, soap-ball.
ballett, 755, 812, ballad.
Banbury (Puritans of), 1148.
Beares-Colledg, 1658, the Bear-Garden.
beat it on the (hard) hoofe, 52.
beckharman, harman-beckage, 56, 695, a constable.
beene, bin, *see* p. 111.
bene bowse, 52, good drink; bene bowsy, 996, drunk.
beside, besides, *see* p. 112.
bit, 914, a bite.
blackmans, 58, night.
blowne wine, 46, stale wine.
bob, 1120, refrain, burden (with pun in next line).
boorded, 843, boarded, lodged.
bowed, 754, 808, bent.
bowse, 52, booze, drink; bowsing, 203, bowsy, 996.
braggatt, 206, bragget, fermented honey and ale.
bralles, 220, brawls, dances.
brest, 954, breast, voice.
bride lace, 746, 818, wedding favour.
britches, put on the, 1036, to domineer.
broake (up), 913, carved.
broken beare, 45, dregs of beer.

cacklers, 60, hens.
calles, 219, summonses.
cant, 561, beg.
carbonado'd, 900, scored and grilled.
chaines, 907, worn as a badge of office.
cheates, 55, 702, stolen goods.
chiballes, 67, stone leeks.
chopt, 914, snapped.

*cippus*, 183, the stocks.
cleanlier, 567, more adroitly.
clowt, 757, 807, handkerchief.
cly, 53, procure, steal.
coacht, 880, in a coach.
Cock-Lorell, 854, 876.
codpieces, B 522, W 590, lads.
come about, 961, come round (to a favourable opinion).
contry, 602, country.
coryphæus, 133, leader.
could, 921, cold.
cove, 121, fellow.
Coventry blue, 750–1, 804, a make of blue thread.
crackmans, 57, a hedge.
crampe-ringe, 183, fetters.

Darby (ale), 204, 933.
dary, 619, dairy.
dells, 605, wenches.
depose, B 345.
deputie, 931, a deputy alderman.
Devills Arse, 90, 840, 848, 874, 939.
dispose, B 345.
divine, 647, prophetic.
diving (pockettes), 154, picking.
dowcettes, 637, the testicles of a stag.
doxie, 481, 605, 1173, a beggar's wench.
drinckalian, 834, ale-drinker.
drinckebragatan, 834, bragget-drinker.

effects, B 8.
elision, *see* p. 114.
em-, en-, *see* p. 113.
errant, 417, errand.
escapes, 657, amours.
estate, B 981, state.
eyne, 1034, eyes.

faery, 231.
farder, 192, further.
fast and loose, play, 139, 1066–7.
fayeries, 538.
file, without a, 1143, unpolished.
firedrake, 235, meteor, will-o'-the-wisp.
fitt, 1149, poem, recitation.
flagonf(l)ekean, 839.
flirt, 1021, a snatch.

## Verbal Index

flirted, 938, blew.
Fortune my foe, 638.
Fortune's wheel, 242.
foxt and furd, 906, trimmed with fox fur.
francke, 464, openly.
Friar (Tuck), 543.

Garter (of the Order), 190.
George, 179, 190, the jewel of the Order of the Garter.
gi'n, B 475, given.
Gowrie, B 908[6], alleged plot against King James.
green sawce, 899, herb sauce.
groate, 592, 754, 808, a coin worth fourpence.
groundes, 1238, foundations.
grudging, 956, longing, desire.
grunters, 60, swine.
grutching, 1180, a twinge.

hall, a, B 919, W 1086, the call for room to dance.
hanche, 917, haunch.
hangs an arse, 664, holds back, is reluctant.
harman-beckage, see beck-harman.
harper, 730, an Irish harp-shilling, worth ninepence.
Hesper, 336, the evening star.
hether, hither, see p. 112.
hey pass, 787–8.
hight, 339, 854, called.
hinch boyes, 911, hench-boys, attendants.
hoary, 923, i.e. white with flour.
hobby horse, 541, 'often forgotten'.
horle, B 339, hurle.
hurly, B 119, uproar, strife.

im-, in-, see p. 113.
importune, B 414, call for; B 440, import, intend.
incle, yncle, 48, linen tape.
intendments, 493, purpose.
invade, 19, encroach upon.

jackman, jarkman, 53 (note), forger.
jan, 53, a purse.
jarke, 53, a counterfeit seal or licence.
John de Indagine, 147.
joylly, 129, jolly.
Jugge, Justice, 33.

ken, 53, 202, B 132, a house (cf. 'libkens').
kine, 1032, cows.
Kitt-Callot, 221, Kit Callet, both terms for a light woman.
knackes, 101, 1037, tricks.
knackets, B 189.

leasure, at, 275, late if at all.
leave by, 138, let alone.
lept, 484, ravished.
libkens, 57, sleeping-places.
lifte, 217, trick, stealing.
line of life, 259, one of the principal lines on the palm of the hand.
linge, 948, 1168, a fish (usually dried or salted).
Lippus, Justice, 181.
loose, 721–2, lose.
Lothbury (metal-workers of), 1147.

maddam, 947, courtesan.
made, 20, been the cause of.
Magna Carta, 215.
Maid Marrian, 543.
mainetainance (pudding of), 909, dignity (punningly formed on analogy of 'cap of maintenance').
major, 908, mayor.
marle, 707, marvel.
marrowes, 768, mates, companions.
mas, B 926, master.
matra, 135, mother (? pretended Gipsy language).
Maudlin, 620, B 690.
maund, B 581, to beg.
mill, 561, to steal.
mill sixpence, 728, 'a sixpence coined in a mill', O.E.D., having a milled edge.
minte, 162, money.
moone, men &c. of the, 552, 993, Gipsies.
mort, 127, 556, a woman.
mutch, 409, much.

Nancies, B 191, girls.
napkins, 540, the kerchiefs carried by morris-dancers.
nimbles, 153, fingers (the only instance quoted in O.E.D.).
nip, 53, to steal.
noise, 835, band, orchestra.
*non upstante*, 673, *non obstante*, notwithstanding.

## Verbal Index

of, off, *see* p. 113.
out cept, 717, except.

*pagina*, 149.
painefull, 51, careful.
paines, 900, bread-crumbs.
Patrico, 59, 224, a hedge-priest.
Peake (of Derby), 89, 212, 840, 877.
peckage, 55, food.
petitoes, 918, toes, (pigs') trotters.
Pharaotes Indus, 146.
Phosphore, 338, the morning star.
pluck, 691, a snatch.
poesie, 1289.
pollcat, 947, punk.
poses, 1040, posies (for the rime).
post and pair, 656, a card game.
poverite of pipers, 570.
*Practise of Piety*, 754.
promoter, 886, informer.
Ptolomee, 30, &c., Ptolemy.
pullen, 1006, poultry.
Pythagoras loft, 143.

quarry, B 205, lair?
quested, 709, barked.
*quinquennium*, 47, fifth birthday.

race (of ginger), 737, root.
ransacled, 717, ransacked, cleared out.
refell, 985, to repulse.
roaring boys, 452, swaggerers, rioters, hooligans.
roome mortes, 127, great ladies.

saffrond, 99, dyed yellow with saffron.
sallet, 895, salad.
salmon, 75, ritual.
scapes, 657, amours.
sent, 490, 942, scent (the old and correct spelling).
serjeant, 901, an officer at law.
shalbe, *see* p. 113.
sharke, 868, sharper, swindler.
sharke it, 136, play the shark.
sillabes, B 11, syllables.
simper-the-cockets, 156.
sin', syne, 415, B 913, since.
skipper, 58, barn, shed.
small-nuttes, 98.
smocks, B 521, W 588, wenches.
sockettes, 155, *pudenda*.
sodaine, 1193, sudden.
spar'd, 1046, spared (for rime).
sped, B 364, rendered pregnant.

spell, 612, speech, tidings ('good spell' suggested by 'gospel').
sprites, 536.
stale, 205, old, strong (ale).
stalke, 635, 1001, walk cautiously.
stand, to a, 86, to a finish.
stauling ken, 53, a receiver's house.
straine, 229, &c., melody, measure.
syne, *see* sin'.

taile, 857, tale.
tall, 74, 921, valiant.
ten, these, B 350, the fingers.
than, then, *see* p. 112.
time, 50, age, years.
to, too, *see* p. 113.
tokens, 758, 807, tradesmens' token coins.
top, 288, 1265, head.
toringe, 1130, turning.
touch, 408, sense, perception, appreciation.
toyes, 1139, trifles.
trace, 23, pair?
trades increase, 218.
trickets, B 192.
tripsies, B 192.
twinger, 790, thief.

uncased, 61, skinned.
undersong, 1201, accompaniment.
undertooke, 817, obtained by craft.

venter, venture, *see* p. 112.
Vesper, 339, the evening star.
vicars wife, 645.
voyce, B 6, word (a Latinism?).

wants his upper lip, 735.
wax, a man of, B 360, a perfect figure of a man.
wet his whistle, 733.
whether, 450, whither.
*Whoop Barnabe*, 750.
wilbe, *see* p. 113.
wimbles, 151, gimlets, augers.
wincke, 208, sleep.
with child of an owle, 117–18.
wittie, 276, wise, learned.
wretchock, 42, weakling.
wusse, B 523, know.

ye, you, *see* p. 111.
yeoman, 902, (serjeant's) assistant.
yncle, *see* incle.

PRINTED IN
GREAT BRITAIN
AT THE
UNIVERSITY PRESS
OXFORD
BY
CHARLES BATEY
PRINTER
TO THE
UNIVERSITY